THE MARY FLEXNER LECTURES

Established in 1928 at Bryn Mawr College
to promote distinguished work in the humanities

Courtly Encounters

Translating Courtliness and Violence in Early Modern Eurasia

Sanjay Subrahmanyam

HARVARD UNIVERSITY PRESS
Cambridge, Massachusetts
London, England
2012

THE MARY FLEXNER LECTURESHIP was established at Bryn Mawr College on
February 12, 1928, by Bernard Flexner, in honor of his sister, Mary Flexner,
a graduate of the College. The income from the endowment is to be used annually
or at longer intervals, at the discretion of the Directors of the College, as an honorarium
for a distinguished American or foreign scholar in the field of the humanities.
The object of the lectureship is to bring to the College scholars of distinction who
will be a stimulus to the faculty and students and who will help to maintain the
highest ideals and standards of learning.

Library of Congress Cataloging-in-Publication Data
Subrahmanyam, Sanjay.
Courtly encounters : translating courtliness and violence in early modern Eurasia /
Sanjay Subrahmanyam.
p.   cm.
Includes bibliographical references and index.
ISBN 978-0-674-06705-9 (alk. paper)
1. Courts and courtiers—Eurasia.   2. Eurasia—Social conditions.
3. Eurasia—Social life and customs.   I. Title.
GT3510.S83   2012
950—dc23   2012015063

In memory of my father
Krishnaswamy Subrahmanyam
(1929–2011)

Contents

Maps and Illustrations

Maps

Illustrations

Preface

This book is an experiment not only on my part but possibly also for many of those who were there at its origins, who encouraged me to write it. I was trained a quarter century ago as an economic historian of South Asia and the Indian Ocean in the sixteenth and seventeenth centuries, but my interests have gradually grown larger and more diverse, both thematically and geographically, over the years. The archives and texts I have used have also naturally expanded, though they usually remained limited to the period between about 1400 and 1850. In this process, I have frequently experienced both excitement and frustration. Many historians of diverse places in Latin America, East Asia, the Middle East, Southeast Asia, and Europe have been my willing interlocutors, sharing materials, questions, seminars, and projects; I cannot name them all here for obvious reasons. Nor will I name the stubborn minority of historians who have ever been (and continue to be) censorious of the newer historiographical trends represented by such projects as "connected histories," preferring instead the comfortable certainties of a history of omniscient and cosmopolitan Europeans roaming the world from the Renaissance to the Enlightenment.

Although I grew up and was educated in India, I spent a good many years in the later 1990s and early 2000s in western Europe, often dining outdoors on spring and summer evenings with friends. Whether in Paris, Oxford, London, Naples, Pisa, or Berlin, we would be approached by young South Asian migrants who hoped to sell us flowers or trinkets but would then strike up conversations with us, using whatever languages were at hand. They were often sobering conversations, as they recounted how they had made their way through Turkey and Greece to the "safer" parts they found themselves in. One of them, a Punjabi called 'Ali, worked in a *döner* joint run by a Franco-Turk near the Gobelins in Paris; I sometimes had to mediate between him and his boss because although they had elements of several languages in common, communication still broke down. This made me feel quite virtuous until the day when 'Ali, finding me at the metro station Censier-Daubenton on my leisurely way to work at noon, said to me reproachfully, "Well, if you're such a layabout, why don't you just teach me French?" *(agar tum itne vele ho to mujhe French kyon nahīn sikhāte)*. Every illusion I had had about mutual complicity suddenly dissolved. Understanding became something much more complicated than just an issue of language or languages.

The lectures that are the source of this book were delivered while I was in residence at Bryn Mawr College over a period of a little more than two weeks in November 2009. It was an enjoyable and thoroughly nostalgic time for me, even if my morning sleep was regularly disturbed by the ominous rumble of the early SEPTA train from Thorndale making its way to Thirtieth Street just past the window of my apartment at around 5:40. As an Angeleno of sorts, I often leapt up from my dreams thinking it was an earthquake. But it was still nostalgic because my first visit to the United States in 1987–88 had been to teach at the University of Pennsylvania, and this was an occasion to visit the Philadelphia area properly again, although so much had changed in the interim. Many faculty and friends, both in

Bryn Mawr and in the broader area, helped make this a very smooth visit. The college's president Jane McAuliffe, herself a scholar of Islam, was at the heart of the invitation and remained a solicitous host throughout. Beth Shepard-Rabadam made sure that everything worked as it should. Members of the History Department, notably Ignacio Gallup-Díaz, Kalala Ngalamulume, Jennifer Spohrer, and Elly Truitt, as well as Christiane Hertel and Steven Levine from the Art History faculty, helped animate the visit and the rigorous follow-up discussions that occurred on the day after each lecture. The brunt of the hosting, including both shopping trips and visits to Center City, was patiently borne by Madhavi Kale, who ironically enough had studied with me at Penn in 1987 and been quite tolerant on that occasion, too. She also helped to host Carlo Ginzburg, who paid me a lightning visit at Bryn Mawr, delivered a wonderful talk on courtly encounters in China, and discussed Mughal painting with Yael Rice and myself at the Philadelphia Museum of Art.

Some historians, like vampires, are wont to look over their shoulders constantly. This professional deformation meant that when I was invited to deliver the Mary Flexner Lectures, I at once looked to see who had delivered them before me. The list of names was at once comforting, because it was so familiar, and disquieting, because it was so formidable. It was not at all easy to stand, as it were, where Arnaldo Momigliano had once stood. But I found comfort too in seeing the name of an old friend who had supported me when I was a young scholar who had barely completed a dissertation, the late Major Charles Ralph Boxer, who had spoken at Bryn Mawr in 1972–73, a year before Momigliano, on "Women in Iberian Expansion Overseas." The work of these two historians is implicitly or explicitly evoked in the pages that follow, as is that of other scholars who have delivered these lectures, such as Svetlana Alpers.

A considerable literature exists on the subject of early modern encounters, focusing on how these provided contexts for the invention of new categories of perception and analysis as well as for the making or remaking of disciplines, including some of the modern social sciences. Histories of ethnology, anthropology, religious studies, international relations, political thought, and a variety of other related disciplines (including a version of world history itself) have a marked tendency to hark back to the sixteenth and seventeenth centuries when they seek the origins of these forms of contemporary knowledge. What is sometimes lost sight of in these considerations is the fact that the encounters usually did not take place between societies or cultural systems as such but between particular subcultures or segments of societies. Some of these were relatively asymmetrical encounters and dealings (as with the Iberian missionaries in their authoritarian rapport with subject populations in the missions of Latin America), others far less so. In these pages, it is my intention to focus on how courtly encounters were the crucial site for the forging of mutual perceptions and representations in Eurasia. This naturally implied a prior recognition of at least a crude parallel morphology, where the so[...]tal agents involved in the encounter saw each other's societies [...] similar political systems, dominated by [...] n possessed systematic rules and [...] Arabic world might be termed a[...] [...] nd eventually translated and rend[...] [...] erhaps apocryphal cartoon figur[...] [...] d, "Take me to your leader," the i[...] [...] ad one.

[handwritten marginal note: based on a three-lecture series]

    All three lectu[...] [...] e illustrated with contemporary vi[...] [...] ced only some of the key images here. [...] uction, Chapter 1 concerns how Muslim and non-Mus[...] n South Asia dealt with one another as court systems in a situation of mutual borrowing as well as intense competition, which sometimes became violent conflict. It will treat the question of the court as a potentially secular sphere, where the religious identities of participants were at times somewhat attenuated or rendered irrelevant, only to rise again to the surface periodically, albeit in unexpected ways. Chapter 2 then turns to the matter of martyrdom, here dealing in particular with the relations between Muslims and Christians (especially Catholics). After considering a few examples from West and South Asia, the chapter moves on to a close reading of select narratives of martyrdom in the context of conversion as well as failed conversion in South and Southeast Asia. Finally, Chapter 3, the concluding chapter, addresses how South Asian states, beginning with the Sultanates of the sixteenth century but largely the Mughals (or Timurids), were depicted in European visual representations, which artfully drew on a combination of "etic" and "emic" devices. This part of the work is thus in part a return to questions of regimes of circulation that I and some of my collaborators have addressed in the past.

Taken together, these chapters attempt to provide a broad-ranging reflection on the worlds of early modern Islam, Counter-Reformation Catholicism, Protestantism, and a newly emergent "Hindu" sphere. They argue—sometimes explicitly, often implicitly—that debates on a variety of matters and concepts of pressing interest for the contemporary world, including secularism and cosmopolitanism, can be subtly illuminated by turning to this earlier phase of interactions and conflicts. In writing and revising these chapters, I have accumulated a number of debts, besides those previously acknowledged. Many long conversations with Muzaffar Alam and Velcheru Narayana Rao animate the core of much that is presented here, and Muzaffar Alam also helped to a great extent with reading the primary materials in two of these chapters. A dry run of these materials was also presented at Serge Gruzinski's regular seminar held jointly at the École des hautes études en sciences sociales (Paris) and the Musée du Quai Branly. Audiences at the Koninklijke Nederlandse Akademie van Wetenschappen (Amsterdam), UC–Berkeley, the University of Chicago, the University of Delhi, the School of Oriental and African Studies (London), the Scuola Normale Superiore (Pisa), and Princeton's Davis Seminar have heard and commented on versions of some of these chapters. With regard to the visual materials, I owe special thanks to Amina Taha-Hussein Okada of the Musée Guimet (Paris) and Susan Stronge of the Victoria and Albert Museum (London), who also invited me to present the Benjamin Zucker Lecture on Mughal Art at the V&A. Jorge Flores and Paulo Pinto were of great aid with regard to some of the materials located in Lisbon. Prachi Deshpande intervened strategically to help me gain access to manuscript illustrations at the Bharata Itihasa Samshodhaka Mandala (Pune). A brief conversation a good many years ago with Girish Karnad at the IIC in New Delhi also stimulated a part of this work that he will possibly recognize. Daud Ali, Whitney Cox, Vasudha Dalmia, Prachi Deshpande, Cornell Fleischer, Finbarr Barry Flood, Claude Guillot, Keelan Overton, Kapil Raj, and Robert Skelton all contributed astute comments on one or the other aspect of the questions addressed here. As always, Caroline Ford gave me sound and timely advice, and helped keep my sometimes flagging spirits up. The reports of at least two of the anonymous referees of Harvard University Press were useful in revising the manuscript, and I am naturally grateful to them.

In December 2009, while visiting New Delhi, I delivered an illustrated evening talk in a popular mode based on the last of these substantive chapters at the India International Centre. My father, remarking that he had never heard me deliver a lecture in all the years I had been doing so, decided suddenly to attend along with my mother. He was apparently somewhat mystified by its art-historical content, since even at dinner afterward we spoke of many subjects but not the lecture itself. I can only regret he is no longer here to read the first of these chapters, which would probably have been more to his taste. My father was my greatest intellectual inspiration during the first ten or fifteen years of my life. So it is to his memory that I dedicate this book.

COURTLY ENCOUNTERS

Introduction

Writing to his monarch, the Stuart ruler of England and Scotland, James I (or James VI) from Istanbul on April 28, 1622, the celebrated courtier and diplomat Sir Thomas Roe reflected ruefully on the ongoing difficulties of dealing with the Sublime Porte even several decades after the founding of the English Levant Company. Roe had earlier been an unsuccessful envoy on the part of the same monarch to the Mughal ruler Nur-ud-Din Jahangir in the 1610s, and he would later perform the same function with a somewhat higher degree of success in various Scandinavian courts. He thus wrote to James:

> The Grand Signor [Osman II] hath sent your Majestie an answer to your roiall letter, which, if you please to oversee the vanity of some phrases, beeing the antient presumptuous style of this court, for the substance, I hope, it will give your Majestie some content, it conteyning a particular reply to every thing, both in your Majesties, and in the propositions made by mee, by your roiall order; and in the generall, I presume, it is as full of respect and observance to your Majestie, as ever was sent to any prince, from those who thinke of no equality.[1]

The idea of "encounters" even—or perhaps especially—between "those who thinke of no equality" has had a powerful hold over both certain forms of the professional historical imagination and its popular counterpart. The past half-century and the exploration of outer space have centered much of the popular trope on variations of the earthling's encounter with the extraterrestrial alien, whether the latter arrives on our planet or humans somehow find their way to other intelligent life-forms. However, it is clear that the vast majority of the literary and cinematic genres of encounters between the human and the extraterrestrial are nothing other than an imagined variant of meetings between humans themselves.[2] The permutations are usually familiar ones: the alien proves to have immense destructive capacities and technologies, resulting in a desperate battle for survival; the alien is a cannibal or can infiltrate the human organism; the alien is superior and godlike, or innocent and childlike, or both; the alien appears to be human, but this is in fact a mere deception. Rarely do we have a scenario where human and alien somehow "meet" but are simply unable for whatever reason to communicate directly because the alien is not just a deformed human entity but a quite other creature or life-form, who—let us say—does not communicate vocally, or has no articulated limbs capable of writing or eyes capable of reading. For the most part, then, our imagined extraterrestrials are simply represented as humans in a distorting or enhancing mirror, just like the gods and anti-gods (*devas* and *asuras*) of the ancient Indian epics and *purānas*, or their Greek and Scandinavian counterparts.

This optimism regarding the relative congruence, as well as the capacity for communication, between humans and as-yet-unknown nonhumans contrasts oddly with the consistent skepticism that has been shown in the past some centuries with regard to communication and cultural commensurability within the human race itself. As is well known, one of the major intellectual consequences of the creation of new long-distance networks of human contact put into place in the later fifteenth and sixteenth centuries—the so-called great discoveries, whether with respect to the Americas or even the larger Afro-Eurasian space—was increased doubt regarding the unity of humanity itself.

The most celebrated versions of these doubts that emerged in Europe in the seventeenth century were pre-Adamite theories, fueled precisely by the encounters between western Europeans and other peoples such as the Inuits of the northern seas and the Native Americans.[3] Less well known, but equally significant, was the fact that intellectuals of the three Abrahamic religions—Judaism, Christianity, and Islam—came in these centuries to have increased contact with other traditions, such as those of the Chinese and Indians, who provided them with a quite different cosmogony, a far longer and troubling time line for human existence itself, and also the view that there had, so to speak, existed "many Adams." The well-known Iranian chronicler and intellectual of the early seventeenth century, Muhammad Qasim Hindushah Astarabadi (better known by his literary alias of "Firishta"), thus wrote:

> The infidels *(kāfirs)* of India like those of China say that Noah's tempest did not reach their country, and instead reject it. . . . They attribute strange and bizarre deeds to Ram, Lakhman et cetera, which do not correspond to the human condition. . . . All this is words and sound which has no weight in the scale of reason. . . . The Hindus say that from the time of Adam more than 100,000 years have passed. This is totally false, and the fact is that the country of Hind, like the other countries of the inhabited quarter of the world, was settled through the descendants of Adam. . . . The oldest son of Ham was Hind, who reached the country of Hind and settled it in his name. His brother Sind reached the country of Sind, and settled Thatta and Multan in the name of his children. Hind had four children: Purab, Bang, Dakan and Nahrawal, and each settled a kingdom, which even today are known by those names.[4]

At the time he wrote this, Firishta (ca. 1550–1623) was a privileged resident in the Sultanate of Bijapur in west-central India, after having spent an earlier phase of his life in the Ahmadnagar Sultanate slightly farther north. These Indo-Islamic courts, even if they did not promote the relatively systematic translations of Sanskrit materials into Persian that the Mughals were to do, nevertheless had a good number of Brahmin savants in their midst, serving as physicians, astrologers, administrators, and the like. Their knowledge and their chronologies, as well as Mughal summary "translations" of texts like the *Mahābhārata*, had thus begun to seep into the Persianate world of the chronicler, and his response was to resist noisily and vigorously.[5]

It may be argued that Firishta's protests should be framed within a far larger global conjuncture, one that could embrace Portuguese encounters in Africa and across the Indian Ocean, the Spaniards in the Caribbean and then on the American mainland, the Russians in Siberia and Central Asia, or the Ming and Qing encounters with their westerly peoples.[6] In all of these instances, expanding empires encountered unfamiliar peoples and attempted to come to terms with them conceptually as well as otherwise, using such varied means as warfare, diplomacy, and ethnography—to name but three among a gamut of options. A powerful argument that has often been deployed by ethnohistorians and others such as Tzvetan Todorov is that, in many of these instances, the central problem was one of a sort of semiotic incommensurability between the parties involved, be it in the Americas or in the South Pacific.[7]

The key notion here is of "incommensurability," rendered famous in the early 1960s in discussions of science by Thomas Kuhn and Paul Feyerabend, and then taken into other contexts—whether explicitly or not. The principal concern of Kuhn in his initial work was with the incommensurability of scientific theories, in which he argued that there was a relation of methodological, observational, and conceptual disparity between paradigms. In a later phase, Kuhn began to argue using—albeit with some looseness—the work of Willard

V. O. Quine that incommensurability was essentially a problem in the semantic sphere, and he further proceeded to argue that the fundamental problem was one of the "indeterminacy of translation."[8] Yet where Quine had argued that there was an indeterminacy between equally good translations, Kuhn seemed to imply that incommensurability was more an issue of a failure of exact translation; this suggested, first, that correct translation was actually possible in principle, and second, that existing translations were not only indeterminate but also bad.[9]

The next step chronologically was the transfer of the idea of incommensurability, used first in the context of the relations between two (or more) "paradigms," to the relation between two or more cultures.[10] This gives us the idea of "cultural incommensurability," which is often itself characterized as a particular form of cultural relativism and one through which anthropology came to influence the practice of historians in the late 1970s and 1980s.[11] The view here is of largely impermeable cultural zones, perfectly coherent in and of themselves but largely inaccessible to those who look in from the outside. To be sure, as Anthony Pagden has forcefully reminded us, the roots of such ideas can be traced back at least to the later eighteenth century, when writers such as Denis Diderot and above all Johann Gottfried Herder produced powerful, and politically volatile, arguments on this subject. For, in Pagden's words, "Herder pushed the notion of incommensurability to the point where the very concept of a single human genus became, if not impossible to conceive, at least culturally meaningless."[12]

Where then does this leave us with respect to the study of encounters and interactions in an interstate and interimperial context in the sixteenth and seventeenth centuries? We know that Herder himself thought very poorly of empires, for he wrote in his *Ideen zur Philosophie der Geschichte der Menschheit*, "A kingdom consisting of a single nation is a family, a well-regulated household: it reposes on itself, for it is founded by Nature, and stands and falls by time alone. An empire formed by forcing together a hundred nations, and a hundred and fifty provinces, is no body public, but a monster."[13] In sum, in this view, empires are already characterized by forms of radical incommensurability even among their constituent parts.

It may be useful here to begin with a simple, even slightly crude, distinction. Some of the Eurasian states and empires of the sixteenth and seventeenth centuries that we shall examine were obviously genealogically related or belonged to overlapping cultural zones; others were not. The former was the case of the three great Islamic states of those years—the Ottomans, Safavids, and Mughals—which seem for many purposes to have even formed a single sphere of elite circulation for calligraphers, painters, Sufi mystics, warriors, and poets.[14] All three used Arabic, Turkish, and Persian in varying measures as languages of communication and culture; all of them thus had a common library of texts, images, and concepts; all of them owed something, either genealogically or conceptually, to earlier Chinggisid and Timurid attempts at state and empire building. This would seem, on the face of it, to provide the grounds for some commensurability. So, for example, we may take the situation in the late 1660s, when the semiautonomous Ottoman governor of Basra, a certain Husain Pasha Afrasiyab, under attack by Ottoman forces from Baghdad for paying little if any tribute to Sultan Mehmed IV (r. 1648–87), decided to go over to the Mughals.[15] The governor was probably somewhat well-versed in Ottoman Turkish, and presumably also had a good command of both Arabic and Persian. We are thus not predisposed to assume that when he arrived in the Mughal court of Aurangzeb-'Alamgir he was like a fish out of water. We also know that the Pasha had prepared his ground for several years before his desertion, and that on his arrival in western India he was escorted with full dignities into Shahjahanabad-Delhi in July 1669, and that—as the Mughal chronicles have it—"by the touch of the royal hand on his back, his head was exalted beyond the sky."[16] In concrete terms, this meant that he received extensive gifts of rubies and horses, a great mansion on the banks of the Jamuna River, and a rather high *mansab* rank of 5,000 in the Mughal hierarchy. Very quickly he also rose to be governor *(sūbadār)* of the central Indian province of Malwa, itself no mean achievement. Two of his sons, Afrasiyab and ʿAli Beg, were also given respectable ranks and taken into imperial service.

Seen from a certain angle, the short Mughal career of Islam Khan Rumi (as Husain Pasha came to be known in India) until his death in battle in late June 1676 suggests how easy it was to cross the boundary between these two empires. The fact that the Mughals and Ottomans shared a Turko-Persian courtly culture is what leads us to this predisposition. We shall have occasion to return to this problem presently, looking to some lesser-known aspects of Husain Pasha's career, but we may state matters here bluntly: there is a tendency to think of cultural incommensurability as particularly acute at moments of encounter, when two disparate (and perhaps historically separated) politico-cultural entities come into contact. We think of Cortés and Moctezuma, Pisarro and Atahualpa, Captain Cook in Hawaiʻi, or Vasco da Gama and the Samudri Raja of Calicut. It is rare to talk of incommensurability in relation to an Englishman like Sir Thomas Roe visiting seventeenth-century Denmark, or when the Safavids send an ambassador to the Mughals.[17] Husain Pasha among the Mughals is thus not what one usually thinks of as an emblematic "early modern encounter." But it is not by showing that, at some times and places, such an issue did not arise that we can wish away the idea of incommensurability itself. Instead, we will try in the pages that follow, with the aid of a set of examples, to explore the issue of incommensurability (and its counterpart, commensurability) in relation to concrete themes such as diplomacy, warfare, and visual representations. Further, rather than look at incommensurability in general, we will focus on the confrontation between courtly cultures instead of the more emblematic (and certainly more romantic) encounters on beaches in the South Seas or their equivalent.

Some brief preliminary reflections may be in order with regard to each of these themes in turn. Diplomacy is, of course, the core of interstate and thus intercourt relations, and we know that the cut and thrust of diplomatic negotiations were the focus of traditional historians throughout the nineteenth and twentieth centuries, including the historians of the celebrated French *École des Chartes* and elsewhere in the world. These studies focused in very large measure on the documents that were produced by diplomacy or around it: texts of treaties, but also instructions given to envoys and ambassadors, and the reports submitted by returning envoys. One great example will suffice to show the crucial significance of such materials. The German historian Leopold von Ranke—one of whose major early works, entitled *Die Osmanen und die spanische Monarchie im 16. und 17. Jahrhundert* (published in 1827), concerned the relations between the Ottomans and the Spanish Habsburgs—used the *Relazioni* of the Venetian ambassadors to the Sublime Porte as a major source for his research. This strategy has since been revived by the French historian Lucette Valensi, with a different purpose in mind.[18] Where Ranke had tended to focus on these reports as sources, crucial in view of his lack of direct access to Ottoman materials, Valensi has tended to use these rather more in the tradition of the "history of representations," even though she shies away from any association with a Saïdian analysis of "Orientalism." Similar attempts have been made elsewhere. The Dutch East India Company's presence in Asia was the basis for a great six-volume collection entitled *Corpus Diplomaticum Neerlando-Indicum*, edited by J. E. Heeres and F. W. Stapel, which dealt with the centuries from 1596 to 1799; in the case of the Portuguese in the Indian Ocean, we have the massive and somewhat haphazard *Colecção de Tratados e Concertos de Pazes*, edited by Júlio Firmino Júdice Biker.[19] These materials have been used sporadically by historians to study relations in a bilateral framework—for example, between the Portuguese and the Mughals or the sultans of Johor and the Dutch.[20] However, a good many years ago, a warning note was sounded by a Sri Lankan historian, K. W. Goonewardena.[21] He argued that if one considered the texts of treaties signed between the Dutch Company and the rulers of Kandy in central Sri Lanka in not the Dutch version alone (as is the case with Heeres) but in both the Dutch and Sinhala versions, it became clear that there were at times massive divergences in content. These divergences can explain why treaties subsequently became battlegrounds, with one or the other side claiming that they were not being adhered to, and the other denying it. What is unclear now was the source of the divergence. Was this merely a case of the interpreter, the Dutch *tolk* or the Portuguese *língua*, being sloppy at his job? Were there in fact deeper issues of translation involved? Whatever be the case, the examples that he produced flew in the face of a view that had gained much ground in the 1950s and 1960s to the effect that the diplomatic experiences of the early modern period allowed for the creation of an unproblematic and quite transparent "Law of Nations," which is to say a set of common conventions or mutually agreed framework within which diplomacy could be conducted.[22]

Contemporaries too were aware of the problem in some incarnation or the other. Thus, a Portuguese chronicler of the 1570s, António Pinto Pereira, described the process of translation between Portuguese and Persian in some detail, and attempted to reassure his readers that the diplomatic materials that he provided them—even if they originated in a distant tongue—were credible. In his *História da Índia*, Pereira thus reproduces the Portuguese version of certain letters of the Sultan of Bijapur, ʿAli ʿAdil Shah (r. 1558–80), to the viceroy of the Portuguese Indies, Dom Luís de Ataíde, and what is remarkable is that he describes the form of the letters as well as his mode of access to them. We may quote him at some length.

> It seemed right to us that these letters should be inserted into this history in the same form that the Hidalcão [ʿAdil Khan] wrote them, for we saw their originals in the possession of the

Viceroy, under the sign and seal *(chapa)* of the Hidalcão, written
in two languages—Persian and Portuguese: primarily in Persian,
in which they write the authoritative version, and on the same
piece of paper, below the same seal and sign, appears the translation in Portuguese by one Bernardo Rodriguez, a New Christian of Goa, who was resident there [Bijapur] as he had fled with
a married woman, and on account of many worse crimes which
among the Moors are [however] not considered strange; and as
he is most able, and fluent in languages, principally in Persian,
and eloquent in that language and in Portuguese, the Hidalcão
makes use of him as a secretary in external matters *(nas cousas de
fora)*, and in his hand they were translated from the Persian script,
which since it is most compendious and comprehensive, one page
(huma lauda) of it occupied more than six in Portuguese, on account of the characters which are all very similar, curved in the
manner of a half-moon, with the differences being on account of
the little points that they carry on the inside and outside, as also
in the part where the body of each letter opens up.[23]

This extensive introduction precedes the verbatim inclusion in the
chronicle of two translated letters, the first undated and the second
dated September 26, 1570. In these missives, which seem to have accompanied the respective embassies of a certain Rodrigo de Moraes
on the Portuguese side and Khwaja Lutfullah on the side of Bijapur,
the ʿAdil Shah complains bitterly of the treatment of his own ships
and those of his subjects by the Portuguese officials at fortresses such
as Hurmuz, Diu, and Chaul, who ransack them and "take away on
land the boys and girls they find there, to convert them by force into
Christians, which include the sons of honored Moors, and their
daughters and wives, and their Abyssinian and Moorish [slave] boys."[24]
These matters, he declares, and in particular the issue of forcible
conversion, are causing much strain to his friendship with the ruler
of Portugal, and it is up to the Portuguese viceroy to resolve the ten-

sion. Other issues dealt with in the letters include the treatment of the vessels of anti-Portuguese Muslim traders in the ports of Bijapur; the free passage of certain crucial goods (in particular opium) into ʿAdil Shahi territories; and the treatment of Christian slaves who flee from Goa to Bijapur—whom the Bijapur ruler agrees to hand over to their masters. Having reproduced them, Pereira in his commentary treats these letters as mere "dissimulation" and as "pretended signs of friendship" when in fact the ʿAdil Shah planned all the while to mount a war on the Portuguese. Yet the presence of these letters in their "raw" form is of some utility, as it already provided sixteenth-century readers with an implicit counterargument to the claims of the Portuguese chroniclers that no real reasons for war existed between the two parties. These then are diplomatic materials that are not necessarily partisan to the Portuguese and cannot be read simply in terms of a conspiracy theory.

Elsewhere, in collaborative work with Muzaffar Alam, I have attempted a somewhat experimental exercise with regard to precisely such diplomatic materials.[25] We have used the original Persian letters (complete with chancellery seals) of another Asian monarch, Sultan Bahadur of Gujarat (r. 1526–37), to establish modern English translations. We have then compared these translations with contemporary translations into Portuguese that were produced in the 1530s and inserted into the Portuguese chronicle of Fernão Lopes de Castanheda. Our conclusions are provisional, but they may be stated as follows. We do not find an enormous divergence in terms of content of the type that Goonewardena found. Further, it is interesting to note that the Portuguese of the translations attempts to hold quite literally to certain expressions in the Persian original. And finally, we note that this lends to the Portuguese of the sixteenth-century translation a certain curious quality, which distinguishes it from the language of the rest of the chronicle in which it is embedded. These conclusions seem to broadly confirm the view of the French historian Jean Aubin with regard to letters exchanged in the context of the

Persian Gulf in the same period.[26] However, he had also noted two features that we must mention here. First, wordplay or double entendre usually does not pass into the translations. Second, the identity of the translator does have some influence on the translation, as was noted also by the Jesuit historian Georg Schurhammer in his analysis of the career and writings of a certain António Fernandes, a converted Muslim in Portuguese service.[27] A translator such as Fernandes tends to write a more ornate Portuguese, and sometimes even introduces phrases into the Portuguese that can only be grasped if one has some background in Persian. The Portuguese historian Luís Filipe Thomaz has made similar helpful comments while recently reediting and translating the Malay letters of Abu Hayat, Sultan of Ternate (in eastern Indonesia) in the early 1520s.[28]

These conclusions may appear somewhat banal to students of translation. But they nevertheless remain somewhat reassuring for the historian when dealing with situations where two versions of the document do not exist, such as a valuable letter from the ruler of Agra and Delhi, Islam Shah Sur, to the Portuguese governor Dom João de Castro dating from October 1546.[29] The long and extremely interesting letter that the Ottoman commander Hadim Süleyman Pasha wrote to Ulugh Khan, the *wazīr* of the Gujarat Sultanate, after his unsuccessful expedition to Diu in 1538 is also a case in point.[30] We do not have the Ottoman original, only a Portuguese version. Yet what then should we make of this text?

A similar problem arises with respect to a quite important, albeit economically written, letter from Vira Narasimha Raya, ruler of Vijayanagara, to the Portuguese governor (later viceroy) Dom Francisco de Almeida in 1505. Here, too, we do not possess the original (which must have been in Kannada, or less probably in Telugu), only the contemporary Portuguese translation. Yet this letter is quite surprising in terms of what it proposes. Before getting to the contents of the letter, it is probably necessary to say a little about its background. The empire of Vijayanagara, or Karnataka, was already known to

Europeans in the fifteenth century largely on account of the writings of Niccolò de' Conti. Yet in their first expeditions, the Portuguese did not seek to establish relations with Vijayanagara, even though this empire had ports on both sides of the south Indian peninsula. They concentrated instead on the kingdoms of Kerala, in the extreme southwest of India, though unofficial contacts were made with Vijayanagara through a Franciscan friar, Frei Luís do Salvador, who made his way to the great interior city of Vijayanagara at the time of a dynastic struggle. Eventually, a powerful warlord, Narasa Nayaka, founded a fresh dynasty, and he left it to his son and successor Vira Narasimha Raya, who seems to have received Frei Luís—though with little knowledge of the European court that the friar claimed to represent. He then sent Frei Luís, accompanied by one of his own representatives and a letter, back to the port of Cannanore in Kerala, where Dom Francisco de Almeida had just landed.

The letter came accompanied by gifts of cloth and bracelets, as we learn from accompanying documentation. Its contents were brief but wide-ranging. It took note that a "Brahmin" from Portugal (*hum teu bramene por nome chamado Frey Luis*, that is, Frei Luís, a priest) had arrived in the court of Vijayanagara as an emissary. He had been well received, and his words had been heard very positively. As a consequence, the king of Portugal was offered an alliance: he could have access to one or more of the ports of Vijayanagara, preferably Mangalore, and the two kings would be allied for the purpose of joint actions on land and sea. And, to seal all this, a marriage alliance was proposed so that the blood of the two royal houses would mingle (*[se] quisereis minha filha ou irmã por molher eu ta darey e asy tomarey tua filha ou irmã ou cousa de teu samgue por molher*).[31] A daughter of the king of Portugal could marry the Vijayanagara ruler and come to India, while a girl of the Vijayanagara ruling family would be sent to Portugal for a similar, and suitable, marriage.

This is a most curious proposal, quite unlike any other that the Portuguese received in the first decades of their presence in Asian waters. In Kerala, they had been treated with hostility, arriving as they did in the form of armed traders with specific demands, such as the expulsion of all Muslim merchants from the port of Calicut. Yet, where Vijayanagara is concerned, we find not suspicion and a volition to keep the distant foreign power at an arm's length but an eager desire to cement an alliance. We know that the proposal reached the Portuguese court, and that a certain excitement stemmed from it. Yet nothing came of it, even though it fitted well enough with certain of the more ambitious claims of Dom Manuel, the Portuguese king. The suspicion one has is that it was the reciprocity of the arrangement that posed a problem in Portugal, even though this very reciprocity was clearly a device to level the playing field. In the political vocabulary of Vijayanagara, simply to give away a daughter would have been to place oneself in a situation of inferiority. This was the reason why the marital exchange had to be mutual. And this was something that the Portuguese court could not countenance: namely, sending a Portuguese princess to a "pagan" court in distant India. There was an interesting and significant asymmetry here between the attitudes of the two courts.

Yet we know that the Portuguese court did entertain marital alliances with other courts in England, Spain, and even Savoy. Vijayanagara rulers did so with other kings in southern India and Orissa. Slightly later, Safavid princesses were married into the Mughal royal family, as indeed were princesses from (subordinate) Rajput households with royal pretensions. In some cases, such alliances involved a measure of coercion, but in others they did not. What defined the limits of such possibilities? Were these limits that we can see as coterminous with the limits of communication as opposed to incommensurability, or would this be too simplistic a thesis?

We may also approach the issue of diplomacy from the other end, namely, that of radical breakdown. We know that in the last years of his life, relations between Amir Timur or Tamerlane (d. 1405) and the Chinese emperors had taken on a problematic aspect. In what must be seen as one of the world's most spectacular displays of the breakdown of diplomacy, Timur had the Chinese envoys sent to him by the Ming emperors Hung-wu and Yung-lo executed in 1395, 1402, and 1403, and letters of insult sent to the emperor, addressing him as "Pig" in a crude play on the emperor Hung-wu's family name of "Chu." This was preparatory to mounting a campaign to the east, which Timur's death in February 1405 eventually prevented him from prosecuting.[32] This must be seen as an extreme case, the equivalent of denying that the source from which the envoys come has any standing at all, though Timur clearly knew this was not the case.

This incident is paralleled in some ways by the fate of the Portuguese envoys from Macao who made their way to Nagasaki in July 1640. They did so in spite of the order issued by the Japanese state council *(rōjū)* in late August 1639 declaring that no further Portuguese vessels would be entertained in Japanese ports, and that any ships attempting to enter would be destroyed and their crew and passengers put to death. Clearly, the Macao Senate did not realize how deadly serious the Tokugawa shogunate in fact was. In a meeting of March 13, 1640, it was hence resolved to send an embassy in a galliot to present a petition asking that the Edict of Expulsion be repealed. The ship left Macao on June 22; as soon as it entered the port of Nagasaki on July 6, it was seized, and the embassy and crew members were imprisoned on the island of Deshima. In early August 1640, a message from Edo arrived accusing them of defying the earlier order. The envoys pleaded that they were not there to trade but to present a memorial to the Japanese government. Despite this, they were sentenced to death. The next morning, those slated for execution were given the choice of renouncing Christianity. Sixty-one refused and were decapitated. Thirteen were spared and returned to Macao in a small Chinese junk with the grim and insulting message to the Senate that the shogunate meant business.[33]

In this instance, as with Timur, we can perhaps argue that the radical breakdown of the diplomatic process was not a breakdown of communication. It was instead a very particular form of communication, a sort of unilateral redefinition of the rules of the game. It was not as if the Japanese and the Portuguese of Macao did not know each other well: they did, and indeed—if one is to follow the historian Jurgis Elisonas—the shogunate knew rather too much about the Portuguese and their possible intentions.[34] What did transpire was that the Macao Senate was desperate to keep the Japan trade open, and willing to take very high risks for this purpose. Disengagement could only take place through a radical symbolic action, and this is what in fact occurred— with both sides reading the "sign" for exactly what it was.

The situation of the Chinese envoys to Samarqand around 1400 was a somewhat different one, for Timur's actions did not in fact produce an end to relations. Rather, shortly thereafter, in 1409, other Chinese envoys arrived at the court of his son, Mirza Shahrukh, and resumed relations, in spite of a further exchange of rancorous missives. In this exchange of embassies, one of the Chinese envoys, an experienced civil servant named Ch'en Ch'eng, was sent to Herat in late 1413. Ch'en even produced a very valuable account of life in the Timurid domains of the southern part of Central Asia entitled "Monograph of the Countries of the Western Regions" to accompany his travel log "Record of a Journey to the Western Regions," which we are told formed the basis of Chinese textual knowledge of certain areas such as Herat and its environs until as late as 1736. The account, a recent analyst remarks, "is remarkably free of bias [except] . . . when his [Ch'en's] Confucian sensibilities were offended," and it even takes time out to praise the quality of the bathhouses and masseurs that he encountered.[35] The incident of the decapitated ambassadors was placed, as it were, within parentheses.

Perhaps our examples so far having come from the world of diplomacy have skewed the argument in favor in commensurability, even when the diplomatic relations break down. Let us turn briefly therefore to a second set of examples, relating to warfare. Here, too, we may start with a radical example, namely, the celebrated hypothesis from half a century ago of the Islamic historian David Ayalon regarding the end of the Mamluk state in Egypt in the 1510s. Ayalon argued that, despite their long cohabitation, the Mamluks and the Ottomans had by the early sixteenth century come to make war in very different ways.[36] The Mamluks were committed to forms of heavy cavalry warfare, to severely limiting the role of firearms, and to a certain composition for their armies. The Ottomans were far more flexible, far less concerned with social hierarchies on the battlefield, and far more exposed—on account of their proximity to and competition with European states—to the use of gunpowder in its various incarnations, from sieges to battlefields. This led, in Ayalon's view, to the rapid collapse of the Mamluk forces in 1516–17, once Ottoman Sultan Selim began a campaign against them. The two styles of warfare were simply not compatible, and no rules of engagement existed to protect the Mamluks. In a certain sense, Ayalon wound up suggesting that the Mamluks faced with the Ottomans were not unlike the Mexica faced with the forces of Hernán Cortés.

A footnote can be added to this. The Spanish chroniclers noted that Hernán Cortés, his sons, and some of his entourage accompanied Charles V on his failed expedition against Algiers in 1541. But despite his age and experience, Cortés was—to his own humiliation— left out of the *consejo de guerra*, and others apparently even made fun of him; a seventeenth-century literary version of these conversations would show the Duke of Alba sneering at Cortés for having "had his battles and encounters with naked people" *(tuvo con gente desnuda / sus batallas y reencuentros).*[37] In short, fighting the Ottomans was not quite the same as fighting in America. The same sort of remark was made by a certain António Real while criticizing the actions of Portuguese governor Afonso de Albuquerque in India. The only serious (and by implication, honorable) warfare was Mediterranean warfare, and all else—or so Real stated—was a matter of "petty wars with naked little unarmed blacks" *(guerrejones com nigrinhos nuus e sem armas).*[38]

To return to our Ottoman-Mamluk example, there are reasons to extend the comparisons further. Ottoman warfare by all accounts did not appear at all compatible with how combat was conceived by the Safavids in the 1510s. The Qizilbash warriors of the latter, initially obsessed with chivalric ideas such as *jawānmardī*, were really no match for the Ottomans in such engagements as the celebrated battle of Chaldiran in 1514. We might argue here that the Ottomans at this moment represented a particularly pragmatic, efficient, and flexible war machine, in comparison with their neighbors and rivals in the Islamic world. Their culture of war was of a different order, it would seem, from that of the Mamluks or Safavids, although the three obviously shared many other cultural traits as well as a common heritage in concepts of state-building and a similar politico-institutional vocabulary. Eventually, as the sixteenth century wore on, the Safavids (who, unlike the Mamluks, did survive the Ottoman onslaught) would adapt their war-machine and take on board many of these newfangled ways of making war. By the end of the century, they would have their own slave-soldiers and mercenaries, were capable of managing cannon and other firearms, and would even participate in the celebrated engagement to expel the Portuguese from Hurmuz in 1622.

We could even return here to the example with which we began: Husain Pasha, who became Islam Khan Rumi in Mughal service in the 1660s. The schematic view presented earlier of his career passed over two matters, one important, the other one less so. To take the less important matter first, it is notable that, after a brief honeymoon period in India, his star began to wane. This was because he came accompanied by two sons, but he had left behind his wives and a third son in Iraq. He apparently did not comprehend that in the eyes of the Mughal court this was seen as a sign of potential disloyalty. In this matter at least, everything was not transparent when one moved from the Ottomans to the Mughals. The second matter is more serious, and it concerns his death. After several years in the wilderness,

Islam Khan eventually managed to return to courtly favor, and he was granted a high post in the Deccan fighting the Marathas and the forces of Bijapur. This required him, however, to fight from the back of an elephant, a common enough practice in India but one that a "marsh Arab" from Basra like Husain Pasha was clearly unprepared for. This is what led to his death in the course of an engagement in late June 1676. The Mughal chronicles report that at the moment of his engaging the enemy, his elephant bolted at the sound of artillery so that he fell into enemy hands and was immediately put to death, along with his son 'Ali Beg. This somewhat ridiculous end (which the Mughal chronicler notes) shows that a quite successful warrior in the Ottoman context could not always transfer his skills to another state, even one as proximate as the Mughals.

Indeed, in the sixteenth century this had been the complaint of Hadim Süleyman Pasha, after his short and disastrous expedition to Diu in Gujarat in 1538. Süleyman Pasha had a very poor opinion of Indians indeed, if we may believe the letter that was briefly mentioned earlier. He thought that they were poor Muslims, who did not care to observe the proprieties of their religion; as he wrote, "When they should be giving thanks to God at the hour of prayer, they do nothing else than dance their dances, and the greater part of them are really infidels and Christians [*cacizes*]." But he also believed that they were poor fighters, unable to meet the testing standards he set them.[39]

How, if at all, does this help us to address the question of the incommensurability (or not) of military cultures when political formations encountered each other in the early modern period? The generalization of Ayalon's hypothesis was made some two decades ago by Geoffrey Parker, in a section of his deservedly celebrated work on "the military revolution."[40] To summarize his main conclusions, Parker argued then that differing culturally inflected conceptions of warfare played a crucial role in most conflicts between Europeans and non-Europeans in the years from 1500 to 1700. His is therefore a somewhat culturalist mode of explanation, though he does not much explore the content of the notion of "culture" itself beyond stating that it was not necessarily a question of "social, moral or natural advantage."[41] The extra-European sphere in this view is further to be divided into three subcategories. First, we encounter those areas where the Europeans had triumphed for the most part by 1650. In areas such as central and northeast America, in some coastal areas of sub-Saharan Africa, in Indonesia and the Philippines, and in Siberia, Parker argued that Europeans "fought dirty and (what was worse) fought to kill," something that went against prevailing norms of those regions. He hence noted that Europeans triumphed because their technology and their modes of war were superior, and above all because their adversaries had "no time to adopt western military technology." He then went on to contrast this situation with a second group of areas, where European expansionary ambitions were stymied until 1700 but not thereafter, namely, in what he termed the "Muslim world" (meaning the Ottoman and Mughal domains principally). In these regions, Parker argued, the local military organization was initially flexible but eventually atrophied, so no significant changes were made after the sixteenth century. In other words, the Ottomans in the eighteenth century were allegedly still fighting "as in the days of Suleiman the Magnificent," and Parker quotes the Maréchal de Saxe, who in 1732 claimed: "It is hard for one nation to learn from another, either from pride, idleness or stupidity. . . . The Turks today are in this situation. It is not valour, numbers or wealth that they lack; it is order, discipline and technique." It is not certain whether Ottoman specialists would agree with Saxe's judgment, and Rhoads Murphey's authoritative work on Ottoman warfare does not in fact discuss Parker's views on the matter.[42] Certainly, writers on the Mughal Empire have in recent times tended to doubt some aspects of this portrayal, and this is an issue to which we shall return.

But let us complete our summary of Parker's portrayal here. His non-European world also includes a third category, one that—he wrote—was "able to keep the West at bay throughout the early modern period because, as it were, they already knew the rules of the game." In other words, this was a part of the world where there was, so to speak, no incommensurability of military cultures, if this is indeed what we should understand by "rules of the game." The reference here is to China, Korea, and Japan, which in Parker's view were regions of the world that—in keeping with the vision in Akira Kurosawa's marvelous film *Kagemusha* (1980)—"were perfectly prepared to take over Western military innovations [but] . . . always adapted them to local conditions in a distinctive way." Why were these regions better able to keep the West at bay? It would seem that, at bottom, it was a question of culture, or of broad cultural conceptions that are also embedded in the institutions of war. East Asia here is seen as the closest to Europe; the "Muslim world" of West and South Asia is some distance off, and Indonesia, parts of Africa, and pre-Columbian America are perceived as having the highest degree of incommensurability, or, in other words, they played by "rules of the game" that were the most different.

This portrayal is not entirely improbable. As late as the eighteenth century, Indian rulers and warlords were often heard to complain about the manner in which the English Company (and the Europeans more generally) made war. Thus, Telugu texts often tell us that the English are characterized above all by "deviousness" *(kāpaty-amu)* and a profound incapacity to keep their promises and agreements. The problem of compatibility or commensurability is also highlighted in certain texts discussing the Battle for Bobbili in January 1757, which ended in the total massacre of a fortified town in southeastern India—aged men, women, and children included—at the hands of a force spearheaded by the French *seigneur de guerre* Charles de Bussy. Here, at least one text tells us explicitly that one of the central problems was that "he [Bussy] does not understand our language apparatus *(bhāshā-yantramu)*, and we don't understand his," and also that the French have a "gibberish-making language apparatus" *(kikkara-bakkara bhāshā yantramu)*.[43] The problem is not one, in this portrayal at least, of a literal lack of translation, for there are indeed translators (or *dubāshīs*) available. Rather, it is a problem of the larger apparatus, which includes a mix of values, notions of admissible and inadmissible conduct, and so on. Indeed, the outcome of the battle was a serious shock to Bussy, and a contemporary European chronicler, Robert Orme, tells us that at the end, "the slaughter of the conflict being completed, another much more dreadful presented itself in the area below: the transport of victory lost all its joy: all gazed on one another with silent astonishment and remorse, and the fiercest could not refuse a tear to the deplorable destruction spread before them."[44]

A general work by Jos Gommans on Mughal warfare has attempted to sum up the contrast between the English Company in the late eighteenth century and the Mughals—two imperial formations locked in a very complex form of combat. In this view, at the heart of the matter was the Mughals and the Europeans having two quite different conceptions of honor. The Mughals, Gommans writes, had ideas on warfare that were characterized by notions of "openness and flexibility" and even "playfulness," all of which were part of what he terms their "fluid politics." He adds that "Mughal policy was usually aimed not at destroying but at incorporating the enemy, preferably by means of endless rounds of negotiations."[45] Contrasted with this are the tactics and strategy of the East India Company under Clive and his successors, which are seen as aimed at monopolizing power and, Gommans argues in a similar metaphor to that used by Parker, "suddenly and unilaterally changed the rules of the ongoing game."

But could the Mughals really not adapt to the new rules? And if they could not, what of the other players, whether the Marathas or the Afghans? Indeed, other work by Gommans has shown clearly how "Afghan innovation" between the time of Nadir Shah in the 1730s and that of the Abdalis in the 1760s significantly changed northern Indian warfare in the eighteenth century, independent of the European presence.[46] In a similar vein, we know that the rulers of Mysore, Haidar ʿAli and Tipu Sultan, adapted their style of war in the 1770s and 1780s, and managed in the process to give the East India Company's armies quite a scare. The Anglo-Mysore Wars were fought with grim earnestness by both parties, rather than being a series of combats between two wholly incommensurable styles, one earnest and the other playful. It is certainly true that such contrasts lend themselves to the stark portrayal seen in Satyajit Ray's film *The Chess-Players* (1977), in which the plot is framed by the East India Company's 1856 overthrow of Wajid ʿAli Shah, the ruler of Awadh. Much ink has been spilt on whether Ray's portrayal lampoons the Awadh ruler by making him excessively "effeminate," and whether Ray himself was in this process buying into colonial stereotypes concerning Indians.[47] But what is clear is that Ray's fundamental intention is to suggest a vast gulf in styles and cultures, and also in conceptions of kingship and warfare, between mid-nineteenth-century British colonialists and "traditional" north Indian aristocrats. In this sense, he too visits the idea of incommensurability, while offering a tantalizing suggestion that there were indeed some "in-between figures," notably the fictitious character in the film of Captain Weston. Though he is English, Captain Weston understands and participates fully in the aesthetics of Hindawi poetry, thus suggesting a greater sympathy for the Awadh monarch than for his own superior, General Outram.

This brings us effectively to our principal point. This is the location of most theories of "cultural incommensurability" in squarely structuralist understandings of culture itself. In sum, it is usually difficult for those who argue solidly in this vein to account for the issue that is central to the historian's concerns, namely, the problem of historical change. In this respect, a final example from early modern military history may be useful: the relatively obscure empire of the

Merina in late eighteenth-century Madagascar, from the time of king Andrianampoinimerina (1745–1810). The rise of the Merina was quite rapid and spectacular over the course of the eighteenth century, and it lasted some four decades, from 1780 to 1820, replacing the earlier dominant power of the Betsimisaraka (literally, the "Great-Never-Divided"), which had been ruled by Ratsimilao and his successors. Both polities arose in a context in which firearms and gunpowder were quite central. Yet they do not fit the comfortable categories that we know of, since they were neither incapable of adapting (and hence doomed to fall by the wayside) nor predestined to adapt and hence capable of riding the crest (as some have viewed the Japanese). Rather, it would seem that the Imerina polity used but significantly transformed the significance of firearms; in Gerald Berg's words, firearms became of "relative technical insignificance in determining the outcome of battle" but held deep symbolic significance in the polity at large.[48] This means that a novel military technology was neither rejected nor simply accepted in order to mimic another polity that was perceived as more successful. Here, then, is the key to the third leg of our argument, which is developed using the field of Eurasian-wide interactions in the field of the visual arts.

First, we may need once more to clear the undergrowth of the weeds of former quarrels. If the intercultural dynamics of the sixteenth and seventeenth centuries must be perceived not through the master-concept of incommensurability but through some theory of interaction, the specter of "acculturation" immediately arises before us. Originating in the 1880s, and given much respectability by Robert Redfield and Melville Herskovits from the mid-1930s to the publication of the latter's influential study in 1938,[49] the idea of acculturation fell into disuse until it was revived in the mid-1970s by French historian and anthropologist Nathan Wachtel, a specialist in the interaction of the Spanish and Inka empires in the Andes. Redfield and others had defined acculturation as "those phenomena which result when groups of individuals having different cultures come into continuous first-hand contact, with subsequent changes in the original cultural patterns of either or both groups." Wachtel was more cautious, pointing out that acculturation could be the result of conquest and imperial domination (as in the Andes), but that groups could also come into "continuous first-hand contact" without any tangible changes being produced. The latter were phenomena of cultural disjunction, as opposed to other situations that he termed integration, assimilation, or syncretism.[50]

The trends of more recent decades have seen a move away from this vocabulary, and instead other key concepts have been proposed such as *mestizaje* (or *métissage*) and "hybridity." At the forefront of those championing *mestizaje* is French historian Serge Gruzinski, a specialist of colonial Mexico, whose work has most recently focused on the imperial Spanish Habsburgs. In contrast, the champions of hybridity draw their examples almost exclusively from the history of the British Empire; moreover, they insist that hybridity should only refer to "the creation of new transcultural forms within the contact zone produced by colonization," which then rules out other, noncolonial forms of contact and interaction as well as their products.[51] No substantive aspect of the interaction between the Portuguese and the Mughals can be dealt with using this vocabulary; indeed, it would seem to rule out most of the history of the sixteenth- and seventeenth-century world outside the Americas from its ambit. Others will want to raise more fundamental objections. Does the concept of "transcultural" escape from any of the problems that dogged "acculturation"? Are we not in the same position of reified cultures, with a "third zone" or a "contact zone" between them, something like Immanuel Wallerstein's unhappy subterfuge of the "semi-periphery," in order to deny that his model was one of binary core-periphery interaction?

It should be noted that we are not the only ones who have considered these problems; they were faced head-on by thinkers during the period under examination. The Jesuit Luís Fróis, for example, in 1585 wrote about them in his *Tratado em que se contêm muito sucinta e abreviadamente algumas contradições e diferenças de costumes entre a gente de Europa e esta provincia de Japão* ("Treatise in which most briefly and succinctly is contained some of the contradictions and differences in the customs of the people of Europe and this province of Japan").[52] Fróis begins by noting that one should not confound the Japanese who live around the Portuguese in Kyushu with the Japanese in general: for "though one may find amongst them some things that may make the Japanese appear like us," it is in fact not so; this is an artificial effect, "acquired through the commerce that they have with the Portuguese." The reality, in fact, is that "many of their customs are so remote, far away and distant from ours that it seems almost incredible that there could be so stark an opposition with people of such culture *(polícia)*, liveliness of spirit and natural knowledge as they have." The point then is neither to divide civilized Europeans from savage Japanese, nor a subjugated people from a conquering one. Instead, Fróis goes about systematically—indeed chapter by chapter and point by point—contrasting what is done in Europe with what is done in Japan. By the end of his fourteen chapters, he has discussed men and women and their apparel; children and their habits; monks and temples; eating and drinking; arms and warfare; horses; medicine and doctors; books and writing; houses, gardens, and fruits; boats and boat-building; plays and music; and with a last chapter on diverse things.

However, Fróis does not say much about an aspect of intercultural (or interpolity) interaction that has of late been the subject of much discussion, namely, visual representation. He thus does not comment on Japanese representations of their own society or of Europeans, or indeed the visual projection in this context of what has been termed *la pensée métisse*.[53] Yet it does not take a great deal of reading to gather that—in spite of what Fróis thought was a vast gulf separating Japanese and Europeans—much interaction did take place. Jurgis Elisonas has written eloquently and persuasively of these changes in the following terms: "The withered and dreamy ideals of medieval aesthetics gave way to an exuberant and forceful spirit. New forms of expression came to dominate in the pictorial, performing, and musical arts, and were introduced into that peculiarly Japanese ritual, the tea ceremony. European traders and Catholic missionaries contributed further novelty to the varied genre scene of Japan. The [sixteenth] century witnessed a dazzling burst of cultural creativity, crowned by the Momoyama epoch, which chroniclers exalted as a golden age."[54]

So the twain could meet, even if only for a time. But we are now increasingly aware that even after the expulsion of the Portuguese, Japan did not close. European influences came to be felt there in various visual fields—as indeed did those from Korea and China. As Ronald Toby reminded us several decades ago, the idea of *sakoku,* the closed country, was not to be taken as literally as the panegyrists of Commodore Perry projected.[55] Elsewhere in Asia and in the Americas, the interimperial sphere produced important innovations. Safavid artists from the mid-sixteenth century influenced key changes in visual representation in both the Deccan and the Mughal courts. In turn, the Mughals in the late sixteenth and seventeenth centuries drew upon elements that were furnished to them by their ostensible adversaries, the Habsburgs, to produce surprising works of art. By the middle years of the seventeenth century, this had been overlaid with the influence of Dutch naturalism, which some have discerned in Mughal masterworks such as the *Pādshāh Nāma,* produced in Shahjahan's reign. In turn, as we shall see presently, Mughal paintings went back to Amsterdam to influence not merely Rembrandt but other painters. This return flow from Asia to Europe certainly repays closer study, and it could also take us well into the eighteenth century.

We are well aware of who some of the agents—the go-betweens or *passeurs*—in the matter were. They include such men as the Venetian Nicolò Manuzzi, who lived in the Mughal domains and farther south for nearly sixty years until his death in about 1720, who never returned to Europe; he ardently projected a European identity but did not always manage to carry it off convincingly.[56] Men like him, and the artists they patronized, did not live between empires, in the interstices so beloved of some recent theorists. Rather, they lived across them, appearing sometimes as subjects of one political power or empire, sometimes of another. But it may be rash to conclude that such characters represent the norm. It is probable that they were statistical outliers; one may even pose them as "anomalies" in the sense that micro-historians have taken to using the term.[57] One may draw upon these historians' ideas that such anomalies are not simply curiosities but enable us to draw some general conclusions as well, in this case on the very possibility of commensurability and also its limits.

Recent work on the Iberian empires of the sixteenth and seventeenth centuries is useful in this context. There have been concerted attempts to look at how visual art forms in such diverse places as Mexico, Brazil, India, the Philippines, China, and Japan changed over the period from about 1550 to 1650 in response to the peculiar conjuncture created by the existence of an Iberian world empire.[58] It can thus be demonstrated clearly that radically new content entered into certain sorts of paintings, woodcuts, and so on, and also that formal innovations took place. In other words, when the art of the Mughal Empire encountered the art of the Portuguese Empire, they did not turn their backs on each other. Each was affected by the other, even if the effects in question were neither symmetric nor continuous. In some instances, as with the Mughal painting from the *Pādshāh Nāma* of the capture of Hughli in 1632 or that of Orchha, a European element (here, the representation of a town) is lifted bodily and transported into a Mughal representation.[59] In other instances, the move is far smoother, as with the incorporation of the halo into representations of the Mughal emperor from the early seventeenth century, or the comfortable incorporation into a Mughal framework of other Christian and secular themes taken from woodcuts and imported objects.[60] In a similar vein, we can see shifts, improvisations, or what some might term traces of *métissage* in paintings produced in Mexico and colonial Brazil. Some of these works were clearly produced in imperial contexts that qualified as "the colonization of the imaginary," rather than in interimperial contexts of a certain equilibrium and balance, as with the Ottoman painters who drew upon a palette that was made possible by their encounter with the Habsburgs.

Time and again we are forced to come to terms with situations that do not represent mutual indifference, a turning of backs, or deep-rooted incomprehension, but rather show shifting vocabularies and changes wrought over time by improvisations that eventually themselves become part of a received tradition.[61] These may be compared in turn to the processes described by historians of science such as Peter Galison that occur in the "trading zones" between scientific subcultures; at a far more general level, they can be thought to approximate a positive intercultural hermeneutics based on deploying concepts such as prejudgments.[62]

Our conclusions in this introductory chapter thus lead us rather close to the views expressed by the philosopher Ian Hacking in a well-known essay entitled "Was There Ever a Radical Mistranslation?"[63] To be sure, it is by no means certain that "radical incommensurability" (or, in Hacking's case, radical mistranslation, which he terms "malostension") never occurred when states and empires encountered one another in the early modern period. However, just as in the cases Hacking investigates, the "amusing fables"—the basis of most claims concerning incommensurability—turn out to be false on closer examination. States and empires were very rarely ships that passed in the night of incommensurability, and every new set of monographic research on the sixteenth and seventeenth centuries makes the hypotheses of yesteryear on the relationship between semiosis and conquest appear less likely. Rather, what usually happened was approximation, improvisation, and eventually a shift in the relative positions of all concerned. The British, once they had conquered India, did not remain—even a single generation afterward—the same British who had conquered it. A Portuguese writer on Vijayanagara in the 1550s cannot simply be confounded with a writer in 1505. Rather, when states and empires—and more particularly their courtly strata—met in historical encounters, there was always learning by doing, even if not a perfect "reciprocity of understanding" in the manner of Diderot. Only an utter devotion to structuralist forms of history and structuralist understandings of culture—and a corresponding neglect of diachronic processes— would force us to regard this as an unnatural or even an unusual outcome. In fact, there were many bridges that led from one culture to another.[64]

At the same time, it is of little use to pose this as a question of compatibility based on a prior congruence. Rather, commensurability had to be made by agents, and bridges between cultures had to be built rather than naturally existing in a state of nature. In equal measure, it is essential to avoid another trap that still besets many historians of early modern encounters: attributing all the initiative in matters of bridge-building to European agents alone. It is still not uncommon to come across works where European travelers (and they alone) naturally comprehend all they see, where Europeans alone are the custodians of all forms of "cosmopolitanism," and where the purpose of analyzing encounters proves to be simply to confirm a picture of the European cultural and intellectual *Sonderweg*.[65] This is usually based in turn on a deeply asymmetrical knowledge of the source materials of the period. Translations, in reality, are always a two-way process. Only an impoverished history will seek to ignore this fact.

In the chapters that follow, we will return to these themes of exchange and intercultural translation using some more obvious and some more improbable (and even frankly paradoxical) examples. The first of these chapters concerns sixteenth-century India and the dealings in the Deccan among a series of states that had been formed between the fourteenth and the sixteenth centuries. These states, which included the sultanates of Ahmadnagar, Bijapur, and Gol-konda, and the more southerly empire of Vijayanagara, had all emerged out of a long historical process that stretched back to the creation of the Delhi Sultanate around 1200. Successive waves of the Delhi Sultanate's expansion had taken it into the southern reaches of the peninsula, even as far as Madurai (where the sultanate of Ma'bar emerged for a time in the fourteenth century). Eventually, an extended bout of political and military conflict led to the creation by the early fifteenth century of rival courtly centers in the Deccan, which were caught in a complex political and diplomatic equilib-rium.[66] The area stretching between the Tungabhadra and Godavari rivers came to host an imposing series of fortified towns that served as the capitals and provincial administrative centers of these polities: Vijayanagara, Kalyana, Gulbarga, Firuzabad, Bidar, Golkonda, Bija-pur, Ahmadnagar, and so on. Chapter 1 is devoted to the conversa-tions, exchanges, and conflicts that took place in the sixteenth cen-tury between the rival centers in this "shatter zone" (as it has been picturesquely termed). It draws upon materials in Persian (as these were highly Persianized polities by the fifteenth century), in the ver-nacular languages of the region, and in Portuguese, for the Portu-guese had arrived and installed themselves on the coasts around 1500, capturing Goa in 1510.

Chapter 2 then takes us to the western part of the Malay world, where once again the Portuguese came to be present from the early decades of the sixteenth century. Their capture of the great port city of Melaka in 1511, which they considerably fortified, once again led to an exacerbated conflict between rival polities. The former sultan of Melaka moved to a series of other towns farther south, and eventually he came to settle in Johor. Yet it was not his state so much as it was a series of other maritime powers—some from as far as northern Java—that challenged the Portuguese frontally. The most significant of these was the sultanate of Aceh in northern Sumatra, which emerged by the middle decades of the sixteenth century as a formidable center of both Islam and trade.[67] Aceh was linked to Gujarat as well as the Red Sea and the Ottoman Empire, and to the east its links extended well beyond Java to Sulawesi and Maluku. The court of the sultans of Aceh attracted numerous traders, warriors, and intellectuals from the west; eventually the court drew on its links not only with the Ottomans and the Hadramaut but also with the Mughal Empire, which had emerged into prominence from the 1570s in the Indian Ocean arena. In turn, this growing prominence of Aceh as a center led to a complex relationship with the Portuguese center of Melaka, which—while never as important to the *Estado da Índia* as Goa— was always perceived as a significant node of power in the Southeast Asian world. These exchanges, once again characterized by a curious and complex mixture of commerce, diplomacy, and violence, thus extend the story eastward from our initial Deccani example.

The third of our examples moves us forward chronologically well into the seventeenth century. It concerns the dealings of the Mughal Empire, which had emerged in fits and starts between the 1520s and 1570s, with a series of other actors in a wider Eurasian space. Here, our focus will largely be on cultural exchanges that were visual in character, that involved the circulation of artists, books, and images across a wide sphere ranging from the Netherlands, Iberia, and Italy to Delhi, Agra, and the Deccan (into which the Mughals expanded in the mid-seventeenth century). The sphere of representation, as well as image making, will be at the center of the analysis here. While less directly conflict-ridden than the two earlier examples, we will note that forms of symbolic dispute were not entirely absent in this case either.

By exploring these three case studies (as well as a number of minor examples that will be mentioned in passing), our intention is to give greater depth to the broad themes set out in this introduction: diplomacy, warfare, and visual representations. To be sure, as a work derived from a discrete set of lectures, it cannot be the ambition of this book to give a comprehensive account of the encounters between courtly cultures in the early modern world (or even the more limited space of Eurasia). Rather, by engaging closely with a diverse set of primary materials, this work continues the conversation between different (and often strangely separated) historiographies, and thus contributes to the growing body of connected histories of the early modern world.

1

Courtly Insults

Why have Brahmins to worship you,
when Sayyids can do it better?
Why have *śāstra*-learned Brahmins to praise you,
when Maulavis can do that better?
Why have *bhaktas* sing for you,
when there are *fakīrs* who shout louder?
Why have pure and principled Brahmins,
when you're surrounded by *pīrzādas*?
We are being thrown out, but cling on to the eaves,
while you've already started looking west.
Quick to kill your enemies,
Man-Lion of the Lion-Hill.

—Gogulapati Kurmanatha Kavi,
Simhādri-Narasimha-śatakamu (ca. 1755)

Kurmanatha Kavi, a Niyogi Brahmin and poet from the temple town of Simhachalam, was clearly annoyed at his god, the man-lion form of Vishnu, Narasimha. He had sensed that, unlike in the good old days when Brahmins enjoyed the favor of both kings and gods, now it was the Muslim "from the west" *(pāschātyulu)* who had the upper hand. The proximate provocation for this taunting verse—insulting the god while simultaneously praising him as *Vairi-hara-ramha simhādri Narasimha*, "Quick to kill your enemies, Man-Lion of the Lion-Hill"—appears to have been as follows. In 1753, the Hyderabad ruler or Nizam, Asaf-ud-Daula Salabat Jang, had been obliged in straitened circumstances to hand over the Simhachalam region to French revenue farmers. However, their entry into the area was resisted by Ja'far 'Ali Khan, the entrenched *faujdār* at Srikakulam, who in turn brought in Raghoji Bhonsle and other Maratha warlords to aid him. A set of skirmishes thus opposed the French and their ally, Raja Vijayarama Gajapati, against this mixed force, which also attacked and plundered the Simhachalam temple and its surrounding villages. Kurmanatha Kavi was later to claim that matters might have been worse still if he had not managed to summon up a miracle: the god eventually sent a swarm of bronze bees, which began stinging the invaders viciously and drove them all the way to the coast.[1]

Familiarity breeds contempt, so runs the somewhat cynical proverb. Moreover, a certain degree of familiarity is the precondition of the deliberate and well-placed insult (as distinct from an inadvertent one) that unerringly attains its target—whether leveled at a man or a god. Once largely the domain of the anthropologist and linguist, the history of insults has possibly fared better in past decades than the history of battles,[2] yet battles and insults are often more closely related than one would suspect. It is widely agreed that a great and deeply significant battle took place in south-central India, or the Deccan, in the latter half of January 1565 C.E., late in the lunar Hijri month of Jumada II 972. But no one seems able to agree on much more than that. Where this battle took place and what its exact date or dates were continue to exercise historians. We can more or less concur on the principal protagonists, but not on their motivations. The battle set the forces of the Vijayanagara (or Karnataka) Empire, which was ruled over officially by its third (or Tuluva) dynasty but controlled in reality by a clan of Telugu warriors—the Aravidu or Araviti clan originally from Palnad—against the forces of four sultanates of varying dimensions: Ahmadnagar and Bijapur to the west, tiny Bidar in the center, and Golkonda to the east.[3] Contrary to what is sometimes claimed, the forces of a fifth sultanate, that of Berar farther north, did not actually take part in the engagement. The action proper possibly did not last more than a few hours. At its end, the chief Aravidu warlord Aliya Rama Raya had been killed, as had at least one of his younger brothers. In its aftermath, the armies of the sultanates marched south to the great city of Vijayanagara and occupied it for a time. However, they eventually withdrew, and for a time the territorial losses of Vijayanagara remained limited. Between 1570 and the 1630s, the rulers of the polity—now officially in the hands of members of the Aravidu clan such as Venkatapatideva Raya (r. 1586–1614)—continued to manage a reduced enterprise, first from a center in the hilltop fort of Penukonda, then in Chandragiri and Velur even farther to the southeast. Eventually, in the later 1630s and 1640s, further campaigns mounted by the sultanates of Bijapur and Golkonda swept away most of the remnants of this kingdom, leaving only a titular monarch of the Aravidu family. In turn, these sultanates were themselves conquered a mere half-century later.

Still, the battle of 1565—like its predecessor some four decades earlier at Panipat—occupies a place of importance in popular histories, school texts in India, serialized television productions on Indian history, and even the works of visiting travel writers.[4] It could quite plausibly be included in any list of subcontinental *lieux de mémoire*, but at a conceptual rather than literal level, as there are at least three rivals for its location: Talikota (the best known but least plausible), Rakshasa-Tagdi (in fact, Rakkasgi-Tangadgi), and Bannihatti. Two of these lie north of the Krishna River: Talikota is located farthest north, on the banks of the tributary Don River, and Rakkasgi and Tangadgi are two distinctly separated villages on the north bank of the Krishna. Bannihatti lies farthest south, at the confluence of the small Maski River and the even smaller Hukeri rivulet (just northwest of Mudenur).

From this viewpoint, it is tempting to compare the battle of 1565 with another legendary battle that took place a mere thirteen years later, on August 4, 1578 (30 Jumada I, A.H. 986), in the Larache region of Morocco.[5] In this instance, the date is clear, as are the protagonists, but much else remains shrouded in mystery. The proximate circumstances involved two rival claimants for power in the region: Sultan 'Abd al-Malik al-Sa'di and his nephew, the former sultan Abu 'Abdullah al-Sa'di. The latter, after having been expelled by his uncle (who had Ottoman aid), appealed directly for help to the Portuguese court, which had had interests and ambitions in the region since the fifteenth century. The young king Dom Sebastião decided on an unusual step, namely, to personally lead an expeditionary force involving a large number of Portuguese noblemen. For several generations, none of his ancestors had entered the field of battle, and many advised him strongly against it. In the battle and its immediate aftermath, all three royal protagonists perished, but Dom Sebastião's death was not an agreed-upon fact: his body never was found, and this became the source of the various "Sebastianist" movements that would follow.

So the "Battle of the Three Kings," as it is sometimes known, has remained deeply contested territory in its own fashion.[6] Termed the battle of Wadi al-Makhazin (Oued el-Makhazen) in the Maghreb, it is known as Alcácer-Quibir (from al-Qasr al-Kabir) to the Portuguese. It is seen as a triumph against European ambitions by a part of Moroccan historiography, but as a national tragedy in conservative Portuguese historiography, since it eventually led in 1580–81 to the incorporation of Portugal into the Habsburg monarchy for six decades. In a classic manner then, rival nationalisms have produced not merely competing memories but competing historical interpretations. One man's national triumph is inevitably another's historical tragedy.

Similarly, melodramatic emplotments of and exegeses on our Deccan battle of 1565 have not been lacking. We may take a relatively recent instance, written in the 1970s, by the best-known historian of the Golkonda Sultanate:

The year 972/1564–65 may be regarded as one of the most important in the history of South India, if not in the history of the
whole country. It was the first time after the downfall of the Bahmanī kingdom that its successor states sheathed their swords
which they had been continuously sharpening against one another, and not merely entered into treaties but actually sealed
them by matrimonial alliances between their ruling families.[7]

We may distinguish here between the notion of rival understandings
of the causes and consequences of the battle, and the concept of radically distinct readings of even its significance. When and why did
this battle emerge into such significance, so much so that the history
of South India is often simply divided into two phases, before and
after "the fall of Vijayanagara (1565)"? There is a natural tendency to
lay the blame at the door of the English civil servant and amateur
historian Robert Sewell, because he is the author of perhaps the most
influential work on Vijayanagara, entitled A *Forgotten Empire*.[8] First
published in 1900, this work has remained in print ever since and
still lies at the center of standard narratives regarding Vijayanagara—
despite several generations of other works with epigraphy and narrative texts since its publication.[9] Sewell was certainly well acquainted
with the South Indian epigraphy of his day, but the novelty of his
work lay in his use of two sets of contemporary Portuguese materials:
the writings of Domingo Paes and Fernão Nunes from the early
1520s and early 1530s, and an early seventeenth narrative by Jesuit
Manuel Barradas.[10] The first two narratives (which had been acci-
dentally discovered and published in 1897 by David Lopes) allowed
Sewell to construct a vision of a "golden age" for both the royal capital and its larger military-political system; the latter account (already
better known, and mostly concerned with succession struggles in the
1610s) he used to set out a picture of the Vijayanagara polity in an
enfeebled state.

Sewell's view of the historical role of Vijayanagara is unambiguous enough. He thus commenced his work with the following words, before developing his thesis of Vijayanagara as "a Hindu bulwark against Muhammadan conquest":

In the year 1336 A.D., during the reign of Edward III of England, there occurred in India an event which almost instantaneously changed the political condition of the entire south. With that date the volume of ancient history in that tract closes and the modern begins. It is the epoch of transition from the Old to the New. This event was the foundation of the city and kingdom of Vijayanagar.[11]

Over the next half-century, a variety of scholars with differing viewpoints attempted to flesh out the picture produced by Sewell, while also casting their net wider for materials. Part of this production became a regional rivalry in the 1930s, between those wishing to assimilate Vijayanagara into the history of the Telugu-speaking region, and those who saw it as more closely associated with the Kannada-speaking areas. Of the former group, the most prominent historian was probably Nelatur Venkataramanayya, whose *Studies in the Third Dynasty of Vijayanagara* is an important attempt to describe the political and fiscal structure of sixteenth-century Vijayanagara rule, undoubtedly drawing inspiration from the work of K. A. Nilakantha Sastri on the earlier Chola dynasty.[12] His main thrust was to produce a systematic listing of the appropriate fiscal and administrative categories in operation, from the imperial treasury down to the level of the individual village, with the temporal focus on the rule of the "third" (or Tuluva dynasty). A far more ambitious work, based largely on Kannada materials, was B. A. Saletore's two-volume thesis *Social and Political Life in the Vijayanagara Empire (A.D. 1346– A.D. 1646)*, which covered a longer temporal sweep, from the time of the polity's foundation to the time of the Golkonda and Bijapur expansion to the south. Finally, a third attempt from the same generation at understanding Vijayanagara (but with a focus on the sixteenth and early seventeenth centuries) was that of Barcelona-born Jesuit Henry (Enric) Heras. After an initial phase of work on the Indus Valley and its script, Heras went on in the 1920s to make use of his command of Portuguese, Spanish, Italian, and Latin sources to put out a lengthy, somewhat turgid work entitled *The Aravidu Dynasty of Vijayanagara.*[13]

Few of these writers contested the fundamental significance of 1565. They merely differed on almost all the details, as well as on the relative reliability of the sources to be used. The matter was further exacerbated in the 1940s with the massive three-volume publication by Venkataramanayya and Nilakantha Sastri entitled *Further Sources of Vijayanagara History.*[14] These volumes included a general narrative, excerpts from a large number of sources, and a volume of translations. By the 1950s, various camps had thus emerged: those who followed Heras (and before him Sewell) in giving central importance to the European (and particularly Portuguese) narrative materials; those who showed a distinct preference for Sanskrit and vernacular materials of the type placed at the heart of *Further Sources* (in opposition to the Persian chronicles of the Deccan); and those who, in turn, defended the primacy of the Persian chronicles, particularly from the point of view of the history of the sultanates and their interactions with Vijayanagara. The arguments followed familiar lines that we can list: the prejudices, or lack thereof, of one or the other religious group in reporting events; the question of chronological proximity to the events reported; and the issue of whether the Sanskrit and vernacular sources were in fact merely "literary" as opposed to genuinely "historical."

But did it all begin with Sewell? There is considerable evidence that Sewell merely drew on a far older British tradition of historiography regarding South India, and that even the idea that the crucial battle of 1565 was fought at Talikota had entered the historiography as a stable notion long before his work. We may consider a brief work entitled *An Historical and Political View of the Decan*, published in 1791 by Jonathan Scott, who had served Warren Hastings as his interpreter. Scott's intention was to evaluate the rule and resources of Mysore's Tipu Sultan, who at that time was locked in an ongoing rivalry with the East India Company. Scott began his text by noting that "until the middle of the sixteenth century, it [the Deccan] formed one great undivided empire called, from its capital on the Tumhbudra, Bejanagur, and sometimes improperly, by travelers, that of Narsinga." He then went on rapidly to sketch the end of Vijayanagara in the following terms:

> It is to be observed also, that about the period now mentioned, the descendants of five Mussulman princes, who had usurped the dominion of their respective governments north of the Kistnah, under the Bamineah [Bahmani] Mahomedan kingdom of Beder, still held in participation that portion of the Decan. . . . Stimulated by the ambition of conquest, and the intolerant spirit of their religion, they waged perpetual war in confederacy, against Ramraje the Hindoo monarch of Bejanagur, who at length was slain in a pitched battle near Tellecottah on the banks of the Kistnah, A.D. 1565.

Scott goes on to describe the emergence of the Nayaka dynasties from the "feeble remains of the Canarine empire," and the eventual conquests in the 1650s by Mustafa Khan and Mir Jumla of the whole region. But the key narrative elements are in place here: the unity of Vijayanagara and its rule over "the two Indian nations of Malabar and Canara"; the illegitimate character of the Deccan sultans; their religious bigotry leading to "perpetual war"; and the dramatic closure provided by Talikota in 1565.[15]

Scott's views in these and other writings in turn had a substantial impact on Colin Mackenzie, as we can see from the latter's extended essay on "the principal political events that occurred in the Carnatic, from the dissolution of the Ancient Hindoo Government in 1564 till the Mogul Government was established in 1687," presented by him to the Asiatic Society in Calcutta in April 1815 but only published decades after his death.[16] Mackenzie, as surveyor and antiquarian, had already "minutely examined" what he termed the "remains of Beejanuggur" at Hampi in December 1800, and by 1815 had a section in his collection of manuscript materials entitled "Memoirs for the History of the Beejanuggur Government of the Carnatic." These included a text that he called the *Rāmarāya charitra*, which he stated contained "the Hindoo account of this memorable battle . . . [and] enters into details descriptive of Hindoo manners, but differing much from the Mahomedan authors in regard to circumstances in the war and battle." Mackenzie is less clear in his narrative regarding the "overthrow of the last Hindoo government of the Carnatic, commonly called the Raia-Samastanum [*rāya-samasthānam*] of Beejanuggur" than Scott, contenting himself with referring to "the celebrated battle with the confederate Moslem princes near the banks of the Kistna," and adding that in the battle "Ram Raaz, and almost all the whole of the ancient nobility fell, the country around the capital was laid waste, and the remains of the great families being dispersed, the city speedily fell into decay."[17]

Scott's views also find echoes in another author of the time, Mark Wilks, who from his base in Mysore sought to construct a history of South India using some of his own materials as well as notes and texts supplied to him by Mackenzie. Wilks for his part suggested that "the early disunion of the Mohammedans of the Deckan gave farther facilities to the growth of the power of Vijeyanuggur," but that this led to hubris on the part of the rulers of that empire. "The success which resulted from the weakness of the enemies of Vijeyanuggur was, in the ordinary course of human arrogance, attributed to its own invincible strength; and the efforts which were made for the extension of its dominions to the north, forced the divided states of

the Deckan into the confederacy which accelerated its fall." Wilks's reasoning here was more complex than that of Scott, and he also noted that there had been a series of "usurpations" in Vijayanagara itself. He concluded:

> But at length, in 1564, the confederacy to which we have ad-
> verted, of the four Mussulman kings of Dowlatabad, Vijeyapoor,
> Golconda and Beder, defeated the Hindoo army on the plains of
> Tellicota, between the Kistna and Toombuddra, in a great battle
> in which Ram Raja the seventh prince of the house of Narsinga,
> and almost all of his principal officers fell. The victors marched
> in triumph to the capital; which they plundered with the most
> shocking circumstances of cruelty and excess.[18]

By the 1810s, despite the divergences, we can see the solidification of a broad narrative tradition among colonial historians. But a little investigation shows that its roots lie not in Scott's brief opuscule published in 1791 but in a far more extensive work. This was his commented translation of a Persian work from the early seventeenth century, the *Tārīkh* or *Gulshan-i Ibrāhīmī* of Muhammad Qasim Hindushah "Firishta." This work had been identified early on by British savants as a key text because it contained a relatively comprehensive account of a variety of regional as well as pan-Indian dynasties. Alexander Dow had first attempted a translation in 1768, which knew some success, including a further translation into German. Scott's own version in 1794, which claimed to better Dow, appeared also in two volumes, and it is a key source for writers in the 1800s and 1810s.[19] To be sure, these writers—including Scott himself—intended to use Firishta not merely as a neutral chronicler but as a witness to and spokesman for Muslim intolerance and bigotry.

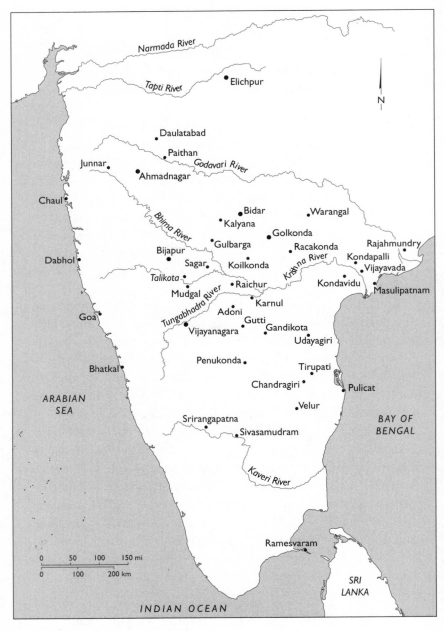

Map 1. The Deccan around 1565.

The Persian Chronicle

Many, if not all, roads lead us to Firishta and his chronicle. If it is not the most cited Indo-Persian text of the sixteenth and seventeenth centuries, it is surely among the top handful, along with the *Āʾīn-i Akbarī* written by Firishta's contemporary Shaikh Abu'l Fazl (in turn a part of his larger work, the *Akbar Nāma*). The phase in which these texts were written, from 1580 to 1610, is indeed the golden age, if ever there were one, of the Indo-Persian chronicle in terms of sheer density and variety of production. Moreover, many of these texts were written in cognizance of, and even in reaction to, the existence of others; Firishta was certainly a reader of Nizam-ud-Din Ahmad Bakhshi's *Tabaqāt-i Akbarshāhī*, for example.[20] Our knowledge of this prolific chronicler is limited, and it is largely taken from his own chronicle, but even so our understanding is not lacking in nuance.[21]

Born in Astarabad in about 1550, Firishta appears to have migrated to the Deccan not long after with his father, Maulana Ghulam ʿAli Hindushah. It is unclear how his father, one of a wave of elite Iranian immigrants to the Deccan, initially occupied himself, but eventually he seems in the 1570s to have become the preceptor of one of the Nizam Shahi princes. His son, Muhammad Qasim, despite a marked inclination for letters, opted for a military career. He became a member—even an important one—of the royal guard of Murtaza Nizam Shah (r. 1565–88). Toward the end of the reign of this sultan, matters became complicated not only in terms of dynastic politics but in the ethnic politics that opposed the "foreigners" from West Asia to the natives of the Deccan, as well as in sectarian religious politics. Muhammad Qasim was thus eventually obliged in the late 1580s to leave Ahmadnagar for the more southerly state of Bijapur, where he was for a time under the protection of a powerful patron, Dilawar Khan Habshi. It was here that his literary talents blossomed.

In around 1594, Muhammad Qasim was brought to the attention of Sultan Ibrahim 'Adil Shah by one of his Iranian compatriots at court, 'Inayat Khan Shirazi. The sultan suggested Muhammad Qasim attempt to write a general history of India on the model of the celebrated late fifteenth-century text of Mirkhwand, *Rauzat al-Safā'*, while pointing to the lack of chronological and geographical balance in Nizam-ud-Din Ahmad's recent work. Incapable of challenging the Mughals in terms of their military might, the sultan seems to have chosen instead to rival parts of their cultural production.[22] Muhammad Qasim took over a decade to complete his text, drawing both on personal experience and a royal library that we know was quite rich in its collections. This text—eventually known by several names, including the *Gulshan-i Ibrāhīmī*, in honor of its patron—was first completed and presented at court in 1606. About four years later, Muhammad Qasim, known by his nom de plume of "Firishta," made a second redaction, and he continued to tinker with the text until 1623, which is often taken to be the year of his death.

Firishta effectively produced a formidable text, made up of twelve *maqālas*, an introduction, a conclusion, and a section of biographies of Muslim holy men. The central parts are divided both chronologically and geographically, and they vary a great deal in terms of their dependence on other recognizable chronicles. He lists over thirty such sources in his introductory section, but he cites at least as many more in various parts of his text. We can see from a comparison of some of these sources with Firishta's text that he was a rather faithful summarizer of received wisdom, but a fair number of the original texts he used are lost to us, leaving his work as their sole trace. These lost works include a good many chronicles of the history of the Deccan under the Bahmani rulers of the fourteenth and fifteenth centuries.

One can thus see why Firishta's text would have attracted from its inception a great deal of attention. Scores of complete and partial manuscript copies were made of the work beginning in the seventeenth century, and abridged versions of it also came to exist by about 1700.[23] This manuscript production continued in the eighteenth century, and this accounts for the dozens of manuscripts that exist in the British Library alone. The first copy that entered a European collection was probably that acquired in the 1750s by Anquetil Duperron during his travels in India, which appears to be from the late seventeenth century. The next decade produced Dow's abridged translation into English, which in turn became the object of considerable controversy: it was read by Edward Gibbon, Edmund Burke, Robert Orme, and Samuel Johnson, but some of these authors— notably Johnson—denounced the text itself as fraudulent, finding it difficult to believe that an "oriental" author could have produced such a work around 1600.[24] To be sure, Dow's style of loose translation and self-indulgent paraphrase was partly responsible for this suspicion, and Johnson clearly did not understand that he was reading an abridgment; his conclusive and damning evidence against Firishta was his failure to mention the Portuguese, whereas they do feature (albeit in a somewhat minor role) in his text.

The central section of the chronicle for our purposes is the third *maqāla*, which deals first with the Bahmanis, and then with the five sultanates of the Deccan: the 'Adil Shahs of Bijapur, the Nizam Shahs of Ahmadnagar, the Qutb Shahs of Golkonda, the 'Imad Shahs of Berar, and the Barid Shahs of Bidar. It succeeds the section on Delhi (ending with the Timurids or Mughals) and precedes that on the Gujarat sultans. At a rough estimate, this single *maqāla* occupies about 40 percent of the entire text, not unreasonable perhaps in view of its author's own subjective positioning. Firishta, we may note in passing, had traveled somewhat in his lifetime but not a great deal. In 1604, he accompanied the Bijapur mission north to Burhanpur to bring a princess-bride to the Mughal prince Daniyal; in 1606, he was sent by Ibrahim 'Adil Shah to Jahangir at Lahore; and also, at an undetermined date, he seems to have visited Badakhshan.[25] These travels may have helped him gather a better sense of the Mughal chronicling world, and they also appear to have had an impact on his writings on Kashmir in his own chronicle. This massive chronicle seems, then, to have consumed much of his time from the mid-1590s, and we know of only one other work he penned, a treatise on medicine entitled *Ikhtiyārāt-i Qāsimī* or *Dastūr al-atibbā'*, in which he does mention his conversations with Indian physicians.

The bulk of modern references to Firishta's work naturally concern the Deccan, a subject on which he certainly tells us more than most of his Mughal contemporaries. There is little doubt that he is the prime source on the wars of the Deccan in the sixteenth century, and by default he also becomes a major source on the history of Vijayanagara itself. His manner of organizing his text by sultanate is inconvenient because it means he often returns to the same events twice, once in the context of the 'Adil Shahs and again in the history of the Nizam Shahs. This is certainly true of his account of the military events of 1564–65 (A.H. 972), to which we now turn before placing them in the larger context of Firishta's narrative strategy.[26]

The first extended passage in which he addresses this matter is in the section on the reign of Sultan 'Ali 'Adil Shah of Bijapur. Firishta's chronicle notes that Sultan 'Ali in the early years of his reign was inclined to alliances with the ruler of Vijayanagara in order to make territorial gains against the Nizam Shahs of Ahmadnagar. However, this strategy eventually led to a dangerous expansion of Vijayanagara power. Firishta continues:

> Ramraj [Rama Raya] continuing to encroach on the dominions of the Muslims, 'Ali 'Adil Shah resolved to curb his insolence and reduce his power by a league of the faithful against him; for which purpose he convened an assembly of his friends and confidential advisers. Kishwar Khan Lari and Shah Abu Turab Shirazi, whose abilities had often been experienced, represented that the King's desire to humble the pride of the Ray of Bijanagar was undoubtedly meritorious and highly politic, but could never be effected unless by the union of all the Muslim kings of

the Deccan, as the revenues of Ramraj, collected from sixty seaports and numerous flourishing cities and districts, amounted to an immense sum; which enabled him to maintain a force, against which no single king of the Muslims could hope to contend with the smallest prospect of success.[27]

The requisite diplomatic contacts thus apparently began, with a first envoy sent from Bijapur to the court of Ibrahim Qutb Shah in Golkonda. The latter was apparently enthusiastic about the idea of an alliance, and he sent Mustafa Khan Ardistani (to whom we shall return at some length later)—who is described as "the most intelligent nobleman of his court"—first to Bijapur and then to Ahmadnagar. Mustafa Khan's presentation to Husain Nizam Shah is summed up by Firishta as harkening back to the days of unity under the Bahmani sultans, and also using the rhetoric of the need to protect Muslims from "the oppressions of unbelievers." The Nizam Shah responded positively, offering his daughter Chand Bibi in marriage to 'Ali 'Adil Shah with the fortress of Sholapur as her dowry, and receiving 'Ali's sister Hadiya Sultana as the bride of his son Murtaza. This double marriage alliance was apparently negotiated on the one hand by Mustafa Khan, and on the other by a certain Mulla 'Inayatullah from Ahmadnagar. Once these marriages had been formalized, the Bijapur ruler sent an envoy to Vijayanagara to ask Rama Raya to give him the fortresses of Yadgir, Bagalkot, Raichur, and Mudgal or face the consequences. Firishta notes that "Ramraj, as was expected, expelled the ambassador with disgrace from his court."

The chronicler now takes us through the essential narrative. The armies of Husain Nizam Shah, 'Ali 'Adil Shah, and Ibrahim Qutb Shah were then joined by 'Ali Barid Shah on "the plains of Bijapur" and set out southward on December 26, 1564 (20 Jumada I, A.H. 972). Arriving at Talikota (the sole mention in the text of the place), they then camped on the northern bank of the Krishna River, while receiving regular supplies from various Bijapur provincial governors.

Rama Raya, for his part, is reported to have first sent his youngest brother Erra Timma (or Tirumala) Raya out with 20,000 cavalry, 500 elephants, and 100,000 foot soldiers, and then his other brother Venkatadri with another similar force. He himself brought up the rear with a third contingent, and these armies then occupied the southern bank of the Krishna, blocking off "all the known ferries and fords" and constructing fortifications that were "strengthened with cannon and fireworks."

Frustrated by this situation, the sultans conceived of the plan of marching along the river in the hope that the Vijayanagara forces would follow them on the opposite bank to block their passage. After marching for three days, they suddenly reversed course at night and returned to the original ford, which they found deserted; the sultan-ates' armies then "crossed the river without opposition" and were able to advance on the south side of the Krishna to the close proximity of Rama Raya's camp.[28]

The Vijayanagara forces fell back and consolidated in three segments. The center was held by Rama Raya against the Nizam Shahi forces; to his right was Timma Raya, who faced the Qutb Shahi and Barid Shahi armies; and to his left was Venkatadri, faced by 'Ali 'Adil Shah and his forces. Rather than ride on horseback, Rama Raya is depicted as being carried initially on a royal sedan chair (or *sing-hāsan*), and then on a red throne "set with jewels, under a canopy of crimson velvet."

Firishta suggests that when the battle began after midday, the Vijayanagara right and left wings were making considerable inroads, to the point that 'Ali 'Adil Shah and Ibrahim Qutb Shah "began to despair of victory and even to prepare for retreat." At this point, however, the Vijayanagara center unexpectedly broke in the face of a concerted Nizam Shahi assault. The chronicler writes:

> The assault by Husain Nizam Shah caused great difficulties to Ramraj's army. Ramraj, who was an old man of eighty years,

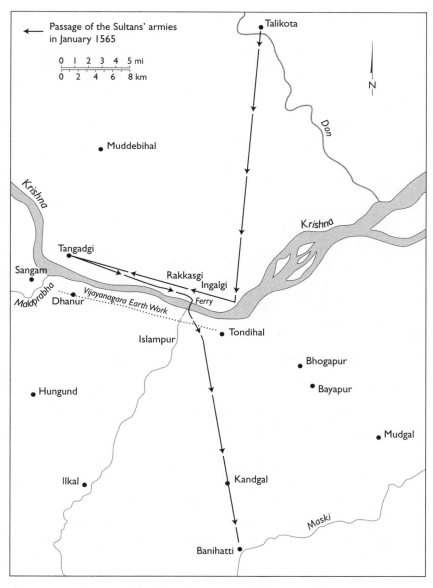

Map 2. The battle of January 1565.

gathered his courage and once more mounted his *singhāsan*.
At this time, an elephant belonging to Husain Nizam Shah
named Ghulam ʿAli approached the *singhāsan*, and attacked
the people around it. Those who were carrying the sedan-chair
were so terrified that they threw Ramraj on the ground and ran
away. Ramraj lay helpless on the battlefield for some instants,
until the glance of the mahout *(fīlbān)* fell on the sedan-chair.
Since he had never seen such an exquisite object, he approached
it and advanced his elephant to seize hold of the chair. A Brahmin was standing there, who was an old servant of Ramraj. He
pleaded with the mahout, saying that it was Ramraj who had
been seated on the sedan-chair. If the mahout brought him a
horse, the king would surely cover him with awards and honors.
As soon as the mahout heard the name of the king, his heart
leapt. He at once seized the king with his elephant's trunk, and
carried him as fast as possible to the chief of Husain Nizam
Shah's artillery, Rumi Khan. Rumi Khan seized hold of Ramraj and brought him into Husain Nizam Shah's presence. The
Nizam Shah at once had the king killed, and had his head separated from his body and thrown on the battlefield.[29]

We also learn that when the head was displayed on the point of a
spear, the Vijayanagara army fled in confusion, and that over 100,000
of them lost their lives in the process. Firishta's own father, Ghulam
ʿAli Astarabadi, apparently composed a chronogram on the occasion:
Nihāyat khūb wāqiʿ gasht qatl-i Rāmrāj ("What an excellent event the
killing of Ramraj was!").

Firishta returns to the battle many pages later in his account of
the reign of Husain Nizam Shah at Ahmadnagar. His account here at
times complements the earlier one in his own chronicle, but at times
also somewhat contradicts it. We learn here that the four sultans, having decided to "crush the rising power of Ramraj," united their armies
and marched south until "they crossed the Krishna and encamped

on the Hukeri river, situated twelve miles from the former." This places the action distinctly south of the Krishna (as indeed does the other passage), and it clearly eliminates both Talikota and Rakkasgi-Tangadgi as possible areas where the engagement might have occurred. Indeed, it seems likely that these sites—on the northern bank of the Krishna—would have been the places where the sultans' armies initially camped, and from which they marched before fording the river. The chronicler adds that Rama Raya, for his part, advanced with an army of 70,000 cavalry and 90,000 infantry, but adds that they were "chiefly matchlockmen, besides archers and artillery-men." He further claims that the size of this army already shook the confidence of the sultans, who "made overtures to him, promising him the restitution of the districts that they had taken from him on the march." But it was Rama Raya who "refused to listen to any accommodation," and instead prepared resolutely for battle.

The Vijayanagara formation is set out in somewhat greater detail: to the left, Venkatadri with 25,000 horse, 500 elephants, and 200,000 foot soldiers opposing 'Ali 'Adil Shah; at the center, Rama Raya himself with 15,000 "chosen auxiliaries" (meaning cavalry), 1,000 elephants, and 500,000 men on foot opposing Husain Nizam Shah; and to the right, Timma Raya with 20,000 horse, 500 elephants, and 200,000 men on foot, facing the Qutb Shahi and Barid Shahi forces. In this manner, according to Firishta, the entire Vijayanagara force now consists of 60,000 horse, 900,000 foot soldiers, and 2,000 elephants, an army of such overwhelming numbers that "the Muslim kings, despairing of coming to any terms with the enemy, resolved to fight desperately."

Their Shi'i religious affiliations are more heavily emphasized here, for it is noted that they "erected twelve standards in honor of the twelve Imams before proceeding to attack." In contrast, it is suggested that Rama Raya took the matter rather lightly, such that he "directed his soldiers to endeavor to take the 'Adil Shah and Qutb Shah prisoners, in order that he might keep them in iron cages during the rest of their lives." His hatred was particularly directed at the Ahmadnagar Sultan: "he directed his own column, if possible, to bring him the head of Husain Nizam Shah."

Firishta's description of the engagement now follows a very different logic, one in which the key role was played by the Ahmadnagar artillery, commanded by the same Rumi Khan who had apparently served in the European wars of the Ottomans. This artillery was made up, the chronicler claims, of some 600 field pieces, which were set out in three rows: first and closest to the enemy, the heavy guns; then the smaller guns (or *zarb-zan*); and finally the swivel guns (called *zambūrak*).[30] This emplacement was, however, concealed behind a force of elite archers, against whom Rama Raya's forces confidently advanced. At the crucial moment, the archers gave way, and the heavy guns then opened up, leading to "confusion with dreadful loss" on the Vijayanagara side. A second Vijayanagara charge then followed after an effort at regrouping, and this time Rumi Khan is stated to have again fired his guns, causing a great deal of carnage.[31] In the resulting chaos, a Bijapur commander named Kishwar Khan Lari (whom we encountered earlier) led a devastating cavalry charge into the central Vijayanagara ranks. Firishta now rehashes the account of the attack by the elephant Ghulam 'Ali while modifying some minor details. As before, Ramraj is carried before Husain Nizam Shah and beheaded by that monarch's order, prompting Ramraj's army to flee toward Vijayanagara.[32]

Leaving aside larger issues of the cause of the battle (to which we may naturally return later), we can see a set of interesting distinctions between these two narrative sequences in the same chronicle. The Bijapur version points to the tactical errors that permitted the sultans to cross the Krishna, and also suggests that Rama Raya was foolish to use the *singhāsan* "in spite of the remonstrances of his officers who wished him to be on horseback, as much safer." Ultimately, credit comes here to Husain Nizam Shah, who remained firm when his allies wavered. This is despite the fact that Firishta is not particularly well disposed toward this particular ruler, whose death soon after the battle in May 1565 (while still in his mid-twenties) Firishta bluntly attributes to "a disorder brought on by excess." The Ahmadnagar version, on the other hand, shifts the focus to a technological disparity between the Ahmadnagar army (and its Ottoman expert) and a Vijayanagara force; though the latter seems to have possessed its own artillery and matchlockmen, it did not know how to deploy them effectively.

We might say that, here, Rama Raya is a relatively early South Asian victim of the "military revolution."[33] But Firishta's methods as a historian are unclear to us in this instance, unlike elsewhere where he closely followed an earlier textual source. After all, these events took place during his own lifetime in the Deccan, and he was certainly acquainted with veterans of the battle, both in Ahmadnagar and in Bijapur. Perhaps it was in using these disparate accounts that he came to entangle himself in a few contradictions, though there is a clear and stable core to both his narratives, especially the ultimate episode regarding the elephant.

The chronicler is also clear enough regarding the consequences of the battle for Vijayanagara.

The kings themselves, shortly after the battle, marched onwards into the country of Ramraj, as far as Anegondi; and the advanced troops penetrated to Bijanagar, which they plundered, razed the chief buildings to the ground, and committed every species of excess. When the allies had destroyed all the country around, Venkatadri, who escaped from the battle to a distant fortress, sent humble entreaties to the kings, to whom he agreed to restore all the places which his brother had wrested from them; and the victors being satisfied, took leave of each other at Raichur, and returned to their respective dominions. The kingdom of Bijanagar since this battle has never recovered its ancient splendour; the city itself was so destroyed, that it is now totally in ruins and uninhabited; while the country has been seized on by the tributary chiefs, each of whom has assumed an independent power in his own district.

For Firishta, there is little doubt regarding the decisive significance of the battle, even if the Vijayanagara rulers as protagonists do not disappear entirely from his chronicle thereafter. He continues to note their relatively feeble activities in areas such as Penukonda and Chandragiri, but also makes it clear that Vijayanagara power in regard to the west coast and its ports had declined substantially, enabling the Bijapur armies progressively to expand to the southwest and capture fortified centers and towns such as Torgal, Dharwad, Bankapur, Harihar, and Chandragutti.[34] A major role in this whole process is attributed to Mustafa Khan Ardistani, the able diplomat from Golkonda, who had by now moved to Bijapur and enjoyed a high position as *wakīl* and *peshwa*.

The Portuguese View

To be sure, we could compare Firishta's views to those of other Indo-Persian chroniclers of his time, such as 'Ali bin 'Azizullah Tabataba, who also have informative comments to make on the battle of 1565 and its context. It turns out, however, that we can find material from a rather different source, which both confirms and at times nuances key aspects of Firishta's account. These are the official archives and chronicles of the Portuguese *Estado da Índia*, which not only had its headquarters in nearby Goa but also possessed a fortress in the port town of Chaul and enjoyed extended dealings with both Bijapur and Vijayanagara. From the very early years of the sixteenth century, Portuguese traders and priests had visited Vijayanagara, and—as we have already noted—left detailed narratives from the 1510s to the 1530s regarding both the empire in general and its capital in particular.[35] The Portuguese were very familiar with the rise to prominence of

Rama Raya and the Aravidu family in the 1540s. In February 1548, the Portuguese envoy to Vijayanagara, Tristão de Paiva, even sent letters to the governor Dom João de Castro detailing his conversations with Rama Raya and his brothers. In his first missive, Paiva mentions not only these discussions but a field review in which Aravidu Tirumala showed him the artillery and fireworks (*a artelharia emcarretada e muitas carretas de bombas de foguo*) that his army could manipulate. A second letter followed regarding their joint plans to place an exiled prince from Bijapur on the throne in place of Sultan Ibrahim 'Adil Shah. This conversation took place in two parts: first, a private talk where Rama Raya had Paiva sit so close to him that "my knees touched his"; second, a discussion involving Aravidu Venkatadri and Dilawar Khan Habshi, a powerful Muslim courtier.[36] Relations were not to remain so cordial in the next decade on account of bitter disputes in 1559 between Rama Raya and the Portuguese settlers at São Tomé de Meliapor on the east coast.[37]

In the early 1560s, the administration at Goa was wary of Vijayanagara, though it still saw a certain commonality of commercial interests. Pepper from the Kanara region, under broad Vijayanagara domination, was beginning to flow in quantity to their rivals in the Red Sea, but the Portuguese thought that they might find a way to divert this flow into their own warehouses. The turn that political events took in 1564 no doubt surprised them. Thus, the incoming governor Dom Antão de Noronha, writing to Lisbon on December 30 of that year, stated the following:

This Idalcão ['Adil Khan] and the Izamaluco [Nizam-ul-Mulk], who in these past years were mortal enemies and made war, in which the Idalcão did a great deal of damage to the Izamaluco, are now friends and allies by means of marriages that they arranged with each other: the Idalcão who is a youth and not very old married a daughter of the Izamaluco, and the oldest son of the Izamaluco married a sister of the Idallcão; and they agreed to this peace between themselves on the condition that they should unite and join together in a single body—and the Verido [Barid Shah] and the Cotamaluco [Qutb-ul-Mulk], two other lords, also joined with them—against the Rajos of Bisnaguá [Rayas of Vijayanagara] who are gentiles. And I have been told that they have resolved to make this peace and this war, and that they joined together in one body, on account of the persuasion of Xatamás [Shah Tahmasp] king of Persia, who through his ambassador and his letters persuaded them to make peace, and reproached them for the fact that despite being such great lords and so powerful, they suffered the presence of gentiles so very close to them, who had no religion (não tinhão ley) and adored the devil, and who were lords with so much land and as great a state as the Rajos are, and that it was a sign of their [the sultans'] weakness not to destroy them and extend the law of Mafamede throughout that gentility. And with this determination, they have all made themselves ready and have placed all their men in the field, and the Rajos too in the same manner to defend themselves from them; and some say that even if they have allied, as they have done on other occasions, the Rajos will be free of them by giving them money; while it seems to others that it will nevertheless end up in a battle, and that there will be a clash between them, given the power and determination with which the Moors have entered into this.[38]

We find direct confirmation here of the marriage alliances mentioned by Firishta and their role in sealing a compact between Ahmadnagar and Bijapur. But a significant idea is that this alliance was in fact promoted by the Safavid ruler, Shah Tahmasp, by means of both envoys and correspondence. Could this have been a mere reflection of Portuguese paranoia of that time, as they were always nervous of large coalitions emerging against them across the width of the Indian Ocean? A subsequent passage in Noronha's letter is helpful in this respect:

It has also been affirmed to me that these Moors have a constant activity of ambassadors in their courts, who continually move and importune them against us, who are Ceides [Sayyids] and relatives of Mafamede, to whom they give much credit for the oppression that they recount is done in this city and in the other fortresses of Your Highness when Moorish merchants come there and pass with their goods, [alleging that] we seize their slaves and make them Christians, especially the Abyssinians who—even if they have no desire to convert—are seized from them, which is something that they resent very deeply, and on this account they tell these kings that they are obliged to make war on us and mobilize their states to this end. And I learnt that this winter [monsoon], the Idalcão and the Izamaluco, who is a very evil Moor and very much our enemy, after making an alliance and friendship, each sent an ambassador to Itimeticão [I'timad Khan], who has the king of Cambaia [Gujarat] under his power and seal, and to Chimgriscão [Chingiz Khan], another lord in Surrate and Barroche, to move them to make war on us and lay siege to Dio and Damão, for he [the Nizam Shah] would attack Baçaim and Chaul, and Idalcão this city [Goa], and in this manner they would place us in dire straits. . . . And it is said that it is the language of these Moors of the Idalcão and Izamaluco, that once they have finished with the Rajos, they will settle scores with us, but be that as it may, they will also receive great losses in doing so, even if they are richer than us and can suffer the losses better.[39]

Who then could these Sayyid ambassadors have been? Was this a reference, for example, to the venerable and influential figure of Shah Tahir Husaini, who had spent a quarter century in the Deccan before dying there in the late 1540s?[40] The dates make this unlikely. Rather, it is important to know that Mustafa Khan, before he held that title, was himself Sayyid Kamal-ud-Din Husain Ardistani.[41] Further, not only did he act as an important political player in Golkonda, then as a go-between in dealings that linked Golkonda, Bijapur, and Ahmadnagar in 1564–65, and finally as a major courtier and general in Bijapur, he also maintained correspondence from the Deccan with Shah Tahmasp. In an important letter to the Safavid ruler from the Deccan, for example, he expresses his continued allegiance to him and also his great regret at his long absence from the Iranian court (dargāh).[42] In another undated letter—this one probably from Shah Tahmasp to 'Ali 'Adil Shah, dating to the early 1570s—we learn that Mustafa Khan had been an "old servant of the Safavids," who still had much concern for his welfare. It is further noted in the same letter that he wrote frequently to the Shahs. Now, after long service in the Deccan, he wished to return to Iran, but it is remarked that the 'Adil Shah has not granted him leave. The Iranian ruler argues that, with the recent victorious end of the war against the Frankish kāfirs (no doubt referring to the war at Chaul in 1570–71), he should be allowed to return home to Iran.[43] We know that nothing came of this request, and that Mustafa Khan eventually died at the hands of assassins in the Bijapur Sultanate in 1580.[44]

Thus, given that the Portuguese could be remarkably well-informed about the politics of their neighbors, it comes as something of a disappointment that their archives for the year 1565—the year of our battle itself—are so sparse. A rare letter, this one from the Portuguese settlers at Chaul to the queen, makes a laconic reference to how "Our Lord has castigated the Inizamaluquo [Husain Nizam Shah] with death," but makes no mention of the wars he has been engaged in.[45] So we must await a somewhat casual mention in December 1566, in a letter from Dom Antão de Noronha to the king, in which he discusses his attempts to regularize supplies of pepper through Kanara (and the hinterland of the port of Bhatkal), using the services of a certain Álvaro Mendes. Noronha writes:

He [Mendes] is leaving in this very ship, since the greater part of its cargo is pepper, and since the service that Your Highness ordered that he should occupy himself this year now cannot take effect, in sending him to Bisnaguá [Vijayanagara] to engage in a contract for the pepper with the Rajo, for Bisnaguá is all destroyed and defeated on account of the victory that the Ydalcão and the Izamaluco had against the Rajos, in which the princes [who were] two brothers died, and the one who survived is hated and a tyrant, and is very insecure in his kingdom. And as the Idalcão is so powerful and he is so weak, he cannot defend himself against him save with a great amount of money that he gives him and other services that he renders. Since the Rajo is in this state, all the lords of this coast, who were his vassals, have rebelled against him and do not pay the vassalage *(páreas)* and tributes that had been imposed on them, on account of which one can no longer deal with the Rajo regarding the pepper, but instead buy them from those [lords] who have them in their lands, as was done through these contracts last year and this one.[46]

Within two years, the same governor would see these very rebellions as an opportunity, going on to seize the Kanara port of Mangalore, after which his successor would attack and seize Basrur and Honawar farther up the coast. These operations in 1568–69 naturally led to the view that the Portuguese were cynical in their use of the battle of 1565 and its outcome.[47]

But this does some injustice to the complexity of the Portuguese response. Against the pragmatism of their governors and viceroys, we must weigh the more complex view set out by their own chroniclers and historians. For the official chronicler Diogo do Couto (1542–1616), in his major text the *Décadas da Ásia*, did indeed provide an account of the battle and interpreted its real meaning for his readers. This, too, is a view that we can usefully set side by side with that of Firishta. Couto's account of the battle is entitled "How the kings of the Deccan conspired against that of Bisnaga, and the power with which they went to seek him out, and of the battle in which they engaged with him, in which they defeated and killed him."[48] It is certainly more economical than the account of the Indo-Persian chronicler, and also places the emphasis elsewhere. It begins by reminding readers of the immense power that Vijayanagara represented.

In many parts of my *Décadas* I have written on how the kings of Bisnaga or Canara were lords of all the kingdoms that lie between the Indus and the Ganges (*intra Indum et Gangem*); whose power and riches were unimaginable things, and of how after the Moors conquered the kingdoms of the Deccan there were always great wars between them, and even in the past year of [15]63, when the Conde do Redondo was viceroy, the king of Bisnaga, Rama Rajo, entered the kingdoms of the Nizamoxa and destroyed and devastated them, and carried great riches away from them; which so afflicted that king that he invited the [other] Moorish kings of the Deccan, the Idalxa ['Adil Shah], Cutibuxa [Qutb Shah], and Verido [Barid Shah] so that they could all set out together against Rama Rajo, and destroy him, and divide his kingdoms amongst them. And for this alliance to be more secure (if there is such a thing as security amongst Moors), the Nizamoxa proposed to have kinship relations with all of them, as he did by giving the Idalxa one of his daughters with a great dowry and the city of Salapor [Sholapur] which he had taken, and to the Cutibuxa he gave another, and he himself married a daughter or sister of the Idalxa, all of which marriages were celebrated with great festivities, and on those [occasions] they swore a League against Rama Rajo.

The account so far is quite accurate, down to the detail regarding Sholapur, even if it considerably exaggerates the total domination the Vijayanagara rulers had once had over all of India. Here, unlike in Firishta's narrative, the initiative for the alliance comes from the Nizam Shahs rather than the 'Adil Shahs, as they have been the principal sufferers from Vijayanagara aggression. Couto now notes the trajectory toward the battle.

He [Rama Raya] had news of this, and got together all his power and all his vassals, and with great speed set out onto the field with his two brothers Vengate Rajo [Venkata Raya] his field captain-general, and Ultima Raje [Erra Timma Raya], his financial intendant. And some Portuguese who were present at this battle told me that this barbarian had 100,000 horsemen and more then 500,000 men on foot, with so great a number of servants, buffaloes, oxen, and elephants that they could not be counted, and that the kings of the League also set off with 50,000 horses, 300,000 men on foot, and some field-pieces, as well as a great amount of baggage. Both parties sought the others out until [the frontiers] of their kingdoms, and one day when Rama Rajo was dining with his brothers, he received news that the enemies' camp had appeared less than two leagues from where they were. At which, he left everything, and leapt on a beautiful horse, and began to set his own camp in order to give battle to the enemies. His brothers and some of the grandees surrounded him and asked him to withdraw with a few men to the city of Bisnaga which was strong, and that they would remain to give battle to the enemies, who, were they to know that he was in that city, were bound to think that he had another larger force with him than that which was there, and on this account might withdraw from fear. The king who was ninety-six years old but had the brio of someone who was thirty, for he was a great cavalier, replied to them that if they wanted they could withdraw and bring up their children; but that he was the king and was bound to do his duty which was to lead his vassals and defend them, and encourage them, running the same risks as they did. They were abashed at this, and said to him that they would all die before him in the defense of his person.

The numbers and figures cited here are very large, but of the same orders of magnitude as those of Firishta with the exception of Rama Raya's age, which is here posed as ninety-six rather than a mere eighty (as in Firishta). We further note that the sultans' combined armies are represented as being far smaller than the Vijayanagara force. A matter of some interest is Couto's claim of eyewitnesses in the form of "some Portuguese who were present at this battle," presumably (but not necessarily) on the Vijayanagara side. Further, a tone of both chivalry, and foolhardy risk-taking has been established in this passage. The Portuguese chronicler continues:

> The king had sent out as an advance party a captain of the royal blood with 12,000 soldiers of the Rajo caste, who are called *rachebidas*, who are of the king's personal guard as the janissaries are of the Turk, in order to scout out the [enemy] camp; when they came into sight of the enemies and their frontline, they were already so placed that they could not turn around without great losses, and so they entered into a formidable battle with them. News of this reached the king, who at once sent his brother Vengate Raje to support them, and he with the rest of the army followed in his train. The brother reached the battlefield, where things were highly inflamed, and entering into its middle encountered the enemies who were forcing back the *rachebidas*, and he fought most valorously with them. And he entered so deeply in their midst that they captured him; here Iltima Raje and his son Rogante Raje [Raghunatha Raya] came to help, and charged at the enemy with such force that they held them back, and even made them yield a good part of the field. And even though he and the son accomplished chivalrous

deeds, the whole weight of the League pressed on them and they were both wounded, and so many of the *rachabidas* were killed that only 1,500 of them were left, for they bore the brunt of the battle. This news reached the king, who pulled out of the position where he was with all his forces, and coming to the battlefield *(lugar da batalha)*, and crying out three times "Goinda" [Govinda], which is their idol in battles there, as we cry out *Santiago*, and caught up in that fury, came up on the vanguard of the conspirators which was led by the Idalxa with 12,000 horse. And at the first assault, he broke him and defeated him and followed him for the space of a half-league in which he killed over two thousand enemies. The *rachabidas*, when they saw their king at their frontline, and in peril, got off their horses and remaining on foot carried out a great massacre of the enemies.

This is a far less orderly battle scene than that in Firishta, where there is a reference to a near classical battle formation, with contingents and their major leaders facing one another almost as in the *Mahābhārata*. Rather, what we have here is a chaotic sequence; an advance party is caught up in a skirmish, and Aravidu Venkatadri rushes to their aid and is captured, forcing Timma Raya onto the scene. Eventually, Rama Raya himself is obliged to intervene by attacking the Bijapur forces. Couto adds two characteristic touches here. One is his use of the term "Govinda" (a name for Krishna), in order to show his familiarity with Indian battle practices; the other is his borrowing of the Telugu term *rāchabidda*, meaning "sons of royalty."

The battle now winds to its climax.

The Inizamoxa, seeing this defeat, rallied his army, and returned with some field-pieces, and found the king of Bisnaga engaged in battle with the Idalxa; and [he] fired the pieces of artillery, at the thunder of which the enemy horses, which were not accustomed to it (for the Rajos did not have artillery), were at once defeated and ran out-of-control, without their owners being able to master them. The poor old man Rama Rajo, in that predicament, found himself captive in the hands of Zamaluco, who was the greatest enemy he had; who, on seeing him, without any respect for his age or majesty, cut off his head with his own hand, saying: "Now that I have avenged myself of you, let God do what he wants of me." The Idalxa had at once had news of his [Rama Raya's] capture, and he arrived with great speed to free him, for he was so much his friend that he called him his father (and I do not know if the sons of these Moors have any greater enemies than their fathers, who kill and blind them each day), and he already found him headless, which weighed on him in the extreme.

Here, we again find an interesting set of intersections with the narrative of Firishta. The Nizam Shahi artillery is credited with the victory, though Couto goes so far as to claim that "the Rajos did not have artillery." Here, too, it is Husain Nizam Shah who is shown to be responsible for the killing of Rama Raya, albeit with his own hand rather than merely ordering it done. Finally, there is the curious matter of the fictive kinship relations between Rama Raya and ʿAli ʿAdil Shah ("he called him his father"), a subject to which we shall return. It remains for Couto then to recount the immediate aftermath of the battle, and its disastrous impact.

With his [Rama Raya's] death, everyone else was routed, and those of the league allowed themselves to rest for three days at the scene of the battle, during which time the sons of Rajos, who were nephews of the dead king, entered the city of Bisnaga, and with great haste carried away 1,350 elephants laden with jewels, precious stones, coins, gold and silver, and trappings, in short everything of worth which they say was valued at well over a hundred million in gold, not to mention the royal throne which they also took which, so it is said, is priceless in terms of its jewels. And with all they went through the hinterland, and took refuge in the pagoda of Tremel [Tirumalai] which is atop an impregnable hill ten leagues from the city of Bisnaga; and even after they had fled with these treasures, the city of Bisnaga which had been abandoned was attacked by the peasants of the villages around it, and they sacked it six times and carried away such enormous riches that I marveled at what I was told. All of which was lost to the kings of the League since they did not immediately follow up in their victory, just as happened to Hannibal who on account of the same negligence was unable to become master of the Roman Empire and of the entire world. After three days were over, the allied kings went to the city of Bisnager to scrabble for whatever was left, and even so some of them became rich on that account; in which [process] they spent five days, at the end of which they retired very rich from the spoils of the army which was enormous; and even today, the Idalxa has a diamond which men who have seen it declare is the size of a hen's egg, which the Rajo had on the headstall of his horse, and another lesser one as a button at the end of its neck-tassels, and still others that he and the others carried off which were of great worth. And the nephews of the dead king, and the brother who escaped divided the kingdoms amongst themselves, and they are still today in the possession of their heirs.

Finally, Couto notes that this was no small matter for the Portuguese either, who implicitly had a major investment in the continued prosperity of both the city and the polity.

From the defeat of the king of Bisnaga the *Estado da Índia* and its inhabitants suffered a great loss, because the greatest and most profitable trade that the inhabitants of Goa had was that with this kingdom, because in it were consumed horses, velvets, brocades, and other merchandise in return for which they brought back precious stones, very fine cloths, and other things in which process the money and the gold pagodas were doubled [in value], so that there came into Goa more than two million in gold to be employed in the ships to Portugal *(nas naos do Reyno)* and in China goods.[49]

Here, he echoes the judgment of the great Florentine humanist Filippo Sassetti, who in a letter written from India in 1586 noted that one of the main causes of the decline of Goa in his time was "the destruction of the city of Bisnagar, seat of the king of all this land of India . . . which was larger than Cairo according to Moors who have seen the one and the other."[50]

However, it is also important to note that neither Couto nor Firishta mention another sort of speculation about the battle that already had begun to circulate in the 1570s. The first author to mention these rumors is the Venetian merchant Cesare Federici, who spent seven months in Vijayanagara in the late 1560s, at a time when Aravidu Tirumala (or Timma) Raya was attempting—as it happened, unsuccessfully—to reestablish the city as a commercial hub. Federici saw Tirumala as a tyrant and a cheat, and he referred to him and his siblings as "three tyrannical brothers, who had kept the real king in prison, bringing him out once a year to show him to the people." Here is his brief account of the battle:

The city of Bezeneger was put to the sack in the year 1565 by four powerful and Moorish kings, who were the Dialcan, the Zamaluc, the Cotamaluc and the Veridi; and it is said that the power of these four Moorish kings was not enough to defeat the king of Bezeneger, who was a gentile, if there had not been treason *(se non vi fosse tradimento)*. Amongst his other captains, this King had two Moorish captains, each of whom commanded 70,000 to 80,000 persons. These two captains (since they were of the same religion) treated with the Moorish kings to betray their own king, and the gentile King, who did not appreciate the force of the enemies decided to come out of his city to engage in deeds of arms against his enemies in the field, which they say did not last more than four hours because the two traitorous captains in the heat of the battle turned their men against their lord and put his camp in such disorder that the gentiles, confused and dismayed, fled.[51]

This narrative, whether derived from Federici or other sources, would eventually become an alternative version (although of relatively minor import) regarding the battle, similar in many respects to accounts of the Ghurid conquest of northern India. A traitor or traitors within has remained a key topos of a certain style of nationalist historiography in India, explaining almost all major political events and in particular military defeats.[52]

Enmity and Intimacy

The Portuguese governor Noronha, we have seen, had a clear thesis regarding what had led to the battle: in ideological terms, it was the hatred on the part of Muslims for gentiles (his equivalent for the Arabo-Persian *kāfir*) "who had no religion and adored the devil," and in diplomatic terms, it was the devious maneuverings of the Safavids behind the scenes. The Portuguese were surely aware, it may be noted, that unlike Ibrahim ʿAdil Shah who had been a Sunni, his son ʿAli ʿAdil Shah had once more embraced Twelver Shiʿism, bringing him closer to the Safavids.[53] Couto, for his part, has no greater explanation beyond the initiative of Husain Nizam Shah to build an alliance after having suffered humiliating losses to Rama Raya; this perhaps accounts for the theme of vengeance at the time of Rama Raya's killing. What of Firishta, and the Indo-Persian chronicling tradition? How do they explain not the outcome of the battle—which, as we have seen, could be accounted for in that set of narratives through tactics, the overwhelming nature of the alliance, Rama Raya's lack of caution, or superior military technology—but its deeper causes? This takes us into less limpid waters—into the manner in which Firishta sees the motors of history in his time.

We have seen that Firishta has had a rather complex reception outside South Asia. The first translations by Dow were met by skepticism, and as a consequence later translators such as Scott and Briggs tended to surround him with a defensive cocoon. Briggs noted that Firishta "seldom indulges in philosophical remarks," and that instead "he has traced the causes of great political events with an accuracy and perspicuity that do him infinite credit; and for fidelity, impartiality, and simplicity, Ferishta is, perhaps, entitled to rank higher than any historian of his country."[54] Concluding the same essay, he then noted that the quality of Firishta was to be "so devoid of fiction, and so free from prejudice" that a British historian could use him with confidence. Reviewing the same work, the French orientalist Jules Mohl focused in particular on Firishta's efficient summary of older texts as well as his capacity to recount the conflict between Muslims and Hindus in the Deccan in a manner that did not always reflect positively on the former. Yet, far more recently, the historian Joan-Pau Rubiés has, by reading Briggs's translation, evaluated Firishta as no more than a relentless advocate of *jihād* and found him in general "extremely unreliable" and characterized by "crude presentations of interactions with the enemy." Rubiés also has written of how, in Firishta, "we find the kings of Vijayanagara playing a stereotyped role which could perhaps be defined as being regularly beaten up by Muslim armies and forced to pay huge ransoms."[55]

In general, it may be useful to divide Firishta's work into three segments: a first set of narratives, where he was able fairly closely to follow a received textual tradition and then summarize it after his own fashion; a second set, where he wrote on matters from his own lifetime and his personal recollections as an adult; and a third, and highly problematic, set, where he had neither a reliable textual basis nor other well-defined means with which to work. It is with respect to the third category that we may compare him, for example, with one of his contemporaries, Sayyid 'Ali bin 'Azizullah Tabataba, author of the *Burhān-i Ma'āsir*, written at the Nizam Shahi court in the late sixteenth century.[56] Because Tabataba also produced a narrative regarding the battle of 1565, this is a useful place to begin a comparison with the version in Firishta's chronicle.

Tabataba's account places the origin of the 1565 battle squarely with Husain Nizam Shah, who decided that it was time to mount a holy war (*ghazā' wa jihād*) against the miscreants in Vijayanagara. The ruler there, pithily termed *Rāmrāj bī ibtihāj* ("Ramraj the joyless"), was both proud and extremely powerful as he possessed a kingdom with sixty ports, extending 600 leagues, and with an enormous revenue. Indeed, the chronicler insists, since the time of the Prophet (*az zamān-i Hazrat Paighambar*), none of the Muslim kingdoms had managed to defeat the Vijayanagara rulers and instead made treaties and accommodations. But Rama Raya for his part "had broken the treaties which he and his predecessors had made with the sovereigns of Islam, and had invaded the territories of Islam and deluged them in blood, and had destroyed the dwellings of Muslims and slain large numbers of them."[57]

In this version, the chief counselors of Husain then advised him of the need for a larger alliance, leading him to approach Ibrahim Qutb Shah. In this chronicle, too, the figure of the Golkonda *amīr* Mustafa Khan now appears in a major role, but largely in order to bring 'Ali 'Adil Shah into the alliance. The marriages between the Bijapur and Ahmadnagar royal houses, with the handing over of Sholapur, is mentioned. Tabataba then tells us that in the following year (that is, A.H. 972) the three sultans and their armies gathered at Sholapur and marched southward. A brief mention is once more made of Talikota on the banks of the Krishna River (*mauza' ke ba Tālīkūta mashhūr wa dar hawāla-i āb-i Kishnā wāqi' ast*), which had yet to be forded. The corresponding movements of the Vijayanagara forces, respectively under Venkatadri, Tirumala, and Rama Raya, are noted, as is their occupation of the southern bank of the river facing the sultans' armies. The next episode, of how the northern armies crossed by subterfuge, once again parallels that of Firishta, save that the entire credit once more goes to the Nizam Shah, who persisted when others advised a retreat. Further, in Tabataba's recounting, Ramraj was now "much perturbed and alarmed," while Husain for his part felt "overjoyed" at the prospect of battle. The Vijayanagara armies were indeed so despondent by this time that they decided "not to fight that day but to make the most of their last day of dominion and power."

By the next day, a Friday by this chronicler's inaccurate reckoning, Rama Raya's spirits had picked up, and he summoned his brothers and other commanders (birādarān wa umarā' wa a'yān) to say that, having reached the age of eighty, "he did not wish to be disgraced by cowardice at the end of his life." He thus is portrayed as foreseeing his own defeat but still determined to go down in full glory. The engagement commenced at noon with a cavalry charge led by an Ahmadnagar amīr, Ikhlas Khan. The Vijayanagara forces now countered this attack, and we learn that both wings of the sultans' armies began to give way, the Qutb Shahis because they were beaten back, and the 'Adil Shahis who ceded ground on account of a secret attachment to Rama Raya, their former ally. But the Nizam Shahi forces stood their central ground, in particular the cavalry under Ikhlas Khan, and the artillery under Rumi Khan, which "kept up a heavy fire on the enemy." Tabataba portrays Husain Nizam Shah then as wholly determined, to the point of conspicuously setting up his great pavilion, or tent of state, to inspire his men to hold firm.

Shortly thereafter, the battle took on a dramatic turn.

In the midst of the engagement, and the heat of the battle, an enormous elephant like the harbinger of death and the terminator of time itself, confronted Ramraj who was wallowing in the dust, and with his spear-like tusks killed his speedy horse. That chief of the accursed people fell from his horse and was now on foot. At the same time, Rumi Khan reached that misguided one with a sizeable and victory-laden force. They wished to remove his wicked and mischievous head from the frame of his torso, for they thought to free the impure body of the beast from its net. At this time, Dalpat Rai, one of the ministers of that faithless and wicked person, appealed to them not to kill him. Rather they should take him to the Hazrat-i Diwan, for he was that unfortunate Ramraj. That leader of the hellish people was tied by the hands and neck and taken to the world's master [Husain Nizam Shah]. When the 'Adil Shah came to know of the capture of that misguided infidel, he set out for the foot of the Caliphate with some companions, to ask for the release of that faithless and damned person. Enlightened opinions however wanted that before the arrival of the 'Adil Shah and his recommendations, the angelic royal heart should contemplate the fate of this wicked infidel, and the face of the earth should be cleansed from the filthy existence of that devilish one. For, if the ['Adil Shah's] recommendation regarding that accursed one was not accepted, then there would be a new sedition and the breaking of agreements; but to release an enemy after having captured him was contrary to the wisdom of the wise people of the world. Therefore, the ruler indicated that that faithless and misguided person be executed before the arrival of the 'Adil Shah. The warriors of the victorious army according to the just king's order separated that tyrant's wicked head from his filthy body and threw it under the hooves of the king's fortunate horse.[58]

Rama Raya's head was now placed on the end of a spear, to be publicly exhibited. The rival army, on seeing this, fled or was put to the sword. The chronicle then notes that the sultans stayed on the battlefield for ten days before proceeding southward to the city of Vijayanagara, where they remained for four months, destroying "infidel temples *(ma'ābid-i kuffār)*" and devastating the country.

While corresponding in some of the broad details with both Firishta and Couto, Tabataba's account also clearly distinguishes itself from them.[59] Rama Raya is the constant object of phrases of abuse, such as "chief of the people of heresy and idolatry *(sardaftar-i arbāb-i shirk wa zalāl)*," stressing the religious orientation of the conflict far beyond its terms in Firishta. To be sure, this is partly the result of the contrast between Tabataba's elaborate style, replete with rhymes and synonyms, and Firishta's far less ornate one, but perhaps style and substance should not be so hastily separated. Further, as might be expected, this chronicler places Ahmadnagar at the center of the action, reducing the other sultans to a minor and even rather dubious role. He notes at the end of the battle that "when the 'Adil Shah and the Qutb Shah became aware of the killing of Ramraj, who was in truth, their support and stay *(fi'l-haqīqat pusht-panāh-i īshān būd)*, they bitterly repented of having entered into the alliance with Husain Nizam Shah." The outcome of the battle, Tabataba makes clear, was really that desired by Husain, and Husain's joy (though cut short by his death) was matched by the other sultans' sorrow *(gham)*.

There is a strong hint here of a deep intimacy between the 'Adil Shah and Qutb Shah on the one hand, and Rama Raya on the other, a relationship that Husain Nizam Shah did not participate in. Tabataba was of course aware that in 1550, when Ibrahim Qutb Shah had assumed the throne in Golkonda, he had done so by returning from Vijayanagara where he had spent an extended period of time as a supplicant and pensioner in the court of Rama Raya.[60] But the relationship apparently went even deeper than that. Though the Aravidu family had occupied a place of some prominence in Vijayanagara politics from the late fifteenth century, it would appear that early in his career Rama Raya had acted as a frontier commander for Quli

Qutb-ul-Mulk in Golkonda, before returning to Vijayanagara and marrying Tirumalamba, the daughter of Krishnadeva Raya.[61]

The move back and forth was not entirely unusual: somewhat later, in the mid-sixteenth century, we have the instance of the formidable warlord Immadi Jagadeva Raya, who, after long years in Golkonda and a base at the fort of Elgandal, fled to Vijayanagara in the mid-1550s and eventually seems to have settled quite far south in Channapatna.[62] In turn, this meant that in 1543, when Quli Qutb-ul-Mulk was killed, his son Ibrahim was able after some wanderings to find a place in Vijayanagara and spend seven of his formative years there; he returned to Golkonda with a marked taste for courtly poetry in Telugu, which demarcates him from the earlier sultans.[63] An anonymous Portuguese text written in about 1580 by an author who knew Golkonda quite well sets the matter out as follows:

> When the Cota Maluco [Qutb-ul-Mulk] was in his pomp, he was killed by his son Xamoxete [Jamshid], from whose pride and avarice his brother Brahemo [Ibrahim] fled to the court of Rama Rajo, king of Bisnaga [Vijayanagara] who was his neighbor, and who welcomed him with honor. When Xamoxete died, his sons were small, and as soon as he died Rama Rajo sent Brahemo with a force and took possession of that kingdom and he killed his nephews, and having become absolute lord he contracted a marriage with a daughter of the Niza Maluco [Nizam-ul-Mulk], which Rama Rajo tried to impede for many reasons that he had, since it seemed to him that the Cota Maluco should not do this on account of the obligation that he owed him. But he [Ibrahim], caring little for that, went to receive his wife at the borders of his kingdom; and when Rama Rajo came to know of this, he sent his captains to besiege the city of Goleconda, the capital of his state, and declared him to be his enemy. The Cota Maluco, wishing to free himself from this siege, had a message sent to

Rama Rajo asking for pardon for the error he had made, and that he should also remember that he thought of him as his father *(o tinha em lugar de pai)*, and that as such he would do what he ordered. When Rama Rajo heard this justification, even though he understood that he [Ibrahim] was making a virtue of necessity, he demanded that as a punishment for the error he had committed and the expenses he had caused, he should give him [Rama Raya] certain elephants, horses, jewels, and other known pieces of great worth which had belonged to his father and brother, ordering his captains that when they had them, they should return.

The reference here is to the campaigns of late 1563, when Vijayanagara forces led by Aravidu Venkatadri, Immadi Jagadeva Raya, 'Ain-ul-mulk Kan'ani, and others had made a sweeping attack on the whole eastern part of the Golkonda Sultanate, as far as Eluru and Rajahmundri. Reduced to dire straits, Ibrahim Qutb Shah had had little option then but to sue for peace, and in negotiations where he was as usual represented by Mustafa Khan, he ceded several fortresses to Rama Raya. Indeed, his nervousness was such that he even ordered considerable strengthening to Golkonda fort itself. Our anonymous author then continues:

The Cota Maluco did [as told] in order to free himself from the travails and peril in which he was, but he was highly aggrieved for they took from him the best pieces that he had. And determined to avenge himself through industry and cleverness, he sent an embassy to Xatamás [Shah Tahmasp] through Mostafa-cam of the caste of Seides, relatives of Mafamede, who at that time was his captain and later that of the Dialcam ['Adil Khan], a Moor well-known [to the Portuguese] in the siege of Goa; and even though the purpose of the embassy was the hatred that remained in him against Rama Rajo, he based it in religion *(fundou-a em religião)*, ordering him to say that as the kings of his sect were continually at war with one another, while they had powerful *cafres* as their neighbors from whom they received great harm, pointing to some instances including what Rama Rajo had done to him, that he [Tahmasp] should order that they should join together and make war on the infidels, particularly Rama Rajo and the Portuguese, from whom the law of Mafamede received the greatest harm. Xatamás thanked him for the gift, and praised him for the zeal he showed for his sect, and send him royal insignia and wrote individual letters to all the other lords, as well as a general mandate to make war on the infidels, for as has been said elsewhere, this is what the name *cafres* means.[64]

This is an interesting overall argument, where intimacy creates indebtedness but royal pride makes it difficult for debts to be paid. Once Ibrahim had returned to Golkonda in 1550 and become "absolute lord *(senhor absoluto)*," he was bound to throw off the Vijayanagara yoke; but, in turn, this would become the start of a causal chain, where religion (or so it is claimed) was a mere excuse to cover a grievance of another sort based on the logic of pride and honor.

And what of 'Ali 'Adil Shah, the main target of Tabataba's suspicion, and who in Couto's words "was so much his [Rama Raya's] friend that he called him his father"? Here, a passage from Firishta's chronicle is interesting for our purposes. He tells us that when Sultan 'Ali came to the throne in 1558 C.E. (A.H. 965), he at once sent ambassadors to both Ahmadnagar and Vijayanagara; the former were met coldly and the latter "with proper honors." The chronicler notes that the 'Adil Shah now saw where his best options lay.

'Ali 'Adil Shah, intent on adding to his dominions, and repairing the losses sustained by his father, entered into a close alliance with Ramraj; and on the occasion of the death of a son of

that Prince, he had the boldness, attended only by one hundred
horse, to go to Bijanagar, to offer his condolence in person on
that melancholy occasion. Ramraj received him with the greatest respect, and the sultan, with the kindest persuasions, prevailed upon him to lay aside his mourning. The wife of Ramraj,
on this occasion, adopted the sultan as her son, and at the end
of three days, which were spent in an exchange of friendly pro-
fessions and presents, 'Ali 'Adil Shah took his leave.[65]

Perhaps to justify the events of 1565, the chronicler adds a final phrase:
"but as Ramraj did not attend him out of the city he was offended,
and treasured up the affront in his mind, though too prudent, for the
present, to evince any sign of displeasure." Once more, we might say,
intimacy brought its own perils.

The Economy of Insults

Though Tabataba's chronicle does from time to time draw on the
insult as a key factor in explaining political events and their logic, the
role that insults play in Firishta's work is really quite striking, something that has been remarked on by historians of the Deccan. A striking early episode is that concerning Muhammad Shah Bahmani
(1357–74), who is depicted as beginning a long and immensely bloody
war against Vijayanagara by means of a gratuitous insult: paying some
visiting musicians from Delhi by giving them a promissory note on
the Vijayanagara treasury (khazāna-i Rāy-i Bījānagar). This results
in skirmishes, then the killing of a Bahmani garrison at Mudgal, and
finally a situation where at the end of years of war together even the
Bahmani Sultan's advisers begin to see the futility of the entire matter,
asking him if "the sultan remembered his promise that in exchange
for 800 Muslims, he would kill 100,000 Hindus, and that the meaning of his oath was not that he should [entirely] put an end to the pride
of the Hindus (takhm-i Hindū)."[66]

These themes of pride, insolence, and the courtly insult surface repeatedly in Firishta's account of the 1540s and 1550s, sometimes carrying a religious flavor and sometimes not. An example of this comes early in his narrative of 'Ali 'Adil Shah's reign, when Firishta notes that 'Ali 'Adil Shah sent a message to Husain Nizam Shah asking him to hand back the fortresses of Kalyani and Sholapur to him; the chronicler notes that the Nizam Shah was so furious that he gave a response contrary to all decency and etiquette, which in turn inflamed the anger of Sultan 'Ali. Not long afterward, the armies of Bijapur and Vijayanagara entered the Nizam Shahi territories. Now it is noted that "the infidels of Bijanagar, who for many years had been waiting for such an opportunity, left no cruelty unpracticed. They insulted the honor of the Muslim women, destroyed the mosques, and did not respect even the sacred Qur'an." The Nizam Shahi forces were forced to retreat, and the city of Ahmadnagar was besieged by a combination of Vijayanagara, Bijapur, and Golkonda forces that all came together against Husain Nizam Shah. Again, Firishta claims that "the Hindus of Bijanagar committed the most outrageous devastations, burning and razing the buildings, putting up their horses in the mosques, and performing their abominable idolatrous worship in the holy places." He then adds a curious passage regarding the problems this presented the 'Adil Shahis.

> The first time that 'Ali 'Adil Shah was troubled by the aggressive intentions of Husain Nizam Shah, he asked for assistance from Ramraj. There was an agreement between 'Ali 'Adil and Ramraj that the Hindus of Bijanagar would not, on account of their old enmity, cause any harm to the [ordinary] Muslims, that the goods and effects of the people would not be seized, and that the honor of the Muslims would not be besmirched. But the Hindus broke that promise, and practised tyrannies on the Muslims of Ahmadnagar, massacred them, stole their goods and possessions, and even defiled their mosques.[67]

The Bijapur sultan was clearly embarrassed by this, all the more so because, in the aftermath of this expedition, Rama Raya allegedly began on a regular basis to mistreat the envoys sent to him by the Deccan sultans, forcing them to stand in his presence and treating them with "utmost contempt and haughtiness." We find an instance of this even in his direct dealings with Husain Nizam Shah, after he had humiliated him militarily in 1561 and imposed a series of conditions on him and his ally Darya 'Imad Shah. The relevant passage from the chronicler runs as follows:

> When 'Imad-ul-Mulk had left, Husain Nizam Shah went to meet Ramraj. At the time of the meeting, Ramraj showed great vanity and loftiness and remained seated, and had Husain Nizam Shah kiss his hand in this manner. Husain Nizam Shah was furious at this improper behavior of Ramraj, and in order to reproach the Raja, he at once, in that very company, called for water and washed his hands. On seeing this, Ramraj was enraged and said in the Kannadi language: "If this man were not my guest, I would instantly cut him to bits with my sword." Thereafter, Ramraj washed his own hands with water.[68]

Here, then, insult was met with counter-insult and then yet another insult, and Firishta makes much of such status jockeying. But rather than seeing it as symbolizing something deeper (such as geo-political rivalry), the chronicler seems to want his readers to understand that this was how royal affairs in the Deccan were conducted.

This chronicler pushed the *topos* of the courtly insult quite far, but we should be clear that he was far from alone in doing so in the Deccani milieu. Even the Portuguese writer Fernão Nunes, writing in the 1530s, makes a point of organizing a part of his narrative around such a theme when describing the combat between Vijayanagara and Bijapur over Raichur in 1520. This includes the triumphant Krishnadevaraya's demand that Isma'il 'Adil Khan should "come and kiss his foot" as part of the peace negotiations; the failure to do so then led to a damaging Vijayanagara attack on the city of Bijapur itself. It has been argued recently that "Nunes's account of the episode respecting Krishna Raya's foot serves to humanize the man,"[69] but we also need to place it within a recurring structure of such episodes in narratives about Vijayanagara and the Deccan sultans.

Indeed, such an insistence on the courtly insult persists even in later vernacular texts. One of these is the Kannada text *Rāmarājana bakhairu* (date uncertain), of which a shorter Marathi version also exists.[70] This complex text retains traces of many of the narrative sequences we have already seen, although it reorganizes them in its own fashion and adds characters and episodes that do not occur in either the Persian or the Portuguese materials. The relevant part of the text deals with the arrival in Vijayanagara of an envoy from 'Ali 'Adil Shah, who bore the title of *mahaldār*. This envoy was received and lodged but was kept waiting by Rama Raya until he sent a petition to him. When the envoy was finally admitted to the *darbār*, things went well at first. But, subsequently, a group of Telugu acrobats appeared in the court, and they were so successful in their tricks that they were rewarded with a herd of pigs. This naturally caused deep offense to the Muslim envoy, who was present and protested; this in turn led to an exchange of insults in open court between him and Rama Raya regarding the relative cleanliness of those who ate pork and those who ate fowl.

Determined to humiliate the envoy, the Vijayanagara chief produced an elaborate mise-en-scène. Large numbers of pigs were confined in a space, and its floor was covered with grains of millet. The next day, a flock of fowl was brought in, and they began to pick at the grain that was by now thoroughly mixed with the pigs' excrement. Rama Raya then brought the *mahaldār* to witness this scene of the fowl consuming grain while "picking them out of the filth of the swine." How clean were those who ate fowl then? he asked sarcastically.

As usual, the minor insult had an enormous consequence. The envoy eventually departed the court furious, and he complained to his master 'Ali 'Adil Shah. The latter refused to act, claiming that he had "attained the status of being called a son of the Narapati [Rama Raya]" and hence had to be loyal to him. This eventually led the envoy to seek help elsewhere, creating the multistate alliance that brought Vijayanagara down (which, in this version, also implicates the Mughals). However, 'Ali 'Adil Shah is shown throughout as playing a reluctant role in all this. When Rama Raya eventually is captured, he turns on the battlefield to the 'Adil Shah, preferring to be killed by him—his adoptive son of sorts—rather than by others. This is accomplished in this Kannada text by a cannonball, or in its Marathi equivalent with a sword.[71]

Such a text cannot be situated in the same temporal or generic context as the work of Tabataba or even possibly Firishta, as both chronicles place themselves squarely in the Indo-Persian tradition of *tārīkh*. The matter grows more complicated when we turn to another important and neglected work that deals with the battle, written in the Deccani vernacular by Hasan Shauqi. This is a text that tears apart all the neat textual classifications normally used in analyzing relations between the Deccani sultanates and Vijayanagara: although the text was produced in Ahmadnagar, it belongs to the category of *masnawī* (narrative poem) rather than *tārīkh* (prose history). Further, it was written not in Persian but in Dakhni, a lively vernacular that was emerging at the time in the region (to be assimilated later into Urdu) (see table).

The work in question is the *Fath Nāma-i Nizām Shāh* ("Account of the Nizam Shah's Victory"), and its author, Hasan Shauqi, remains quite obscure. He appears to have been active in the later sixteenth and early seventeenth centuries, and he is briefly mentioned by some other poets from the mid-seventeenth century as their predecessor. Like other Deccani intellectuals of the time, he moved between courts; though he spent the first part of his career in

Primary sources for the events of 1564–65

Text	Author	Date	Genre	Language
Gulshan-i Ibrāhīmī or *Tārīkh-i Firishta*	Muhammad Qasim "Firishta"	Ca. 1610, revised until 1623	*Tārīkh*, or chronicle	Persian
Burhān-i Maʾāsir	Sayyid ʿAli bin ʿAbdullah Tabataba	Ca. 1590	*Tārīkh*, or chronicle	Persian
Da Àsia, Década Oitava	Diogo do Couto	Ca. 1600	Chronicle	Portuguese
Fath-Nāma-i Nizām Shāh	Hasan Shauqi	1560s or later	*Masnawī*, or narrative poem	Dakhni
Taʾrīf-i Husain Shāh	Aftabi	1560s or later	*Masnawī*, or narrative poem	Persian
Primor e Honra	Anonymous	1580/1630	Secularized hagiography	Portuguese
Viaggi	Cesare de Federici	Late 1560s	Travel account	Italian
Lettere	Filippo Sassetti	1580s	Epistolography	Italian
Letters from 1564–66	D. Antão de Noronha	1564–66	Viceregal correspondence	Portuguese
Rāmarājana bakhairu	Anonymous	Post 1670	*Bakhar*	Kannada, with later Marathi version

Ahmadnagar, he then shifted to Bijapur, where he composed another *masnawī* text, the *Mīzbānī Nāma*.[72] It is generally agreed that the composition of the *Fath Nāma*, of which two manuscripts exist, considerably preceded the high point of Dakhni literature under the sultans—namely, Nusrati's texts such as the *'Alī Nāma*, which date to 1665 (A.H. 1076). The *Fath Nāma* is also almost certainly older than even the *Ibrāhīm Nāma* of 'Abdul Dihlawi (1603/A.H. 1012).[73] Though the text was clearly written in Ahmadnagar and is presented as though the battle of 1565 had happened just yesterday, we cannot discount the possibility that this was really a literary device. In short, we cannot rule out that the *Fath Nāma* was written as early as the 1560s, but this view needs a firmer basis than we presently have.

The text, around 600 verses, is entirely organized on the idea of an exchange of insults leading to war. It begins conventionally with praise of God and the Prophet (a *hamd* and *na't*) and then has a number of subsections. At the very outset, the poet describes in seven brief verses the alliance between the four sultans and the reasons for the war. It is clear from the start that the deeper underlying cause was not religious difference but that Ramraj felt a deep enmity toward Husain Nizam Shah, as we see when an insolent envoy from Vijayanagara appears in Husain's court. Here, the poet insists that in every community, be it among Muslims, the ancient Persians, or even the Hindus, excellent rulers have existed—but Ramraj, for his part, is evil incarnate. Shauqi writes:

> Excellent behavior is the hallmark of the man
> as fragrance is the hallmark of the flower.
> In every country, good deeds can be found,
> in every community, good words can be found.[74]

The scene then shifts to the *darbār* of Ramraj, where a conversation is in progress. The Vijayanagara ruler brings in his *wazīrs* to prepare for the fight against the Nizam Shah. Having first praised the courage and intelligence of Husain, Ramraj then unveils his plan. It has been weighing on Ramraj that while the whole world calls him a king, only this "Turk" denies him such a tribute. Ramraj now cynically provokes the religious sentiments of the *wazīrs* against the Nizam Shah, saying that he does not acknowledge the Vedas or Puranas, only the Qur'an. The *wazīrs* become enthusiastic about the prospect of war, and say:

> How can one compare Ramraj to Shah Husain?
> Or compare the Red Sea with two cups of water?

The Vijayanagara court decides that the best way to go about starting a war would be to demand an elaborate and insulting tribute from Husain Nizam Shah: this would include camels from Kabul, ambergris, aloes, musk, a large silver bell, a golden flute, cash and precious goods, powerful maces, and Bahmani daggers. So Ramraj composes an insolent letter making these and even more outrageous demands: jade pitchers, ruby cups, diamond cubes, and the foot bracelets of Malika Khunza Humayun, the wife of Husain Nizam Shah (in what is potentially a sexually loaded reference). He also asks that some of the principal Deccani notables such as Rumi Khan, Makhdum Khwaja Jahan, and Asad Khan be sent to him. Finally, he demands that Husain stop eating beef, turn away from Mecca, and instead pray to the Saiva ascetics or *jangamas*. If Husain does not do this, Ramraj threatens the direst of consequences.

> I'll spare neither Turk nor Turkish bow
> If there's a Rustam in this time, I dare him to come forth,
> From the Bhima's waters to the Narmada's edge
> I'll spare neither the rich nor the poor.
> I will not spare the brides of Hind
> Nor will I spare the brides of Sind
> I won't spare a single Maulana or *faqīr*

Neither aged nor youth, neither young man nor old.
I'll expel the foundations of Islam far off
Only those who accept Ram will be spared.

Na turkān ko chhorūn na turkī kamān
Agar gyo Rustam hāzir zamān
Ze āb-i Bhimwar tā lab-i Narbadā
Na chhorūn tawangar na chhorūn gadā
Na chhorūn kidhain kadkhudāyān-i Hind
Na chhorūn kidhain kadkhudāyān-i Sind
Na chhorūn mulānā na chhorūn faqīr
Na barkā na larkā na barnā na pīr
Karūn dūr buniyād Islām kī
jo māne dorāhe jagat Rām kī.

The last line is, of course, a play between the name of the Vijayanagara
ruler and the name of the god after whom he is called. What is striking besides are three features of this verse: its aggressive intent against
Muslims, the sexualized language that is used (against the brides of
Hind and Sind), and the geographical ambitions on display—which
extend far to the north of the Krishna (the usual boundary between
Vijayanagara and the Deccan sultans) and all the way to the very
banks of the Narmada River.

This message is then sent to Ahmadnagar with an envoy by the
name of Haridas, and it is received with suitable annoyance. Husain
Nizam Shah now calls in his council and expresses his disgust at
Ramraj.

He knows neither your holy men, nor your nobles,
He knows neither your diplomats, nor your scribes.
He tears down your mosques and makes them desolate
He harasses your muezzins and kills them too.
He never acknowledges those Muslims who are praying,
And describes Fakhr-i Razi as a mere madman.[75]

The implication is that Ramraj lacks the basic attributes of a cultured ruler: not only does he attack mosques and people at prayer, but he has no respect for the unmarked and generally acceptable knowledge of diplomats, scribes, or even great scholars of the past. The Ahmadnagar *wazīrs* hear this and are naturally enraged. They assure the sultan that he is great and is capable of great deeds—even to the extent of conquering distant Transoxiana. While he is a lion, Ramraj is a mere pig; while he is a diamond, Ramraj is just a rock.

Encouraged by these words, Husain Nizam Shah drafts a suitable response through his own head of chancellery (or *mīr munshī*). In this letter, he swears on all that is holy and invokes all that is heroic—a long series of names from the pre-Islamic Iranian past to the Old Testament—to assert that he will destroy Ramraj. His insulting letter of reply treats Ramraj as a mere speck of dust, and says that he will light a torch to destroy him that will illuminate the land all the way to Sri Lanka (or Singaldip).

Ramraj in turn is enraged to receive this letter, and the wordy combat escalates. He, too, replies with further insults. His new alleged missive improbably states:

I, Ram, am the real Dajjal [Anti-Christ],
I'm from the lineage of Shaddad son of 'Ad,
I'm not just Ram, but Ram and Lakhman combined,
If Bahri [Husain] is one maund, why I'm a lakh of them.

Now that these elaborate insults have served their purpose and are out of the way, the scene is set for a battle. The Nizam Shahi army of *ghāzīs* marches to the Don River and beyond, as swift as a python on the move. The armies of the other sultans are barely worth a mention for the poet, focused as he is on Husain Nizam Shah. Ramraj's army that confronts them, on the other hand, includes groups such as Bedas, Khatris, and Tadpatris, and Nayaks and Payaks (the last pair no doubt in the interests of the rhyme). The Vijayanagara ruler is not even above employing jungle people, who eat lizards and other vile things, as well as cannibals. Among the other Vijayanagara leaders, particular mention is made of the ruler's brother Venkatapati.

The combat begins on the banks of a river to the sound of various instruments (drums, trumpets, and the like). Firearms play a somewhat prominent role in the poet's version, too.

> Cannons and falconets sent off their shot,
> And the sound of rockets was to be heard everywhere.

In the midst of all the smoke and dust, a certain Asad Khan distinguishes himself. Many of the Vijayanagara notables *(rāy-rāyals)* on horseback are cut down, as are countless foot soldiers.

For his part, the evil Ramraj deliberately seeks out Husain Nizam Shah, but instead it is he who is himself eventually seized and brought before the sultan. The poet recounts the scene in brief:

> With heavenly help for his victory,
> Ram was brought before the Shah.
> When the Shah's gaze fell on him
> He at once ordered his execution.
> The justice of his faith was pronounced,
> and the Pearl of Faith spoke thus:
> "O God! By the grace of the Prophet and saints,
> And the grace of 'Ali, King of Men,
> You bestowed victory on me at this time,
> You gave me the key to triumph in my hand.
> I had this tyrant's head cut off
> I threw it down in a dozen pieces.
> Reward me for this patient deed,
> For I punished such a faithless man."
> A heavenly voice said in response:
> "Your wish is fulfilled in advance,
> For you are the foundation of the faith of Islam,

> And contained in your sword was the death of Ram."
> The infidels made trouble, and God gave glory,
> So Ram's head was severed from his body.[76]

Shauqi tells us that that the head was promptly stuck on a lance and then eventually sent to Ramraj's son, Tufalya (possibly an error for his brother, Tirumala).

Once the victory was complete, the Ahmadnagar army marched south and entered Vijayanagara. Husain Nizam Shah was greatly impressed by the city and its prosperity, comparing it in his own mind not only to Transoxiana but to the prosperous Gokul of the Hindu god Krishna. But this did not prevent the inevitable sack of the city.

> The Shah ordered the plunder of the city,
> The order was given to both noble and commoner,
> They then rendered the city desolate,
> They harassed and killed the *jangamas*,
> . . .
> Both open and hidden wealth were revealed,
> Treasure was brought up from beneath the ground,
> . . .
> People came to acquire riches and wealth,
> Full of merriment, happiness and delight.
> . . .
> Boxes of jewels in the thousands,
> Gold and silver beyond count.[77]

The *Fath Nāma* then concludes with a long set of praise verses in the name of Husain Nizam Shah, its hero and the victor of the battle.

It is undoubtedly a curious text, which even though it was known to scholars of literature from at least the 1920s has never attracted the attention of historians. In its adherence to many of the elements that

characterize the Indo-Persian historiography of authors such as
Firishta and Tabataba, it leaves open the intriguing possibility of some
form of intertextuality between *tārīkh* and *masnawī*. At the same time,
it formulates the plot of the battle in ways that are its own. Though the
rhetoric of Islamic (and even specifically Shi'i) triumph is brought
in at the close, when Husain declares his new title to be *Bahrī kuf-
fār-shikan* ("Bahri, the destroyer of infidels"), Shauqi poses the opposition between Husain and Ramraj in ways that would certainly
have been entirely alien to Tabataba and even perhaps to Firishta.
Husain, he states, combines the qualities of bravery, generosity,
and justice found in ancient Persian, Muslim, and Hindu heroes,
whether Kayumars, Jamshid, Dara, Sikandar Zu'l-qarnain, Mahmud
Ghaznawi, or even Rama, Arjuna, and Krishna. In contrast, Ramraj
is likened to the Pharaoh, Shaddad (enemy of the ancient prophet
Hud), and the evil Ravana, besides the Anti-Christ (or Dajjal). The
insults exchanged are curiously wide-ranging and nonsectarian. In
the end, the cause of the quarrel is Ramraj's sense of inferiority and
the feeling that he was not adequately respected. Was Shauqi aware,
as Firishta certainly was, that Rama Raya was not in fact from the
Vijayanagara royal house (or Tuluva dynasty)?[78] The war here thus
does not begin at the initiative of the Nizam Shahs, the patrons of
the text and of Shauqi; rather, they are simply obliged to respond in
the face of the barrage of insults to which they are subjected from an
arrogant but inferior actor.

Boudoir and Battlefield

A last piece remains for us to be able to complete the puzzle of 1565.
This is another intriguing *masnawī* text, also originating in Ahmadnagar. But unlike the work of Hasan Shauqi we have just discussed,
this work—written by a poet of distinctly Shi'i inclinations with the
pen name of Aftabi—is in Persian, and is entitled *Ta'rīf-i Husain
Shāh Pādshāh-i Dakan* ("Praise-Poem for Husain Shah, the Ruler of
the Deccan").[79] Further, as verses from this text are quoted both by

Tabataba and Firishta in their works of history, we can be confident that it preceded them; it may be speculated that its sole manuscript—currently lacking a colophon—was first in the Ahmadnagar royal library and then passed on to the Mughals (as a stamp exists suggesting it was owned by a Mughal notable in around 1720). Also important is the fact that this is an illustrated manuscript, with six of the twelve extant paintings concerning the battle of 1565; the other half deals with Ahmadnagar court life.[80] Though they are often quite naïve, hardly matching either later Deccani painting or the products of the Mughal atelier, these paintings remain of considerable interest, both from an art history and a documentary viewpoint.

The text of Aftabi's *Ta'rīf* as we know it today is made up of some 341 verses, though some more have almost certainly been lost. Slightly less than a third of these comprise the rather elaborate initial praise verses: the *hamd* in praise of God, the *na't* in praise of the Prophet, and the specifically Shi'i praise of the Prophet's cousin 'Ali, *amīr-i 'arab shahryār-i 'ajam*, as he is termed here. It is thus only in the fifth canto that we turn to matters having to do with Ahmadnagar itself, and more specifically with the rule of Husain Nizam Shah, here given the exalted status of a *shāhinshāh* and the "Refuge of the World" (*'ālampanah*). The charged rhetoric of the poem also has it that he was ruler of the entire Deccan, indeed extending "to the borders of China, Cathay and Khotan" (*az sarhad-i Chīn wa Khitā wa Khotan*). Comparable to the noonday sun in his capacity to illuminate the world, we learn that this ruler in turn had a wife of unsurpassed beauty, Humayun Shah. The poet devotes a good number of the succeeding verses to praising her charms, facial beauty, grace, and the sweetness of her speech.

To accompany these verses, we have the first two of the twelve paintings found in the manuscript, one depicting Husain and his wife seated in a pavilion with some women attending them, and the second showing the royal couple seated in a garden, once more with female servants. The suggestion is that Humayun Shah (or Khunza Humayun, as she is known to the chroniclers), the daughter of a notable man, had caught the Nizam Shah's eye.[81] He sent an envoy to her family with rich gifts, at the same time preparing to receive her in a suitable manner, to offer her nothing less than the Deccan (*mulk-i Dakan*) itself as bride-price.

The verses that follow are marked by considerable eroticism, which would have been all the more remarkable to contemporary readers if indeed—as has been claimed—the queen was living at the time of the poem's composition. Not only her face with its shapely moles, but her breasts like "fresh pomegranates" (*anār-i tāza*) and various other physical attributes are set out in loving detail in verse after verse. (The figure of the queen was partly or completely painted over by a censorious hand in the centuries after the manuscript's production, to the extent in one painting that she appears as a large smudge.[82]) Even after the wedding festivities are over, the king seemingly never tires of her, and he orders yet another elaborate banquet in her honor. Everything points so far in the direction of Husain Nizam Shah's reputation, which the chroniclers also confirm, as an inveterate *bon viveur*, which we see also depicted in a scene where he oversees a performance of singers, musicians, and dancers (Figure 1).

Two further paintings accompany these passages, and they show Husain and Humayun together in their private chambers. In one, they are surrounded by attendants with fruit and one offering the sultan a wine glass. Between this intoxication, and that produced by his love for her, we see the ruler in the next painting pleading with his wife not to leave for her own rooms just yet. Despite the large choice of women at his disposal, we learn from the poet that he preferred her above all others. In turn, this leads us to the relatively brief ninth canto, "in praise of speech, love and love making" (*dar taʿrīf-i sukhan wa ʿishq wa ʿāshiqī gūyad*). Poems, Aftabi tells us, should be about lovers and love (*ʿāshiqī wa ʿishq*), and thus far in the poem, he holds to his premise—even if there has been little by way of a plot or even a narrative sequence in evidence.

Figure 1. Husain Nizam Shah observing court dancers. Bharata Itihasa Samshodhaka Mandala, Pune, Ms. *Ta'rīf-i Husain Shāh*, Miniature 3. Photograph by Prachi Deshpande.

As we enter the tenth canto—and by now we are well over two-thirds into the extant text—the tone and content suddenly shift, as "Husain Shah makes military preparations with the intention of making war on the Kafir and marches on Bijanagar" *(lashkar ārāstan-i Husain Shāh ba 'azm-i ghazā'-yi kāfir wa rawān shudan ba jānib-i Bijānagar).* No particular reason is given for this expedition, nor has Vijayanagara (or indeed any other kingdom) merited any mention in view of the poet's single-minded preoccupation thus far with the royal couple. Yet we are suddenly transported from the boudoir to the battlefield, as the king's martial qualities are brought to the fore.

> Husain Shah, that brave king,
> before whom the lion is like a fox,
> chief of exalted and mighty men,
> on him mortals and angels bestow praise.
> Lord of the sword, the throne, and crown,
> in honour and dignity, like the glorious sun. (vv. 258–60)[83]

Unlike the version in Hasan Shauqi's text, there is no elaborate exchange of insults. Rather, it is righteousness alone and his innate sense of justice that make Husain Nizam Shah act.

> In his heart, he cherished no desire,
> nor was he inclined in any other direction,
> than to combat the infidel Rao of Bijanagar,
> and subdue that sedition and wickedness,
> For at the hands of that wicked infidel,
> many Muslims had met their end. (vv. 264–66)

The march of the sultan and his incomparable army is thus announced, and we have the first of the warlike paintings, showing Husain on a prancing horse, with all the royal insignia, accompanied by other horsemen, elephants, and foot soldiers (Figure 2).

Figure 2. Husain Nizam Shah rides into battle. Bharata Itihasa Samshodhaka Mandala, Pune, Ms. *Taʿrīf-i Husain Shāh*, Miniature 7. Photograph by Prachi Deshpande.

This leads us into the penultimate canto, concerned with the military engagement itself, which is entitled "Husain Shah wages war on Ramraj, who was the king of Bijanagar, and is victorious" (*jang kardan-i Husain Shāh bā Rāmrāj ki Pādshāh-i Bijānagar būd wa fath kardan*). The poet evokes the beginning of the battle's clamor, the beating drums and the marching hooves and feet. The two armies rush at each other, with lines of soldiers and horses and the charging of "furious and intoxicated elephants" all adding to the deafening noise. But the losses of the infidels are far greater than those of the armies of Islam; under the relentless attacks of Husain and his army, their hearts began to melt like wax in a furnace (*chū az kūra-i ātishīn mom rā*).

The paintings that accompany this section are careful to distinguish the two armies, even in the midst of the combat. While both employ a mix of horses, elephants, and foot soldiers, the weaponry in use mostly consists of spears and swords. Though the occasional mounted archer may be found, no artillery is in evidence in these depictions. Further, many of the Ahmadnagar horsemen wear distinctive coats and headgear of mail. Less well-protected, the Vijayanagara cavalry are distinguished by their pointed *kullāyi* caps. Indeed, Rama Raya himself is shown in two paintings wearing one of these caps, mounted on a horse, and accompanied by servants carrying a royal parasol (Figure 3).

The end of the battle is now near, though the poet has not chosen to render any military details of the engagement as such. The conclusion comes quite expeditiously.

> Victory became the guide of Husain Shah,
> as the routed enemy sought refuge.
> Adversaries caught up in defeat,
> even the bravest infidels called out for help.
> The infidel Ramraj was wounded with a spear,
> his head struck the ground, as did his crown.
> That *kāfir* fell, struck by a mortal blow,

Figure 3. Rama Raya in the midst of battle. Bharata Itihasa Samshodhaka Mandala,
Pune, Ms. *Ta'rīf-i Husain Shāh*, Miniature 12. Photograph by Prachi Deshpande.

And that, you might say, was Resurrection *(rastkhez)* itself.
The king made a sign to someone,
and his head was severed and stuffed with straw. (vv. 312–16)

The painting that accompanies these last lines is arguably the most dramatic of the dozen of which we dispose (Figure 4). The bottom section shows an assortment of Nizam Shahi troops on foot and mounted on horses and elephants. The top right of the composition is occupied by a royal figure on horseback (with a parasol), who is recognizably Husain Nizam Shah from the other paintings. As in the poem, he gestures with his hand to a servant, who is in the process of decapitating Rama Raya, who lies supine and stripped to the waist. To the left, there appears another somewhat portly royal figure on foot, also with a parasol, who is making a pleading gesture with his hand as if to stop the decapitation. With his white beard, he is far too old to be ʿAli ʿAdil Shah and must therefore represent Ibrahim Qutb Shah—also linked in his own way, as we have seen, to Rama Raya.

Yet the closing verses of the *masnawī* manage to surprise us. The battle is followed by plunder and the gathering of considerable treasure, but in Aftabi's version, Husain Nizam Shah is troubled by the senseless carnage of the battle: "apparently he laughed, but wept inwardly." Perhaps this was the poet's way of reconciling the lover of the first part of the poem with the sword-wielding warrior of its later sections. Husain eventually returns to his capital Ahmadnagar with his army, carrying an enormous booty.

Here, the poem ends abruptly, though we may gather from the heading to the last canto that Aftabi must have written some concluding verses regarding the sultan's death, which occurred not long after. We know from the Persian chroniclers that this death led to deeply troubled times in Ahmadnagar, characterized by the succession of Husain's son Murtaza Nizam Shah, during whose reign the *Taʿrīf* was probably completed.

Figure 4. The killing of Rama Raya. Bharata Itihasa Samshodhaka
Mandala, Pune, Ms. *Taʿrīf-i Husain Shāh*, Miniature 11. Photograph by
Prachi Deshpande.

Conclusion

A generation ago, when cultural historians examined the endless history of medieval European battles and combats that had fed and largely contented their predecessors in the profession, they turned to anthropology for answers and the prospect of distance. They sought the possibility of "a sort of ethnography of the military practice of the early thirteenth century," and to "situate the battle in relation to war, to truce, to peace, as a means of circumscribing in a more exact way the field of what we call politics, as well as to see how the sacred, at that time, was inextricably mixed with the profane." The reference here is to the celebrated battle of Bouvines in Flanders, which occurred on a Sunday, July 27, 1214, and around which a copious body of materials had accumulated. Bouvines, which opposed the rulers of France and Germany, had over 750 years "suffered a progressive deformation, on account of the play, rarely innocent, of memory and forgetting."[84]

Though we are more than 300 years closer to the battle of January 1565 than to that of Bouvines, some of the same problems undoubtedly beset us. Men like Firishta, Tabataba, and Couto had all lived through the time of the battle, and all of them surely had a personal acquaintance with participants. This constitutes a first sediment for us, which in turn stands in complex relation to other works, such as those of Hasan Shauqi and Aftabi. But less than a generation later, memory and forgetting had begun to play tricks. The traveler and gem merchant Jacques de Coutre from Bruges would write of how he had visited the city of Velur in the 1610s, where "the emperor of Bisnaga who was called Ramarraja [once] had his court. . . . So great was his power that the kings of Bengal, Sind and Cambay, who are powerful kings, were tributaries of the empire." Coutre added that "many authors have written [about Rama Raya] rather variously, giving him the title of king and not of emperor. I do not doubt that in the beginning it may have been a kingdom, but it is said that he has always been known through all of the Orient as emperor, just as that of Germany was known in Europe and the whole world."[85]

With the passage of another three quarters of a century, the Venetian Nicolò Manuzzi could regale his readers with how "more than two hundred years ago, there reigned an emperor called Ramrajo, who was so generous that it is remarked in the chronicles that he never refused any favour asked." It was he who had created the Deccan sultanates, by handing over "his principal provinces to his servants and slaves" such as a certain Yusuf 'Adil Khan, "carver at his table, a Georgian by race."[86] Rather than his opponents or rivals, the Deccan sultans thus became the successors of Rama Raya.

It has certainly not been possible here for us to respond to the ambitions of a Duby, in part because of the relative poverty of the historiographical context.[87] But there is also a fundamental difference; that is, all the participants in the battle of Bouvines were Christians, subject to the same anathemas and to excommunications by bishops and popes. To a large extent, that elite political culture— even if it could indeed be circumscribed through several logics— can properly be seen as contained within a single religious culture. This was certainly not the case with Deccani politics of the sixteenth century. The sultans, as we have seen, were usually Shi'i Muslims, but there were important exceptions such as Ibrahim 'Adil Shah (r. 1534–58). Their courts harbored a number of well-placed Hindus and—as with Ahmadnagar in the 1540s and 1550s—even the odd Christian or Jewish savant (such as the celebrated Garcia da Orta).[88] Correspondingly, Rama Raya apparently employed a fair number of Muslims, including those who were disgruntled with the religious policies followed at Bijapur in the late 1530s. Thus, despite the retrospective attempts by certain Telugu and Kannada textual traditions to present the sultans as wholly alien, mere "drunkards and opium eaters," the radical opposition between Vijayanagara and its northern neighbors was never a political, diplomatic, or even familial reality.[89]

A number of authors in the past have sought to show how these different South Asian polities between the thirteenth and eighteenth centuries shared many aspects of court culture, from literature and music to architecture and even traditions of painting. The effort has thus been to argue for the production of what has been called a "composite culture" in terms of the creation of an Indo-Islamic synthesis.[90] Yet the sphere of politics itself (and its counterpart, diplomacy) has remained curiously absent for the most part from this discussion. But the very nature of the encounters we have discussed in this chapter—and the effective deploying time and again of invective and insult—is suggestive of the deep intimacy that existed among these courts. It is quite another matter whether these were the real motivations underlying events (as many contemporary observers thought) or mere symptoms for other processes. In January 1565, Aravidu Rama Raya may have been many things to the sultans, but he was certainly anything but a stranger.

2

Courtly Martyrdom

The captured soldier ought to be most constant in faith,
patient in travails, keeping hope in God that he will remedy them,
for Solomon says: Better to be patient than a strong man,
Melior est patiens viro forti. [Proverbs 16:32]

—Anonymous, *Primor e honra da vida soldadesca
no Estado da Índia* (c. 1580)

Late in 1557, an envoy from the court of the Sharifs of the Muslim holy cities of Mecca and Medina set out for Istanbul to the Ottoman court of Süleyman the Lawgiver. The Sharifs were aggrieved for they felt constantly disrespected and even insulted by the Ottoman garrison commander at Medina. Some forty turbulent years had gone by since the Ottoman conquest of the region from the Mamluks, and it seemed that matters had still not quite settled down.[1] The man appointed to head their mission was an intellectual from Gujarat who had been a long-term resident of Mecca, Qutb-ud-Din Muhammad Nahrawali (1511–82). He was middle aged or even older, by the reckoning of the times, and was an accomplished scholar, even if many of his major works—such as a chronicle of the Ottoman conquest of Yemen, and a general account of Mecca—were still to be written.[2] Moreover, he had already visited Istanbul some two decades before to accompany an embassy from the Sultans of Gujarat to the Ottoman ruler. Nahrawali was a Sunni of the Hanafite school and also a Qadiri Sufi; he was fluent in Arabic and Ottoman, and perhaps a little less so in Persian. He was, it has been written, "Indian by birth, Meccan by adoption, Arab in culture, and Ottoman in political adherence . . . dismissive, even contemptuous, of others and their work, while unabashedly boastful of his own accomplishments."[3] Perhaps he was not the best choice of emissary, but then—as we have seen—diplomacy was in those times (and still is in ours) not always about self-effacement.

To be sure, the circumstances of the embassy were not the most propitious. The sultan's favorite wife, Hürrem Sultan, had died in April 1558, throwing the court into turmoil and rendering all negotiations infinitely more difficult.[4] The eleven-month trip must have been counted not merely by his principals but by Nahrawali himself as a failure, since at the end of it the Sharifs merely received a stern reprimand from the court. But late in May 1558, as Nahrawali—penniless and embittered—was preparing to return from Istanbul to Mecca, a curious incident occurred which he recounts at some length.

> On the 8th of Sha'ban [May 26, 1558] the grand vizier ordered the execution of Shaikh Zain-ud-Din [from] Jabal 'Amil. He was brought to the council (*dīwān*) and wasn't [even] questioned before being ordered onto the scaffold, where he was decapitated. With a sword they split the soles of his feet, and while his head was being severed he was uttering the two Islamic attestations of faith. His story was the following. He was at Damascus when Hasan Beg Efendi was *qāzī* there, and was suspected of being a Shi'i heretic. So he was apprehended and taken before Hasan Beg. When the latter asked him about the Islamic school of law (*mazhab*) to which he adhered, he said that he was a Shafi'i.[5]

Both the central figures in this episode are curious indeed. Hasan Beg was a German, captured and converted, who had acquired an excellent education, permitting him to become a prominent Muslim jurist. On the other hand, Zain-ud-Din ibn 'Ali al-Hajjah was a celebrated Shi'i intellectual of his time, who was here practicing the time-honored strategy of concealment.[6] Nahrawali continues his narrative by noting that in the first instance, Hasan Beg was convinced that the other was a Sunni and released him, but that he then came to regret this. He subsequently encountered Zain-ud-Din again in Mecca and had him arrested and confined. Not only this, he even embezzled the money of those who tried to have him set free. Nahrawali passes no particular judgment on Zain-ud-Din himself, beyond noting that he was "a man who outwardly was extremely upright . . . , had abundant virtue and was possessed of excellent conversation and a graceful manner of speaking." The clear implication for the reader is that this upright man was a probable victim of Ottoman greed and injustice.

Yet with Zain-ud-Din we are dealing with a personage known as the *Shahīd al-sānī,* or "the Second Martyr" in Shi'i terms. What the episode recounted above makes clear is that martyrs were often produced not in the clash between religions but in the sectarian clash within a religion: thus, between Sunnis and Shi'is, or Catholics and Protestants. Further, even if this case is relatively clear, others are far less so. Shi'is in South Asia are apt to claim as their "Third Martyr" *(shahīd al-sālis)* the Iranian immigrant Nurullah Shustari, allegedly killed at the order of the Mughal ruler Jahangir at Agra in 1610. This jurist had held prominent positions over several decades in the Mughal domains, and the circumstances of his death remain remarkably obscure, even contested: if some argue that he may have been put to death for concealing his Shi'ism, others suggest more directly political motivations.[7] Further, Shustari's case is often considered together with that of a "martyr" from quite a different tradition, namely, the fifth guru of the Sikhs, Arjan, who was killed in 1606, also early in the reign of the emperor Jahangir. Arjan's conflict with Jahangir is well attested, including in the latter's own memoirs, where he is accused of notionally abetting the ruler's rebellious son Khusrau. But the precise circumstances of his death as a martyr (or *shahīd*)—while an abiding article of faith for Sikh believers—remain unclear.[8] The elaborate account in a contemporary letter by the Jesuit Jerónimo Xavier posits that he died of mistreatment for failing to pay back his guarantors a substantial monetary indemnity, but that the Mughals were not directly responsible.[9] Because Xavier based his account on hearsay, we may make of his complex and admittedly devious narrative what we will.

That said, once the precedent of Arjan's martyrdom had been established in the seventeenth century, the Sikh tradition seems to have embraced the idea of the *shahīd* with enthusiasm, making it a central tenet of the constitution of the tradition itself. The central notion of the martyr, as indeed the *shahīd*, that they literally—and etymologically—bore witness to the truth of a faith, was thus absorbed into this conception.[10] Thus, in the later reign of Aurangzeb, their ninth guru, Tegh Bahadur, is said to have been killed at the emperor's orders in 1675. Again, obscurity surrounds the actual event, which is mostly described in somewhat later texts. But plausibility is often lent to it by the fact that, as with Arjan, this is a case of paired martyrdom: the other half of the pair was the celebrated Sarmad, executed early in Aurangzeb's reign (in 1660) for insisting on his public nakedness and other forms of "extreme" comportment. The French savant François Bernier referred to him in one of his letters dating to 1667 as follows: "I have seen a [*faqīr*] who was famous for a rather long time in Delhi called Sarmet, who wandered about all naked on the streets, and who in the end preferred to have his neck chopped rather than dress himself, [despite] some promises and some threats that Aurangzeb made him."[11] Sarmad's shrine in Delhi continues to attest to his popularity, even if as an extreme mystic (or *majzūb*) he was sometimes an object of ongoing mockery in Mughal court culture. As we know, the mature Mughal period not only created its own martyrs but showed a marked interest in martyrs—real and imagined—from earlier times.[12]

A First Context

In short, the sixteenth and seventeenth centuries had their share, and more, of martyrs and martyrologies. Among the most celebrated of such texts is John Foxe's *Acts and Monuments* (1563), popularly known as his "Book of Martyrs," which marked the turning away of England under Elizabeth I from the Catholic faith and its attendant persecution of Protestants.[13] Yet for all its production in the middle of the century of the "great discoveries," the conception of Foxe's work did not for the most part include what we might term "interfaith martyrs" beyond those of the ancient past, perhaps because the English had yet to mark their presence firmly at that time in either Asia or the New World.[14] The great "royal martyr" of the next century, Charles I, was long thought to have gone to the scaffold on January 30, 1649, leaving the bishop of London, William Juxon, with the enigmatic word "Remember!" But who was ever a martyr for the cause of forgetfulness? For courtly encounters and intercourt tensions—as we have seen in the preceding pages—did not end at their worst with mere insults. They could lead to the shedding of blood, even royal blood, and the making of martyrs, whether within a tradition or, as with Dom Sebastião in Morocco in 1578, in the encounter with another all-too-familiar courtly milieu.

Martyrology could in turn spill over into other genres. One of the most popular and widely read works produced in the course of the first two centuries of the Portuguese presence in the Indian Ocean was the *Peregrinação* of Fernão Mendes Pinto (ca. 1511–83). First published in 1614, about three decades after its author's death, this rambling work deals with his adventures over some two decades or more in Asia, including the claim (or perverse boast) that he was "thirteen times made captive and seventeen times sold."[15] There is little consensus today among scholars regarding how we should read Mendes Pinto's work. One strand of scholarship, most forcefully represented by the late Rebecca D. Catz, would see it above all as a literary work and social satire, embodying a moral critique of empire as conceived by some sixteenth-century Portuguese who participated heavily in it themselves.[16] Another would still see it as containing a core of verifiable "fact," covered with layers of imaginative elaboration and several coats of final varnish that may have been applied after the author's death when the work was being brought into print. The most recent attempt to produce a balanced evaluation of its ethnographic value, including a nuanced critique of Catz's overly schematic reading, concludes that while it "is not the most accurate, nor the most penetrating, contemporary account of peoples of the East . . . it still remains that Mendes Pinto presents some key dimensions of the Portuguese Empire more effectively than the humanist-educated poets and historians who wrote elegant apologies for national and religious expansion."[17]

A key element on Mendes Pinto's narrative is the role played by captivity. This should give the reader pause, for the purpose of such an insistence on captivity is surely to make the Portuguese actor appear to be not merely the perpetrator of empire (with all its moral ambiguity) but also its victim—and very nearly a martyr.[18] This is not surprising in view of Mendes Pinto's markedly Christian vocation and his proximity to the Society of Jesus, in particular to the figure of St. Francis Xavier. This is an aspect that is carried forward into other captivity narratives of a more secular flavor. There has been a recent revival of such narratives, as telling a sort of "history from below" of empire from the point of view of the underdog, particularly with respect to early modern British expansion. We have been reminded of the sorry fate of the British captives held by the rulers of Morocco or by Tipu Sultan of Mysore, who were obliged to acculturate and at times even to convert to Islam.[19] Inevitably these exercises, carried out by historians of the British Empire, tend to forget or at least downplay their Iberian precursors in matters of such captivity narratives, whether those of the so-called *chrétiens d'Allah* in North Africa or ones involving states in South and Southeast Asia in the sixteenth century.[20] They certainly say little about the case that will mainly concern us here: a curious narrative from Aceh in western Indonesia.

The foundation and consolidation of the Sultanate of Aceh in northern Sumatra in the sixteenth century had significant direct effects on the history of the western edge of the Malay world, and also spread far wider ripples that extended from eastern Indonesia to the Red Sea. There were several contexts for Acehnese expansion: rivalries with other kingdoms in northern Sumatra and the Malay Peninsula; political, economic, and cultural links to Sunda and the ports of the Javanese *pasisir* such as Jepara and Gresik; commercial and other contacts with Bengal, Gujarat, and southern India; and complex, murky connections with the Ottoman Empire. The dealings with the Portuguese *Estado da Índia* were also of considerable importance.[21] The early struggles of Aceh's founding sultan, ʿAli Mughayat Syah (d. 1530), involved the Portuguese both at Melaka, which they had captured from its own Sultan in August 1511, and for a time at the northern Sumatran port of Pasai, where the *Estado* had founded a short-lived fortress. Acehnese opposition to the Portuguese gained even greater significance in the next major phase, which corresponds *grosso modo* with the reign of ʿAla-ud-Din Riʿayat Syah al-Qahhar (1539–71), when the activities of *il rè d'Assi* against "the Portuguese, his greatest enemies" *(li Portoghesi suoi inimicissimi)* even came to the regular attention of the Venetians.[22] This was the period that Charles Boxer perspicaciously identified in a brief but classic essay written four decades ago as the moment when the commercial contacts between Aceh and the Red Sea port of Jeddah came to be fully consolidated.[23] In the past two decades, the diligent archival researches of a number of younger historians have further developed the nuanced, important analysis of Boxer and have enabled us to gain a far better understanding of Aceh in the years before its traditionally defined apogee under Sultan Iskandar Muda (1607–36) in the early seventeenth century.[24] Elsewhere, it has been demonstrated how the image of Aceh as a political and commercial center came to develop in these years in Mughal India, particularly through a text written just after 1600 by Tahir Muhammad Sabzwari, a Mughal intellectual.[25]

The work of Boxer and others tended to lay great stress, undoubtedly with reason, on the commercial side of the Portuguese-Acehnese rivalry. After all, the main problem with Aceh, as the Portuguese saw it, was that it was a center for the collection and transshipment of pepper and spices, the pepper coming from the Sumatran west coast, Sunda, and the Malay Peninsula, and the spices coming much farther east from Maluku. However, it is almost impossible to speak of this struggle without looking at its religious dimensions. The Portuguese were undoubtedly motivated in some measure in their early empire building in Southeast Asia by religious stirrings, at times providentialist in character and at others downright messianic in their coloring. In this they were not unique, for the world in which the likes of Vasco da Gama and Afonso de Albuquerque were brought up was not entirely distinct from that of Savonarola or Columbus, both notorious for their politically flavored and quite muscular Christianity. However, as the sixteenth century progressed, the nature of Portuguese religious activity in Asia also changed. The major Catholic religious orders all entered the fray; with the advent of the Counter-Reformation in midcentury, the Jesuits came to play a prominent role, joining the earlier Franciscans, and soon to be followed from the 1560s and 1570s by the Augustinians.[26]

It has been common enough in the literature to pose this expanding Christianity side by side with an expanding Islam, propelled by the "missionary" activity of Muslims from West Asia and the Indian subcontinent in Southeast Asia. In at least one celebrated and iconic episode involving the ruler of Makassar, Sultan ʿAla-ud-Din, in the early seventeenth century, the two—Islam and Christianity—even appear as rival suitors for the hand of an undecided "heathen" bride.[27] In an early account of his conversion in 1605, the ruler allegedly sends out to Aceh and Melaka for representatives of the two religions who could present their rival arguments; the Acehnese arrive first, and he thus accepts Islam. Indeed, as Anthony Reid has written, "the intense competition between the two sides certainly sharpened the boundary, not only between themselves, but between each of them and the surrounding environment of traditional beliefs."[28] If the Portuguese deployed the notions of crusade and of holy war *(guerra santa)*, certain Muslim *ʿulamā* for their part made appeals to ideas of *jihād*, as much in Southeast Asia as on the Indian west coast, where a celebrated text written in the 1570s by Shaikh Zain-ud-Din Maʿbari boldly titles itself *Tuhfat ul-mujāhidīn fī baʿz ahwāl al-Burtukāliyyin* ("A gift to the holy warriors in the form of some tales of the Portuguese").[29] In reality, however, we know that the Portuguese had extensive trading contacts for a good part of the sixteenth century with both the Mappilla Muslims of Kerala and merchants from the Iranian plateau, so their religious zeal was always tempered by a certain pragmatic spirit. In turn, even the ʿAdil Shahs of Bijapur—notionally among the fiercest opponents of the Portuguese in India—periodically opened up dealings with Goa, though such episodes could at times appear to be no more than maneuvers intended to lull the *Estado* into a false sense of security before a further set of hostilities.[30]

Another way of posing the problem of Muslim-Christian relations in the sixteenth-century Indian Ocean might be to say that some groups and parties more than others were interested in stirring the pot and keeping the religious rivalry fresh. Underlying this was an awkward fact. Much of the conversion to Christianity and to Islam in the period was of individuals and communities with a third location— neither Christian nor Muslim—such as the Paravas of southern

India or the peasants and hill-men of eastern Bengal. Over a century and a half before the Portuguese arrived in the Indian Ocean, the Moroccan traveler Ibn Battuta briefly visited Pasai in the 1340s, and described its ruler, al-Malik al-Zahir, as "a most illustrious and open-handed ruler, and a lover of theologians [who] is constantly engaged in warring for the Faith and in raiding expeditions." In this view of the apparently ceaseless war between Muslims and *kuffār*, obviously it was the Muslims "who have the upper hand over all the infidels in their vicinity, who pay them a poll-tax to secure peace."[31] But in the sixteenth century, there was also the problem of Christians who became Muslims and the other way around. By all accounts, this was a somewhat asymmetrical process, for Muslim states in Asia had far more resources and prestige to offer at this time than their relatively modest Christian counterparts.[32] Faced with this reality, it is not entirely surprising that we see the production of a set of exhortatory texts in the second half of the sixteenth and early seventeenth century that are intended to urge Christians to hold firm to their faith, even to prefer the goriest forms of martyrdom to the temptations of Islam. That missionaries might be seen as potential martyrs is not entirely unexpected, but it is interesting that this odor of sanctity is also extended to secular actors such as soldier-martyrs, whose deaths seem to provide a conceptual link between Portuguese activities in North Africa and the *Estado da Índia*.[33]

An Author

One of the oddest personages in the intellectual history of the Portuguese *Estado da Índia*—and there is avowedly no shortage of them—is Manuel Godinho de Erédia, who was born around 1558 in the great Southeast Asian entrepôt of Melaka, and who died in 1623. Erédia was a Luso-Asian, termed a *"hijo de la India y mestiço"* by the powerful Italian Jesuit Alessandro Valignano, who seems to have known and heartily disliked him. His father, João Erédia, was in all likelihood a Portuguese soldier of Spanish and Italian descent in the Melaka garrison; his mother was either Malay or Bugis, probably from the Makassar region of Sulawesi.[34] Manuel Godinho was the youngest of four children, and his two older brothers constructed religious careers for themselves, one—Francisco Luís—with a certain degree of success.

After an education with the Jesuits in Melaka, Manuel Godinho, who was apparently the most ambitious of the three brothers, moved in his early teens to the Portuguese Asian capital of Goa, where he seems to have been accepted by the Jesuits into their order as a novice in about 1574. But things really did not go well for him in this context. After ten years at the fringes of the Society, Erédia was asked to leave, accused by superiors of doing no more than "troubling and disturbing others," and also of having no serious religious vocation. He may have equally been a victim of the discriminatory policies that the Jesuits such as Valignano and Mercuriano came to formulate in Asia from the mid-1570s against natives (*naturales*) and those of mixed blood (*mestiços*), something of an irony in view of the tolerance that the same order showed in regard to New Christians in Europe.

Nevertheless, Erédia had demonstrated by then that he possessed a certain number of other talents, notably in geometry and mathematics more generally (which he taught), and above all as a draftsman and painter. These, together with cartography (and what he liked to term "cosmographia"), were the skills that he would deploy with some measure of success throughout the rest of his life, living first in Cochin (where he married Violante de Sampaio in about 1586), then in Melaka, and eventually in western India.

Manuel Godinho de Erédia was a characteristic intermediary figure or go-between when seen from several points of view. As a *mestiço* who affirmed rather than denied his dual heritage, he was an "in-between" even before he was a go-between. The manner in which he used this heritage was quite typical of many such figures, in that he inflated the weight and prestige of his genealogy. Thus, on his father's side he claimed some relationship with the noble Italian family of Acquaviva; in a self-portrait from 1613, he showed himself with the admittedly ill-defined arms of a noble family (*escudos de sua nobreza*, as he himself put it), and he suggested that his father was in fact a *fidalgo*. But he gave as much if not more importance to the notion that his mother belonged to the Southeast Asian aristocracy; in this sense, the distinguished Portuguese historian Luís Filipe Thomaz has noted that "Erédia was, in effect, not just a physical *mestiço* but a cultural *mestiço*, a *topaz*, as used to be said in Portuguese in at the time in the East: the term . . . etymologically signifying 'bilingual', but better translated by the notion of what we might as a neologism term 'bicultural'."[35]

Here, the reference is to the Portuguese version of the Indian term *dubāsh* or *dubāshī*, literally meaning he (or she) of two *(du-)* languages *(bhāshā)*.[36] An early nineteenth-century French colonial official in India would define these *topazes* or *dubashes* as follows: "they come from the mixture of Europeans with the women of the land, and from Indians who have renounced their caste." This means that such a group was made up of a mix of acculturated converts and Eurasians, and was in none-too-good a shape by then, for we learn from the same source that "the *topas* population is the most miserable in India, and with the exception of some individuals who are employed as scribes in offices or who have shops, the others have no profession and no employment."[37]

Unlike those who were being referred to in the early nineteenth century, Erédia manifestly did not see himself as belonging to some *topaz* community but as pretty much *sui generis*. He also strongly asserted his attachment to a learned culture, that of the Catholic Iberian world. His Jesuit education had brought him into contact with classical authors from Aristotle and Ptolemy to Pliny, and he also had gained some acquaintance with Copernicus and Girolamo Cardano as well as Petrus Plancius and Mercator. This was a written culture, quite unlike his Asian heritage. Erédia did have some notions of

Konkani, the vernacular language of Goa, as we note from works on botany where he uses terms from that language to designate plants. However, he had a far deeper immersion in Malay, which probably stemmed from a childhood spent in Melaka, and perhaps from the direct influence of his mother. But his access to both these languages was manifestly through the world of orality, bodies of stories and legends as well as the life experiences of mariners and others. Further, he tended to use such materials quite pell-mell and in a credulous manner whereas he reserved a somewhat more critical spirit for his readings of European materials.

Erédia is known for having written about ten works of a quite diverse variety; if, on the one hand he was a scholar, the other aspect of his life was as a man of action, notably as a prospector, explorer, and military engineer. But in reality these two sides of his life were inextricably mixed up. One set of his works thus concerns the plans of fortresses and settlements of the Portuguese, and shows off his (admittedly limited) skills as a draftsman.[38] A second, and quite diverse work, dating from 1612, is his "Summary of the Trees and Plants of India *Intra Ganges*," accompanied again by illustrations from his hand. Then there are works of geography or pseudo-geography, ranging from his "Discourse on the Province of Indostan, Termed Mogûl" from 1611, to the spectacularly confused "Declaration on Malaca and Meridional India, with Cathay."[39] A further set of works concerns one of his principal obsessions, namely, the search for sources of gold in the vicinity of Portuguese Asia and especially in the broad region of Melaka. These include the earliest of his known works, from 1599–1600, the "Information on the *Aurea Chersoneso*, or Peninsula, and Auriferous, Carbuncular and Aromatic Islands." It is clear from this last lot of writings that Erédia viewed himself as an explorer; we know that in the 1590s he importuned a series of Portuguese viceroys to allow him to explore the gold-bearing potential of Southeast Asia, in a conception that paralleled the El-Dorado projects of his contemporary Walter Ralegh. What is interesting, however, is the source for this drive, for it is mixed. In part, it derived from classical works such as that of Ptolemy and their construct of the "Golden Chersonese," but Erédia also drew fully on a range of Malay legends that spoke of a place called *Pulo Mas,* an island where the beaches had golden sands that could be harvested easily. In a similar vein, he developed the idea of a great southern land lying beyond Java that could be explored, drawing it would seem on a mix of tales carried by Malay sailors and maritime communities (or *orang laut*), and rumors that stemmed from the first Dutch sightings of the north coast of Australia. We need not revisit the rather futile controversy here concerning the "secret discovery of Australia," but rather point to how Erédia was able to produce a curious synthesis of classical Western, oral Southeast Asian, and contemporary European knowledge, tempered of course by a large dash of his own ungovernable imagination.[40] Further, as we see from his autobiographical *Sumário da Vida,* he was much given to exaggeration regarding his own knowledge, achievements, and connections, something that places him within easy reach of the category of trickster as well. For example, the royal grant that he allegedly received from Philip II in 1594 to promote his explorations in Southeast Asia seems to have been either an outright fantasy or a major exaggeration on his part.

A Work

Our central concern in the pages that follow is none of the works we have previously cited, but rather a peculiar work entitled *História de serviços com martírio de Luís Monteiro Coutinho, ordenada por Manoel Godino de Erédia, mathemático, Anno 1615* ("History of the services and martyrdom of Luís Monteiro Coutinho, set in order by Manoel Godinho de Erédia, mathematician, in the year 1615").[41] There is some significance to the choice of the word *ordenada,* in place of *escrita* (written) or *composta* (composed); it seems to place some distance between author and work. What the work (henceforth

abbreviated as *HSMLMC*) intends to explore is the life and death of
a minor Portuguese nobleman, who met his end in 1583 after serving in Asia for an undefined period of time, possibly something under fifteen years. It exists, so far as we know, in a single manuscript
copy in the Biblioteca Nacional in Lisbon and to date is yet to be
published. It is carelessly put together, and may not be in the final
form that Godinho de Erédia intended to give it; for example, it lacks
a proper conclusion. It is also accompanied by seven rather interesting watercolors from the hand of Erédia, as well as the arms of the
Monteiro Coutinho family.

The hero of Erédia's work is a rather obscure figure, hardly one
of those who feature regularly in the great chronicles or texts of the
second half of the sixteenth century. He is mentioned only once in
Diogo do Couto's *Da Ásia*, in regard to a naval combat that led to his
capture, and in this mention he is simply called Luís Monteiro. We
might say that his capture and death are the most remarkable features of his biography, and that even to produce a relatively modest
text of some thirty folios requires a certain amount of embroidery on
the part of Erédia, with extraneous contextual passages (usually with
geographical and historical ramblings) being introduced on more
than one occasion.

We begin with the framing, which is in the form of a short dedication to Augustinian prelate Dom Frei Aleixo de Menezes, former
Archbishop of Goa, who in 1615 (at the time *HSMLMC* was completed) was Archbishop of Braga and Viceroy of Portugal on behalf
of the Habsburg Crown.[42] The dedication runs as follows:

> Amongst authors, it is a very common matter to dedicate their
> works and offer their writings to princes and illustrious persons,
> so that under their protection and shade they might be esteemed;
> and in this way, this small work [too] might gain worth under
> the shade of Your Lordship, particularly on account of the great-
> ness of the martyrdom of Luís Monteiro Coutinho, which his

brother Nuno Monteiro Coutinho wished to publicize amongst
the Christians *(publicar entre os Christãos)*, as it has been forgotten through negligence, [especially] that new mode of martyrdom which was through the firing of a cannon *(tyro de hum
basalisco)* by which means he decorated his own services and
the services of his brothers: And he [Nuno Monteiro] encouraged us to pursue this act of impudence of offering this work to
Your Lordship so that the populace might not despise this work
of praise, confident in the notion that the great nobility of Your
Highness would act as a shield to defend this small work offered
to Your Highness, whose person God be pleased to preserve for
many years, with the greatest and happiest state, for the protection of this servant of his. In Goa, on the 11th of November of the
Year 1615, Manoel Godinho de Heredia.[43]

A few minor aspects of this dedicatory text are worth remarking.
The first is the explicit notion that the text is meant to "publicize
amongst the Christians" a moment of martyrdom, and thus goes
beyond the simple limits of the Portuguese or Luso-Asian sphere. A
second point is the situating of the martyr not as an individual but as
a member of a noble family, which is collectively exalted by his death
and prior services. A third point is Erédia's use of a slightly obscure
technical term, *basalisco* or "basilisk," to describe the weapon that
was used to execute the hero of the text.[44] The novelty of the martyrdom, he implies, lies as much in its technological means as anything
else; rather than being stoned, decapitated, pierced with arrows,
skinned alive, or crucified, Monteiro Coutinho is very much a martyr
of his own times. The same fact is emphasized in the following passage, a brief address by Erédia to his reader (*"Ao Lector"*):

The martyrdom of Luís Monteiro Coutinho not only caused
amazement *(pos em admiração)* to the King of Achem, Raia
Mançor, and to the grandees of that court, when they took

note of his constancy and very great willpower *(esforço)* in the very act of dying, but this martyrdom also astonished all those nearby Moorish kings and satraps. And to the Christians it was a cause of great consolation, because Luís Monteiro Coutinho was martyred with a new [type of] martyrdom through the shot of a *basalisco*. Since it was an example for others to follow as a good and prudent captain of Portugal, and since it was a notable act, it seemed to me that I should not allow such a glorious death and so many and such distinguished services, which have been taken into account in the Divine Tribunal *(tribunal da glória)*, to be forgotten. Therefore, only he and his services, as well as the services of his brothers will be dealt with summarily in this history, without taking account of the other events of the time, or mentioning other persons besides Luís Monteiro Coutinho and his brothers who followed him in service. And may this martyrdom be for the honour and glory of God, and an example for all Christians; it occurred on the 24th of March, in the presence of the King of Achem, and the grandees of his court, and all of the princes of Samatra, the relatives and vassals of Raia Mançor, and the ambassadors of the Grand Turk, and they were all present at that most happy death *(naquella felicissima morte)*, for on that account his soul was able to enjoy eternal glory in the year 1588.[45]

We already see here the first signs of carelessness on the part of Godinho de Erédia in respect of the year of martyrdom, which was considerably earlier than 1588. The Sultan of Aceh referred to here is ʿAla-ud-Din Mansur Syah, a prince from the Perak Sultanate who had been brought during earlier wars to Aceh and had married into the royal family there, eventually succeeding to the throne in 1579 at the death of Sultan Zain-ul-ʿAbidin. Mansur Syah appears to have died in 1586 and could manifestly not have been the ruler in 1588 if the martyrdom indeed took place in that year.[46] Malay texts from the region carry a concrete and fairly well-defined image of this ruler, suggesting that he was firm, just, and pious as well as a rather *sharī'a*-minded Muslim, unlike his somewhat playful predecessor. He is reputed to have supported a number of learned *'ulamā'* from West Asia, notably Syaikh Abu'l Khair ibn Syaikh ibn Hajjar al-Makki (a specialist in *fiqh* and author of the text *as-Saif al-Qāti'*) and his Yemeni rival Syaikh Muhammad Yamani. The period also saw the arrival of at least one prominent *'ālim* from the Rander region in Gujarat, Syaikh Muhammad Jilani ibn Hasan ibn Muhammad Hamid Quraishi.[47] It is also possible, as Erédia's text suggests, that Mansur Syah had Ottoman representatives regularly present in his court. But the Portuguese text of the *HSMLMC* is not particularly helpful in these matters. In contrast, Jorge de Lemos's account of the sieges of Melaka published in 1585 does give us a hint of the Portuguese perspective on this reign. He writes that "one should not allow this occasion to pass since there is now no king in Achém. And the kingdom being in such a state that some captains suspected that there were thoughts of rebellion and uprisings amongst the most powerful, they worked to calm things down and invited the ruler of Perak (*o Régulo de Pêra*) to govern the kingdom: [but] he is poorly obeyed."[48] Since, in Portuguese writings of the period on Asia, weakness and tyranny were often seen as two sides of the same coin, one can see how such a portrayal might go together with one of a Sultan inclined to blow up brave Portuguese captains from the mouth of a cannon.

By the time Godinho de Erédia set out to write his work in the 1610s, a number of possible models for such texts already existed in the context both of Portuguese Asia and the wider ambit of the Portuguese Empire. He would have known of the major chronicles of Fernão Lopes de Castanheda and João de Barros, as well as the continuation of the latter's work by Diogo do Couto (1542–1616), a personal acquaintance of Erédia in Goa. Besides these, there were works that focused on the trajectory of a single figure, such as a viceroy, a governor, or even a simple captain. Afonso de Albuquerque's son had

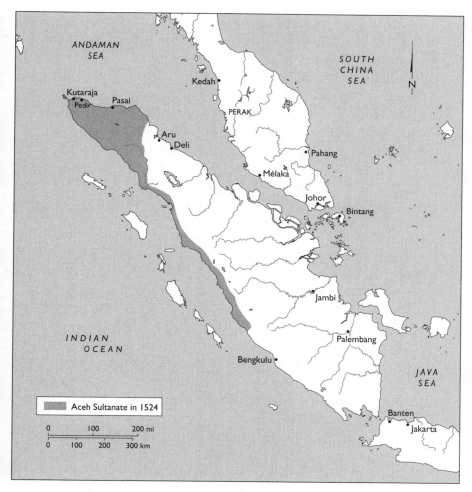

Map 3. Aceh and the Malay world.

written a work about his father and published it in two versions in the latter half of the sixteenth century; other works existed for example on the mid-sixteenth century figure of Dom João de Castro by authors such as Leonardo Nunes and Dom Fernando de Castro. Closer to the object at hand, Diogo do Couto himself had written the *Vida de Dom Paulo de Lima Pereira*, concerning the life of a *"fidalgo*, soldier and captain, who in this *Estado da Índia* fought for many years, during which time he always enjoyed great and famous victories"; Pereira (1538–89), the illegitimate son of a northern Portuguese nobleman, eventually died after a shipwreck on the African east coast while on his way back to Portugal.[49]

Couto possessed significant advantages that Erédia did not. As an official chronicler and archivist, he had access to written documents as well as a privileged position from which to gather oral testimonies. Erédia, on the other hand, seems to have been very largely dependent on Luís Monteiro Coutinho's own family, and in particular his brother Nuno who lived in Melaka, for his material.[50] He thus begins his text in a somewhat vague tone, once he has delivered to the reader what he possesses by way of genealogical information. We know that most Portuguese soldiers of status in Asia tended to build their own dossiers in the expectation of future rewards, and Luís Monteiro Coutinho must certainly have done the same. This dossier included letters and certificates *(consultas de partes)* from those under whom the soldier in question had served, which would eventually be summed up in a central narrative document *(carta de serviço)* wherein the soldier set out the principal steps of his military *curriculum vitae*.[51] However, it is clear that this dossier was not available to Erédia, inducing a certain imprecision in his narrative.

We thus learn that Luís Monteiro Coutinho was born in Lamego, just south of the Douro River in northern Portugal, on August 25, 1527, and was hence named for Louis IX (or St. Louis), the king of France and saint for that day. There is a certain obvious irony in this, for St. Louis embarked on at least two crusades against the Muslims in the thirteenth century; while in Egypt, he was defeated by the Ayyubid Sultan Turanshah at Fariskur in April 1250, taken prisoner, and eventually ransomed at considerable cost.[52] Our hero's father was António Monteiro Coutinho, his mother was Lucrécia Luíz, and he was the oldest of four brothers, the others being Domingos, António, and Nuno, all of whom (as Erédia assures us) were "of merits and great services" *(todos de merecimentos e grandes serviços)*. The milieu was clearly one of the middling nobility; both parents counted themselves as *fidalgos* and numbered connections with houses such as the Monteiros, Coutinhos, Mouras, and Pereiras of Lamego on the father's side, and the Luizes and Vazes of neighboring Penajoia to the north on the mother's side.

The first quarter century of Luís Monteiro Coutinho's life is left a mystery by Godinho de Erédia. He contents himself by noting that Luís Monteiro Coutinho was baptized in the parish of Almacave in Lamego, and that during his "childhood and young age continued his studies in Lamego for some years until he attained the age of twenty-seven years."[53] This was in fact a rather advanced age until which to remain at home, and many sons of the nobility embarked for North Africa or Asia at a far earlier age. Perhaps it was the privilege of the oldest son to remain in the parental abode longer. At any rate, we learn that he developed a taste for adventure at the age of twenty-seven.

And being capable of military action *(capax de melicia)*, in order to show his force and his high spirits, he left his patria of Lamego and embarked in Lisbon for India in the company of Francisco Barreto, conqueror of Monomotapa, who was governor of the *Estado da Índia* on the death of the governor Pêro Mascarenhas in the year 1554. And Luís Monteiro Coutinho in the company of the said conqueror disembarked in Moçambique from where he passed on to Soffalla, and with his men went marching into the interior *(o certão)* of the Rio de Cuama as far as Monomotapa.[54]

This is, to put it mildly, a rather confused little narrative sequence. Barreto (1520–73) had been interim governor at Goa in the mid- to late 1550s, after having first arrived there in 1547. Thereafter, he had returned to Lisbon after a tortuous and complex voyage, to eventually be named by Dom Sebastião as head of a massive expedition to discover the sources of gold in east-central Africa. However, this large body of men left Lisbon in April 1569 and arrived over an extended period in Mozambique. If Luís Monteiro Coutinho was in fact a member of this expedition, we still cannot account for the period between 1554 (when he was twenty-seven years old) and 1569, when he embarked for the Indian Ocean. In any event, it does not appear that Monteiro Coutinho accompanied Barreto on his long and fruitless trek up the Zambezi River valley, in the process of which (after a further return sortie to the coast) he eventually died at Sena in July 1573.[55] Rather, he was despatched to Goa sometime in the early 1570s: "and the said Francisco Barreto wished to inform the Viceroy Dom Luis de Atayde of his arrival and the conquest of Monomotapa, and to this end despatched Luís Monteiro Coutinho with letters in order to voyage from Moçambique to the port of Goa the capital, in a *pangayo* [*sic*: for pangajava], and on his arrival that whole court rejoiced."

In 1570, Erédia reminds us, "the Moorish kings of India" had constructed a major alliance in order to attack the fortresses of the *Estado da Índia*, and each had decided to besiege one site. The viceroy thus called on Luís Monteiro Coutinho to serve in one of the most hard-pressed of the fortresses, namely Chaul in the Northern Province, which was under siege by Murtaza Nizam Shah (1565–88) of Ahmadnagar.[56] The Portuguese had built a fortress there in 1521, but we are informed that by 1570 the larger Portuguese settlement was "open without any defence in terms of walls, or bulwarks, nor any people in it save the *cazados* who were very few in number to resist the great power of the Nizamaluco who from Adenager [*sic*: for Ahmadnagar] in the Balagate advanced with two hundred thousand infantrymen and cavalry and with them attacked Chaul several times." Coutinho accompanied the captain of the expeditionary force sent from Goa, Dom Francisco Mascarenhas, later himself to be the viceroy of the *Estado* in the 1580s. His hagiographer underlines Coutinho's courage and valor in this first military operation: "he was the first on the frontline in assaults, and sorties and attacks on the [enemy] camp, in which he visited destruction on the Moors, and in the fight he was stabbed mortally six times, and God permitted that he should regain his health and life, so that he could later attain glory through martyrdom."[57]

This account is confirmed in its broad details by the chief Portuguese source for that period, namely António Pinto Pereira's *História da Índia*. Pereira mentions the bravery of the cousins Nicolao and Luís Monteiro at one point in his account of the siege of Chaul, and then adds further interesting details in regard to another episode. Writing of Fernão Pereira de Miranda and his actions, he notes that "in everything, he was followed by Luís Monteiro, a very honorable soldier and one of his clients (*de sua criação*), who in this and other combats always followed and helped him greatly, and on this occasion was pierced by a lance through his mouth."[58]

Recovering from his wounds, Luís Monteiro Coutinho seems to have followed the regular pattern of newly arrived soldiers from Portugal, serving on the coastal fleets that were sent out annually from Goa to patrol the west coast against the Mappilla Muslim adversaries of the Portuguese. According to Erédia, he accompanied Matias de Albuquerque in 1572 when the latter was sent out against Calicut and Chaliyam; the next year, he was part of the coastal fleet that made its way to the Gulf of Cambay and Surat "to impede the arrival and departure of ships from Mecca, so that they do not carry out voyages without a *cartaz* from the viceroy." The year was 1573, and Gujarat had just been conquered with relative ease by a Mughal army.[59] Relations between the Mughal dynasty and the Portuguese were about to enter a new footing, and Luís Monteiro Coutinho would play a minor (but hitherto unnoticed) role therein. Erédia writes:

> And since the King Equebar of Mogor wanted to see Portuguese in his court at Agra, he asked the captain-major Fernão Telles de Menezes to send some Portuguese so that he [Akbar] could make him some grants: and to this end, the said Fernão Telles de Menezes chose Luís Monteiro Coutinho and his cousin António Teixeira Pinto, and having been supplied with all that was needed, they left Surrate and through Amadava [Ahmadabad] arrived in the court of Agra, where they were well-received and fêted by the King Equebar.[60]

Further, if we are to believe Erédia, Coutinho made a particularly favorable impression on the monarch on the occasion of a fencing tournament *(hum desafio de espadas pretas)* that was held at the Mughal court in which he "overcame all the Moors with his sword [so that] everyone was astonished, and it was a great cause of honour for the Portuguese, and at once the king Equebar gave him grants of money and sent him back to Cambaya."[61]

Coutinho thus seems to have returned via Gujarat to Goa around the time of the great administrative disputes that broke out in late 1573, leading to the setting aside of the viceroy Dom António de Noronha and his substitution by António Monis Barreto in December of that year.[62] Noronha was apparently accused of having neglected the affairs of the south *(negócios do Sul)*, and in particular the ongoing dispute between the Portuguese and the Aceh Sultanate. The new governor Barreto, it is claimed by Erédia, was well aware of the valor and enterprise shown by Coutinho at Chaul, Calicut, and elsewhere; he hence chose him to participate in a small maritime force to help shore up the position of the Portuguese in Melaka. Coutinho was thus given command of a galliot, and his brother Domingos Monteiro of another; they accompanied some rather more substantial vessels, including one carrying the incoming captain of Melaka, who according to Erédia was Dom João da Costa, brother of Francisco da Costa who had been captain of Melaka in the years 1570–73 and died in office. This is, however, rather difficult to reconcile with the extant record, which shows that the incoming captain of Melaka at the time was Tristão Vaz da Veiga, who took over from the interim captain Francisco Henriques, and who arrived in the great Southeast Asian port probably in early June 1574. Whatever the confusion with names and precise dates we find in Erédia's text, it is nevertheless clear that Coutinho had no particular desire to remain in Melaka; rather, his chief ambition was to take his galliot and move eastward to Ambon because he had a letter naming him Captain-Major of the Sea of Ambon (*capitão-mor do mar de Amboino*), to eventually be succeeded in that post by his brother Domingos.

But the administrative confusion and disputes that characterized Goa at this time seem to have had an effect lower down in the administrative hierarchy of the *Estado* as well. Thus Dom João da Costa (or Tristão Vaz), having assumed the post of captain of Melaka, insisted that he could not spare any vessels because he needed them all to protect the straits around Melaka and secure them from attack. Both Coutinhos were thus obliged to serve in the seas around Melaka, and Costa/Vaz eventually may have persuaded the governor Barreto in Goa to confirm this decision. Erédia claims to have had access to the original orders *(regimento)* given by Barreto, and produces a copy of it. It runs as follows:

On account of the good information I have of you, Luís Monteiro Coutinho, and of your services and of the good manner in which you have carried them out, I decided to employ you in this aid that I am sending to Malaca, giving you a galliot in which you can better serve the King, my lord, thus adding new merits to those of the past for which I hope you will soon be rewarded, so that setting your prow against all the travails of the

sea and the land, you will set sail together with your brother in
the company of the *nao* of Francisco de Souza Tavares . . . and
you will make for the island of Pulo Pinam [Pulau Pinang], and
there you will wait for the galley and for the captain of Malaca
Dom João da Costa so that you may all go together to the port
of Malaca, and without him you will not move from Pulo Pinam for I am informed through letters that arrived in this mon-
soon that the [king of] Achem was out with his fleet against the
fortress [Melaka]. And these two galliots and the galley are to
go on to Maluco with Diogo de Azambuja, or whoever else is
named in his place if he cannot go. However, I order you and
your brother should go with that galley to Maluco, which is in
great need of assistance, and when you return your brother will
take charge of that post of captain-major of the sea of Amboino,
which I have granted him and charged him with. And nothing
should prevent you from going to Maluco, or from making that
voyage. May Our Lord be pleased to make you prosper in it,
with tail winds and a calm sea, and may He give you the victory
in those parts that I desire for you. Jorge de Lemos composed it
in Goa on 13 April 1576. António Monis Barreto.[63]

We may suspect Erédia here of gilding the lily somewhat; perhaps
he even invented this document entirely in view of its unlikely mention of Dom João da Costa. The language in the latter part of *regimento* is rather suspicious; governors of the *Estado* did not normally
use such phrases as "May Our Lord be pleased to make you prosper
in it, with tail winds and a calm sea" (*que Nosso Senhor volo queira
prosperar, com vento a poupa e mar bonança*). In any event, the chief
purpose of this is to show how, despite his considerable service to the
Crown and the *Estado*, Coutinho was still hampered by the mean-
spiritedness of a *fidalgo* such as Dom João da Costa.

In any event, Erédia assures us that in the succeeding years,
Coutinho continued to act vigorously in the seas around Melaka,

initially in the company of Dom Pedro de Menezes, captain-major of the fleet there. There was a new ruler in Aceh, Raya Mançor, and he apparently wished to put together a new league between the Acehnese and the Malays against the Portuguese, through a marriage alliance between his family and that of the Sultan of Johor, 'Ali Jalla 'Abdul Jalil Shah (whom Erédia terms "Raja Ale Rey de Jor e Viantana").[64] Later, Coutinho also participated in a naval battle between a Portuguese fleet commanded by Matias de Albuquerque and a very large Acehnese fleet *(huma grossa armada de 150 vellas)*, including forty galleys allegedly commanded by Turks with crews made up of "lascarins, Turks, Arabs, Deccanis and Acehnese."

This engagement apparently took place at sunrise, when the Portuguese fleet—which was sailing southeast from Melaka toward the Straits of Singapore—chanced on the Acehnese fleet as it was entering the Johor River.[65] Some of the Acehnese vessels, including the two chief ones *(a almiranta e a bisalmiranta)* were driven onto sandbanks and into mangroves, somewhere in the vague region between Baru Bukit and Tanjung Pura. Coutinho is again said to have engaged in hand-to-hand combat in boarding these galleys, and once more he was wounded seriously; as usual, however, "God granted him life so that he might accomplish marvellous works."

By the time of this engagement, which allegedly took place on January 1, 1578, but really occurred a whole year before on January 1, 1577, Erédia would have it that Coutinho's old nemesis Dom João da Costa had been substituted in the captaincy of Melaka by Aires de Saldanha. (The reality is that Aires de Saldanha became captain in 1576 in place of Miguel de Castro, who had briefly taken the place of Tristão Vaz; we see here that administrative detail and its chronology are clearly not Erédia's strong points.) Saldanha thus permitted Coutinho to return to Goa in late January 1577 (or perhaps 1578), carrying letters for governor Barreto and the king, Dom Sebastião. It was an occasion for Coutinho to insist once more at the capital of the *Estado* on his earlier grant to be captain-major of the seas of

Ambon and the Moluccas, and this was in fact reconfirmed for him by the governor. Barreto apparently also gave him a certificate *(certidão)* mentioning his tireless services on the sea, in particular the combat in the company of Matias de Albuquerque; this, together with another document signed by the city-council *(câmara)* of Melaka, is again copied by Erédia into his text.

However, if Luís Monteiro Coutinho intended to make his fortune in eastern Indonesia, he had chosen the wrong time to do so. The presence of the Spaniards in the Philippines from the 1560s onward was a major reason for the growing problems that the Portuguese faced in that area. In addition, they had mismanaged their relations with the sultans of Ternate to a very great extent from the mid-century on, and the assassination of Sultan Hairun by Portuguese *casados* in 1570 confirmed a rapidly deteriorating situation.[66] The brothers Coutinho thus left Melaka for the eastern seas in a situation where military resources were desperately needed by the Portuguese outposts there. But luck did not favor at least one of them. Domingos Monteiro in his galliot managed to arrive safely at the Portuguese fort of Ambon in time to aid the captain there, Sancho de Vasconcelos, in his bloody inter-island raids in the course of which (according to Erédia), he "captured a great *coracora*, and burnt many other places, favouring friends, and castigating enemies and rebels."[67]

Luís Monteiro was caught in a storm and was eventually shipwrecked, losing his galliot near Pulau Ende on the south coast of Flores. The captain and a number of his companions managed to survive, eventually making their way from Flores—very likely on local vessels—farther east to Solor, where the Portuguese had a fortified settlement.[68] Here they found that they had fallen out of the frying pan and into the fire. This is how Godinho de Erédia describes the situation:

> And Luís Monteiro Coutinho, after that shipwreck, he and his companions passed on from Ende to Solor, and on finding that

fortress of Solor besieged by Moors and renegades in a battery, so the said Luís Monteiro Coutinho with those people from the galley formed a squadron of rescue *(hum esquadrão de soccorro)* and went marching up the beach to a camp with over two thousand renegades and Moors, who were blockading the supplies by sea and by land so that that fortress, which was already at its limit, would surrender from hunger. And Luís Monteiro Coutinho when he was at the distance of an harquebus-shot, opened fire with his harquebusiers *(sua arcabusaria)* with such a fury that he caused great destruction in that encampment; those who escaped from it died at the point of a sword, so that they attained a victory, and freed that fortress of Solor, the capital of that [part of] Christendom from its travails, and also took six *coracoras* as a prize.[69]

Erédia claims that Coutinho and his men went on to build on their momentum and consolidate this victory, marching a league off to Lamakera, which was at that time fortified and defended by a force of 2,500 "renegades and Moors" (Figure 5). This fort, too, was taken by escalade, and all the defenders were massacred; the fortress was razed to the ground, after which Coutinho spent four further months on the island mounting raids and attacks on enemies, while also building alliances for the Portuguese garrison. In short, Erédia concludes, "that shipwreck was a boon for that fortress of Solor" *(antes aquelle naufrágio foi o remédio daquella fortaleza de Solor)*.

This is a curious and interesting narrative section. We note that Erédia himself in his text is fairly vague regarding the identity of the Moorish opponents of Coutinho in these combats in the Lesser Sunda Islands. They might well have been part of a growing shadow of Islamization extending from the western part of the Malay world to the eastern archipelago. Or they might have represented disgruntled groups from areas such as Ternate, which had by now had over half a century of bittersweet dealings with the Portuguese. What is

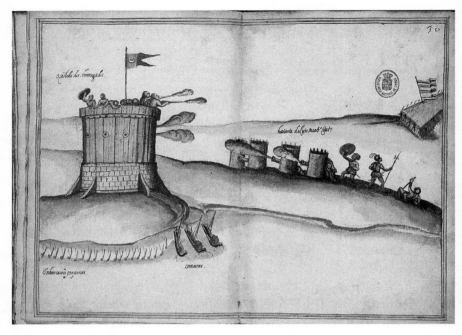

Figure 5. Luís Monteiro Coutinho's attack on a renegade castle in Solor. Biblioteca
Nacional de Portugal, Fundo Geral, Reservados, Codex 414, ff. 29v–30r. Photograph:
Biblioteca Nacional de Portugal, Lisbon.

equally of interest is Erédia's insistence on the presence of renegades
(arrenegados) in the affair, who may have been either Portuguese
or Luso-Asians like Erédia himself. At any rate, what is of crucial
importance for the narrative overall is the constant confrontation
between the figure of Luís Monteiro Coutinho and Islam in its various manifestations: the Mappillas off the Kerala coast, the Mughals
in northern India, the Acehnese off Singapore, and the mysterious
"Moors" as far east as Solor. We may equally note a particular aspect
of Erédia's text, namely, his inclusion of documents, many of which
clarify the matters that he himself is rather vague about. This includes a letter from Frei Amador da Victoria, a priest and vicar *(vi-*

gairo) resident in Solor of the Provincial of the Order of the *Prega-dores de Portugal.* He writes:

> The last year of 1581, Luís Monteiro Coutinho was lost in these parts of Solor through a storm, while he was on his way to aid the fortresses of Maluco and Amboino, as the captain of a galley with 80 soldiers, and it would seem that God brought him to this fortress of Solor with these people to aid us, for we were in such tribulations that I cannot stress those travails enough in this [letter]: for the fortress was besieged, and there was nothing there to eat, since no-one dared to send out for supplies or water by sea or by land, as Solor was wholly besieged by two thousand renegades who had been Christians, and on the sea by six *coracoras* from Maluco. And when Luís Monteiro Coutinho arrived, he attacked them and killed many people. And not satisfied with this, he went on to attack a fort that was at a league's distance, and which had in it more than two thousand five hundred warriors *(homens de peleja),* amongst whom there were Moluccans; and by the force of arms he took this castle from them as well as thirty small vessels and three *coracoras* from Maluco, and six large pieces of metal artillery. So that, on account of his arrival, Solor was liberated, and during the time that he was in this fortress which was four months, he was forever occupied in service, patrolling the coast with an armada, [and] visiting Christian communities. And for this reason, we ask Your Paternity, both we and the *cazados* of Solor, that you may want for the love of God to remember this Christianity. From Solor, on 24th of April 1581. Frei Amador da Victoria.[70]

In Frei Amador da Victoria's letter, matters appear in terms that are far clearer. The source of the difficulties, it would seem, stemmed essentially from the Moluccas and not from western Indonesia. The problems in Solor appear to be above all a fallout of the affairs of

Ternate, and the renegades may have been as much converted Catholic Moluccans as Portuguese or Luso-Asians.

There now follows a hiatus in the text of the *HSMLMC*, suggesting that Erédia had not quite completed drafting it. We are left adrift in Solor, without quite knowing how or when Luís Monteiro Coutinho returned to the western Malay world. The next passage (on folio 18r) returns us abruptly to Melaka in 1582, at a moment when Roque de Melo Pereira had succeeded Dom João da Gama as captain of that fortress. (Here, as usual, Erédia's chronology is incorrect, for he tells us that "Roque de Mello Pereira . . . succeeded Dom João da Gama in that fortress in the year 1581.") This new captain, we learn, sent Luís Monteiro out as captain of an excellent galleass, accompanied by several lighter vessels, to patrol the Straits of Singapore and in particular to accompany the Great Ship of Amacon *(a nao de trato)* as it made its usual stately way to Macau.[71]

Not long after, a message arrived for Coutinho from Roque de Melo stating that Melaka was once more under attack by the Sultan of Aceh with an enormous fleet, comprising seven large and well-armed ships *(sette naos grandes)*, forty royal galleys, and another 150 lighter vessels *(embarcações de galeotas, fustas e lancharas)*. Coutinho prepared to enter battle, after having reinforced his own galleass with elements taken from the other vessels.

Godinho de Erédia portrays his sudden appearance and attack as being an enormous success: "in that encounter, the galleass fired its artillery with great fury, with which it caused great damage to the armada, sending some galleys to the bottom and destroying others."[72] However, the combat eventually came to be close, and the galleass itself was boarded (Figure 6). This was when an unfortunate accident occurred. One of the soldiers dropped a pot of gunpowder *(huma panella de polvora)*, which fell into the gunpowder magazine of the ship. The whole galleass quickly caught fire and exploded, going down with the bulk of the crew and the soldiers on board. According to Erédia, only twelve Portuguese escaped this tragedy, and

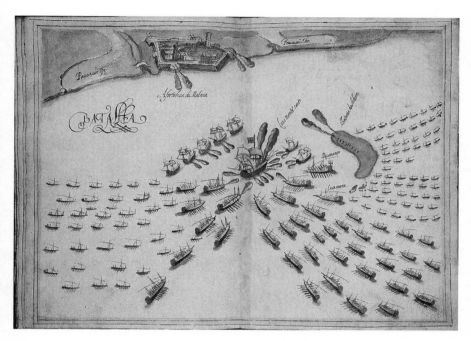

Figure 6. A naval battle off Melaka. Biblioteca Nacional de Portugal, Fundo Geral, Reservados, Codex 414, ff. 12v–13r. Photograph: Biblioteca Nacional de Portugal, Lisbon.

among them was Luís Monteiro Coutinho because he had been defending the stern *(o castello de poupa)* as it was being boarded by the Acehnese. Violently thrown into the water and nearly drowned, these Portuguese were "at once taken prisoner by the Acehnese of the chief galley *(da galle almiranta)* which was to the stern of the galleass and [then] taken to the king Rayamançor who handed them over to the general Laksamana *(Lacamana)*."[73] The sea engagement, he notes, took place on February 6, 1583, "in the presence of the captain of Malaca Roque de Mello Pereira, and all the people in that fortress, who were deeply heartsick to witness such an unhappy and lamentable event, with no-one being able to remedy the travails of that galleass that was lost and burnt."[74]

The official Portuguese chronicler Diogo do Couto in his *Década Décima da Ásia* offers us a somewhat different account of the incident. He notes the arrival of Roque de Melo Pereira from Goa in Melaka on June 20, 1582, and the rather difficult transition between him and the previous captain, Dom João da Gama, who insisted on holding on to a part of his privileges for some time at least. Shortly thereafter, a significant new threat loomed on the horizon: "on 22nd of August [writes Couto], there appeared before that fortress an armada from Achem of one hundred and fifty sail, which included seven great ships *(náos de alto bordo)* and eleven bastard-galleys *(galés bastardas)*." A siege now began, and various residents of Melaka are said to have distinguished themselves in the defense of the city. Couto then adds that he will describe a "very saddening case, and very deeply felt" *(hum caso muito lastimoso, e muito pera sentir)* that occurred.

At the time that the enemies appeared, Luiz Monteiro was employed as the captain of a galleass in the Straits of Sincapura and he had with him about sixty soldiers who were mostly sons of Malaca, to whom Dom João da Gama quickly sent information about the armada from Achem, ordering him to go beyond the Straits of Sabão to be farther away from the enemy, and that he should not budge from there for he would advise him of all that was happening; and that he should on no account allow any Turks or *juncos* with supplies to pass through but rather detain them, for otherwise they would fall into the hands of the enemies and they would supply themselves; and not being content with just one message, he sent him a second and a third, and Roque de Mello did the same after he took command of the fortress with threats of severe action *(penas de caso maior)* if he did the contrary. But since he [Luís Monteiro] was very energetic, and he had so many sons of Malaca with him, it seemed to all of them that they were not doing what they ought to do unless they went to the aid of that fortress, and since they believed that the galleass alone could fight against the whole armada, they all came to an agreement, and ignoring the orders and the insistence of the Captain *(não dando pelos mandados, e protestos do Capitão)*, set sail towards Malaca, and appeared in the sea [before the town].[75]

There is a certain superficial ambiguity here in Couto's version, but it can be cleared up. It is certain that direct orders were disobeyed, but was this with Luís Monteiro's complicity (after all, he was "very energetic," *muito esforçado*) or against his will? It seems that Couto means us to understand that Luís Monteiro Coutinho was in part to blame, and he is certainly in no doubt that the action of Coutinho and his crew was deeply foolhardy. He also reports that as soon as Roque de Melo saw the vessel, he sent out a boat with a certain Nuno Vieira, "whom he ordered to tell Luiz Monteiro that he should at once return to the Straits, under threat of severe action, but he paid no heed to him." Instead, the galleass advanced into the midst of the Acehnese fleet, which divided itself into two parts and surrounded the Portuguese vessel. There is again no doubt in Couto's account concerning the spirit and valor *(animo e valor)* of Coutinho and his companions in the close combat that followed. In his version, they might even have succeeded in making their way through the opposing armada and to the safety of the fortress but for the fact that the sails of the galleass caught fire; a flaming piece then fell down a hatchway where the bombardiers were loading the cannon, and it set fire to barrels of gunpowder. There was a tremendous explosion as the ship blew up: "from the fortress that spectacle was seen with such deep sentiment that all the people were moved to laments, for the greater part of the residents *(moradores)* had sons, and brothers and nephews on board." Couto notes that "some of those who were thrown by the fire into the sea were captured alive by the enemy and taken away as captives," but he mentions no particular names. His moral conclusion is a somber one: "God permitted that with that sort of death they should pay for their disobedience to their Captain [Roque de Melo] for against his repeated orders they came to seek him out in that place."[76]

The Martyrdom

It is possible, even likely, that Erédia was aware of Couto's as yet unpublished official narrative when he wrote his own work, for he certainly was personally acquainted with Couto in Goa. In a sense, therefore, Erédia's purpose may have been to counter the official version; he equally wishes to reassure his reader that all this bravery was not in vain. For, as he tells it, ʿAla-ud-Din Mansur Syah ("El Rey do Achem Rayamançor"), realizing that he had no hope of capturing Melaka in the face of such fierce resistance, packed his bags, called off his men and ships, and returned rapidly to Aceh. The only problem was that he also carried off with him Luís Monteiro Coutinho and his twelve companions (a conventional and rather convenient number), who were thrown into prison where they "endured many troubles from hunger, and thirst, and ill-treatment, all of which they suffered with patience, while each day awaiting the sentence of martyrdom." Erédia continues:

> The King Rayamançor, coming to know that he [Coutinho] was a noble, and a very energetic cavalier, wished to attract him to his service. But he did not wish to show his desire without first ascertaining if he wanted to return to Malaca. And as he came to understand that he was determined not to remain in Achem, he had him secured in prison with his companions.[77]

The implicit comparison may have been with other Portuguese, who—when faced with such adverse circumstances—would have willingly switched sides. But, as Erédia would have it, in Coutinho the Acehnese Sultan had no ordinary prisoner:

> But Luís Monteiro Coutinho, not being able to suffer those intolerable travails of the prison, wished to gain his liberty even at the risk of his person and that of his companions, to whom he communicated regarding this affair in secret, and together with them he concluded that it was necessary to liberate themselves from that captivity. And immediately, that very night, Luís Monteiro Coutinho and the soldiers broke down that prison, and from the gaol they passed to the coast of Pedir [Pidie] in order to freight a vessel in that port for Malaca. But the affair could not be concluded with sufficient secrecy and rapidity, before they were found out by the guards, and in particular by the prison officials. When the King of Achem was informed of that flight of the Portuguese, he sent an Acehnese captain on a powerful elephant with all the guards that were needed, to search out Luís Monteiro Coutinho and the Portuguese, who were concealed in the forest of Pedir, where the Acehnese captain found him with his arms in hand. And when he wished to capture him, Luís Monteiro Coutinho attacked the elephant with his sword and shield with such force that he cut off a piece of its trunk. And the elephant who was constrained by that pain retreated to the settlement. However, the men in the guard captured Luís Monteiro Coutinho and the Portuguese and all of them were taken back to prison. But when the King of Achem Rayamançor was informed of how Luís Monteiro Coutinho had cut the trunk of the elephant without the Acehnese captain being able to kill him while he resisted, the King was filled with rage and he called for the Acehnese captain to be seized and he cut off his head.[78]

The story is an interesting one, as it reflects both Southeast Asian and South Indian tales of individual heroism, where a single hero

Figure 7. Coutinho in combat with an Acehnese elephant. Biblioteca Nacional de Portugal, Fundo Geral, Reservados, Codex 414, ff. 15v–16r. Photograph: Biblioteca Nacional de Portugal, Lisbon.

resists an elephant as a sign of his royal potential (Figure 7).[79] Here it has been transformed into an act of resistance, even if it is a futile one. Coutinho, it seems, is a sort of untamed force of nature, and this leads to the inevitable *dénouement* of the text.

Erédia, like most Portuguese authors of the period, sees the Acehnese Sultans as heavily under Turkish (which is to say, Ottoman) influence.[80] In his account, then, when faced with someone like Coutinho, it was to his Turkish advisers that Mansur Syah was obliged to turn; they advised him to attempt further negotiations.[81] So approaches were once more made to the Portuguese captain;

"that they would give him a life with much money, and he would be given honorable posts in the court at Achem if only he would care to change his faith *(mudar ley)* and accept the sect of Maffamede, but if he refused this offer, then he would be most rigorously punished and killed through the firing of a cannon *(tyro de bombarda)*." It is unclear whether the threat that accompanied the blandishments is supposed to also have been part of the *conselho de Turcos*. At any rate, the response that is placed in the mouth of Coutinho by Erédia is a highly exalted and religious one.

> To this Luís Monteiro Coutinho responded with great joy, saying that he was a Portuguese Christian, baptized in the church of Our Lady of Almacave in Lamego, his Patria, and at that baptism he had been called Luís; and later he received Confirmation in the same parish, and had always lived as a Christian. And that he hoped to die a martyr for the faith of Christ in order to attain eternal glory, and on this account he did not care for mortal life or the riches of the body, for he only desired the salvation of his soul.[82]

He is also supposed to have told his companions that it was a great honor to be in that prison, for they had not been sent there for evil deeds "but only because they defended the Patria and State of Portugal." Coutinho's response is reported by Erédia to have enraged the sultan, who ordered Coutinho to be blown up by a cannon, and his companions to be trampled by elephants, quartered, and have their hands and feet cut off and their throats cut. Furthermore, this was to be carried out as a public spectacle before a crowd.

Erédia continues:

> And on the day following the sentence, the King Rayamançor ordered Luís Monteiro Coutinho and his soldier-companions to be taken from the prison to the fortress on the seafront *(a*

fortaleza da barra) which was two leagues away, where all of them were to be martyred in the presence of the king. And in order to witness this spectacle, the King Rayamançor set out with his grandees from his palace to the fortress by the sea, situated on the edge of the shore, at the mouth of the river, and mounted on an elephant he placed himself in that public square *(terreiro)* to see that martyrdom and if by chance Luís Monteiro Coutinho changed his mind. And to terrorize the said Luís Monteiro Coutinho, they began first to carry out justice on his Portuguese companions, and in front of him they threw a few to the elephants who were at once smashed to bits; and another few were quartered and cut to pieces, with their hands and feet cut off, and others had their throats cut, and while they were in these agonies, Luís Monteiro Coutinho consoled them. And the executioner *(o Algos)* brought Luís Monteiro Coutinho to the mouth of a cannon *(hum bazalisco)* which was on the beach, and without their making a great effort he came to the mouth of the cannon that was to blow him up, where with a great joy he went down on his knees facing the mouth and turning his eyes to the Heavens, and raising up his hands, asked God to pardon him for his sins, since for love of Him he was offering himself for martyrdom [Figure 8].[83]

The soldier is now transformed into the Soldier of Christ, repeating certain of the joyful gestures of the Messiah without the final moments of doubt, ambiguity, and regret that appear in the Gospel. The text continues, drawing the suspense out:

And the executioner once again laid the conditions before Luís Monteiro Coutinho, asking if he wished to accept the sect of Maffamede, to enjoy his life, money, posts and many honors from Rayamançor. And the said Luís Monteiro Coutinho always responded with lucidity that he did not care about the mortal

Figure 8. Coutinho prepares to be martyred. Biblioteca Nacional de Portugal, Fundo Geral, Reservados, Codex 414, ff. 22v–23r. Photograph: Biblioteca Nacional de Portugal, Lisbon.

life when he was about to enjoy eternal life. And hearing this clarity, the executioner pretended to fire the cannon to terrorize him, and he did this several times to see if he changed his faith. And since Luís Monteiro Coutinho disillusioned him saying that they should not waste their time in vain, since neither for promises nor for threats would he abandon the faith of Christ his God, and that they should quickly fire the cannon since what he wanted most of all was to die for the Faith. And when the executioner saw his constancy, and that each time [he responded] with greater warmth and greater boldness, and with total clarity that he would accept nothing from Rayamançor, then the executioner really set fire to the primer of the cannon, and with the setting off of the gunpowder, that glorious body was blown into pieces in the air. And his fortunate soul was joined with his God whom he loved so much while on earth, so that for his faith and love he died. And they found nothing of his flesh, for the gunpowder blew everything into the sea in the northerly direction. And the martyrdom happened on the 24th of March on the eve of Our Lady of the Annunciation, for the greater glory of God, in the year 1583.[84]

Here the text of Erédia effectively ends, having at least clarified the chronological confusion that appears at its outset. Two final documents are copied to provide a solid documentary base for this concrete claim of martyrdom. The first is dated May 1595, and is signed by Dom Leonardo de Sá, the Portuguese Bishop of China, who had not long before been held prisoner in Aceh for three years. He recounts the immediate events surrounding the death of Coutinho, his willing martyrdom, and his being blown up by a cannon (bombarda); he also adds that he learned of all this "from persons who were present there, and there still are three or four eyewitnesses (testemunhas de vista)."[85] A second certificate follows from the Augustinian Frei Hieronimo da Madre de Deus who had been in Aceh as the representative of the Bishop of Melaka, Dom João Ribeiro Gaio. The Augustinian for his part certifies that while in Aceh he interrogated some "local Moors and a renegade" (alguns mouros da terra e a hum arrenegado) and was told the story of Coutinho and his constancy in the face of a spectacularly violent death.[86]

Some Framings

As was noted earlier, the text of the HSMLMC exists in a single manuscript copy, and there are clear indications that it was not wholly completed. Among other matters, a gap exists in the narrative between the events in Solor and the return to Melaka in 1582, which Erédia probably hoped to fill. It is, besides, a rough text, often approximate in its syntax and repetitive in its vocabulary. But it is a work in which Erédia clearly invested something of himself, to the point of drawing several highly stylized and curious illustrations for it. I will list these illustrations, noting that they are somewhat disordered and do not follow the proper sequence of events in the text itself.[87]

- The arms of the Monteiro Coutinhos (fl. 2r)
- A gory scene of martyred Portuguese in Aceh (entitled "Portuguezes martyrizados"), which should correctly be at the end of the text (fls. 10v–11r)
- A bird's-eye view of the naval combat between Coutinho in his galleass and the Acehnese armada (fls. 12v–13r)
- The combat between Coutinho and the Acehnese captain atop an elephant near Pedir (fls. 15v–16r)
- The combat at Solor after the shipwreck in Pulau Ende (fls. 19v–20r)
- "Martírio de Luís Monteiro Coutinho," showing him kneeling before the cannon (fls. 22v–23r)
- Naval combat between Matias de Albuquerque's fleet and the Acehnese fleet near the Johor River (fls. 25v–26r)
- Attack by Coutinho on the renegade fortress in Solor (fls. 29v–30r)

There were at least three distinct possible framings to the writing of the *HSMLMC* that are worth bringing up. The first of these, which we mentioned briefly earlier, is its curious and anomalous place as a commissioned work in the overall oeuvre of Erédia himself. Nuno Monteiro Coutinho, the brother of the text's hero and its patron, was himself a *casado* in Melaka, and it may have been his solidarity with a fellow citizen that led Erédia to accept the compilation of a work like this that allowed him to hark back to his days as a religious novice. A second framing is that of the captivity narrative, a genre that was no doubt gaining a certain popularity at the time in the Portuguese Empire. To be sure, in Erédia's version, Coutinho's captivity was a relatively short one: about seven weeks from the day of the naval combat (February 6) to the day of the execution (March 24). But it could still be read in relation to other narratives that had made a place for themselves in Portuguese literature, particularly after the Battle of Alcácer-Quibir in North Africa, where—after the death of the Portuguese king Dom Sebastião on August 4, 1578—a large number of his followers were captured by their Muslim enemies. Notable among these narratives was the spiritual work of the Augustinian Frei Tomé de Jesus (or Tomé de Andrade, 1529–82), whose work *Trabalhos de Jesus* (significantly, itself written in captivity) was published with much success in the early seventeenth century.[88] In its preface, we learn the circumstances of the text.

[In the battle] he was wounded by an arrow in the shoulder: he was afterwards taken by a Moor, and sold to a *Morabut*, which is the name given in that country to the Mahometan monks. This *Morabut* treated him at first very mildly, and promised him great things, that he might engage him to renounce Christ; but seeing this artifice did not succeed, and that on the contrary he had great difficulty himself to resist Fr. Thomas, who urged him to embrace the Christian faith, by shewing him clearly the absurdity of that of Mahomet, he had recourse to violence; he stript him of his cloaths, loaded him with chains, and threw him into a frightful prison, where he caused him to be cruelly beaten, and allowed him no more food than what was necessary for keeping him alive. It was there that Fr. Thomas of Jesus composed this book of the *Sufferings of Jesus Christ*, for the support and comfort of his captive brethren, whom he could not help in any other way.[89]

This view of things may still have been in the mind of the best-known hagiographer who took up the cause of Luís Monteiro Coutinho, namely, Francisco de Sousa. This Jesuit priest, born in Bahía in 1649, moved to the *Estado da Índia* at a relatively young age after a short stay in Lisbon. In 1710, not long before his own death, and a century and a quarter after the death of Coutinho, he published his celebrated work *Oriente conquistado a Jesus Cristo pelos Padres da Companhia de Jesus.*[90] In it, he devotes some pages to the case of Coutinho, whose martyrdom he dates to 1584. Sousa is well informed indeed, in ways that are astonishing if not suspicious. He provides us details that even the sixteenth-century writers do not seem to have at their disposal, and claims that his main source was the account of "António Ribeiro, a Portuguese, who was captured on the same galleass and was present at everything." Here is how he narrates matters. He begins with how the captain of Melaka, Roque de Melo, had sent Luís Monteiro Coutinho to the straits (of Singapore) in a galleass on June 12, 1582, with orders not to return to Melaka on account of the threat of a large Acehnese fleet. He then informs us that despite these orders, Coutinho chose to return with his forty-two soldiers and made his way back to the sea of Melaka on September 6. However, in the course of the combat (in which 600 enemies were slaughtered), a sail caught fire, which led to an explosion of gunpowder. Coutinho and nine (rather than the formulaic twelve) of his soldiers were captured and carried off to Aceh.

The Sultan of Aceh is here called "Alaradim" (which is not incorrect), and it is noted that after he was defeated before Melaka in 1582, his fleet went on to attack Johor for about three weeks. Sousa's narrative, wherever it comes from, thus manifestly owes nothing to that of Erédia. He also goes on to note that on returning to Aceh, the sultan "divided [the prisoners] in various places in the interior of his kingdom." Several individual Portuguese names are mentioned, including Mateos de Andria and Domingos Toscano (both natives of

Melaka), and Gaspar Gonçalves, the master of the galleass. Sousa tells us that after a year and a half of being incarcerated, Coutinho, Andria, and Gonçalves decided to break out of prison, and they made their way to the seashore, where they managed to get hold of a vessel. But they were not able to get the sails going and did not have the strength to row; as a result, they simply hid in the woods until they were captured. Brought before the royal presence, they were subject to summary justice: Gaspar Gonçalves and Domingos Toscano had their hands and feet cut off, and they were thrown into the sea. Another prisoner, Francisco de Freitas, was thrown under an elephant. As for the young boy (mancebo), Mateos de Andria, he too had his hands and feet cut off, and his body was thrown into the river; Sousa suggests that in this place, the water acquired miraculous and curative properties and that it became a holy spot as a result.

Only Luís Monteiro Coutinho remained to be dealt with. Sousa writes: "One cannot explain the hatred that the tyrant conceived against this Cavalier of Christ, and wanting to give him an exemplary punishment, he ordered that he should have such a death that it would serve as an example to all the Catholics who might find themselves in similar battles." He thus ordered a special cannon (called "Avê") to be brought forward, which was as wide as a great church bell, and had it filled with gunpowder; shortly before sunset, he then gave Coutinho the option either to convert to Islam or to die.[91] The Portuguese responded that he wanted to enter heaven and be united with Christ, and went and sat down in the mouth of the cannon (se foi sentar na boca da bombarda). The cannon was discharged, and "he flew through the air transformed into smoke." Sousa reports that several Christians searched for his relics afterward, but all they could find was a small part of his entrails (entranhas) atop a dried-up tree. The other captives were apparently released and returned to the Estado da Índia, since the tyrant's bloodlust had been satisfied. Oddly enough, Sousa and Erédia do not even have the same date for the martyrdom: the latter suggests March 24, 1583, and the former April 1584, implying a far longer captivity.[92]

A third and final framing in which the work by Erédia can be read is provided by a significant anonymous work published in Lisbon in 1630 (but initially drafted about half a century earlier) entitled *Primor e honra da vida soldadesca no Estado da Índia* ("Excellence and honor of the soldiering life in the State of the Indies"), which we briefly discussed in Chapter 1. This work, like many of those we have surveyed, was closely linked to the Augustinian order; we learn from its title page that it is an "excellent book, composed earlier in the same parts of the East Indies, without an author's name, and now put into order to see the light with an eulogy about him [the author] by P. M. Friar António Freire of the Order of St Augustine, deputy of the Holy Office of the Inquisition in Lisbon." The work is then divided, after a dedication, a note to the reader, and a brief introduction *(fundamento da obra)*, into four symmetrical parts. The first is entitled "Of the obligation that we have to spread the Faith and Christian Religion" and comprises fifteen chapters. A second part is headed "On the service of the King, and of the common weal," and once more is made up of fifteen chapters. The third part, "Of the credit of the nation and of the *Estado*," contains the same number of chapters, and leads us to the final section, "Of the particular excellence of the life of each one," the fifteen chapters of which contain moral and practical lessons for the common soldier. The work has a mixed tone, which may mean that it was the work of more than one hand, namely an anonymous author (possibly himself an old soldier who had served in Asia), and the Augustinian "editor," who may have interfered with the text far more than he admits. On the one hand, it is full of classical citations in Latin, both from religious texts and from lay Greek and Roman authors. On the other hand, its greatest interest lies in its proliferation of concrete examples, drawn for the most part from the middle decades of the sixteenth century, in the years after the foundations of the *Estado da Índia* had been laid. Two of these are particularly relevant to us, both appearing in the first part of the work.

Chapter 9 of Part One of the *Primor e Honra* is entitled "Of what transpired with Diogo de Mesquita in Cambaia, and of the death of seventy soldiers in the same kingdom as well as of Simão Feo." The incident is supposed to have taken place during the governorship of Lopo Vaz de Sampaio (1526–29), when Mesquita, his brother Jorge, and several other Portuguese were captured during a naval battle off the west coast and were taken to Sultan Bahadur of Gujarat (r. 1526–37).[93] The text continues:

> The King of Cambaia wanted to make use of them, in particu-
> lar of Diogo de Mesquita, as he was the chief person, and they
> were all warriors *(todos homens de guerra)*. And so he told him
> that he should become a Moor, and that he would give him
> many honors and benefices; and since Diogo de Mesquita re-
> sponded to this with words against the sect of Mafamede,
> and besides said that there was no great enough honor that he
> [the Sultan] could do him compared to what he as a Christian
> would receive from the Portuguese, so he [the King] ordered
> him to be greatly tortured. And since he showed great forbear-
> ance and constancy in our faith, and great contempt for the sect
> of Mafamede, the King ordered that he should be placed in
> the mouth of a great cannon *(grossa bombarda)*, and that they
> should fire it. Once he had been placed there, they said to him
> that he should pay some attention to the great peril in which his
> life was, and that he should become a Moor, and that if not they
> would fire as the King had ordered and he would be smashed to
> pieces. To which he responded: "O accursed people, ministers
> of Satan! Go ahead, fire away, fire away *(ponde fogo, ponde
> fogo)*, for I am not a man who will negate the true law of God in
> order to accept the false sect of Mafamede." When the King saw

the great spirit and constancy of this man, he was astonished, and wanted even more to have him in his service; and since the other companions had told him [the King] that they would do whatever Diogo de Mesquita did, the King ordered them all thrown in a hard prison, where they were very badly treated, until God organized matters in such a way that they were freed.

While the sequence here is the same as that of the narrative of Erédia to a point, the narrative would have us believe that Mesquita was able to call Sultan Bahadur's bluff. But the author (or authors) does not want to leave the reader with the impression either that things will always end well: they follow this section with other extremely gory stories, such as that of the slaughter of Simão Feo and his men in the 1540s, or of a "young Portuguese, a gentleman, who was crucified and skinned alive since he would not agree to the abominable sin [*pecado nefando*, i.e., sodomy] with that accursed king Soltão Badur."[94]

The next chapter of the *Primor e Honra* is, in some sense, of even greater relevance for it deals with Aceh at the time of Sultan 'Ala-ud-Din Ri'ayat Syah al-Qahhar ("Soltão Aladim, rei do Achém"). It recounts how, in the mid-1560s (a date we can infer from some contextual details), a certain number of Portuguese in the eastern Bengal port of Chittagong (Porto Grande) began to have profitable trading relations with Aceh. These included Cosme de Magalhães and his associate Fernão Viegas. But on a subsequent trip, Viegas, his son, and Álvaro Ferreira were seized in Aceh, perhaps because they had had a quarrel with an Ottoman ambassador (*um mouro embaixador do Grão Turco*) there. Given the options of conversion or death, they were tortured by being stretched out naked on the sand, with heavy beams on their legs; Ferreira was then skinned alive (*esfolado vivo*). The text then narrates a touching conversation between Viegas and his son, where the father urged the boy to convert and save himself, and the son steadfastly refused. But there is more to the tale: soon after, Cosme de Magalhães, entirely innocent of what had happened to the others, appeared in Aceh and was seized in turn, despite the fact that he had a royal *farmān* (or *formão*) to protect him. The sultan pointed out the damage that had recently been done to his ships by a Portuguese fleet under Gonçalo Pereira Marramaque; after a brief but violent exchange of words, the sultan had Cosme de Magalhães and his companions stabbed to death with spears (*às azagaiadas*).[95] Finally, in the same sequence, Pero Lobo, a Portuguese merchant from the Coromandel coast, was also seized with his companions (including a cowardly Fleming from Bruges) and brought before the sultan, who asked him what useful service he could render. Lobo is reported to have replied "that he knew how to make munitions for muskets, and kill many Moors with them"; he had his eyes torn out for his insolence. The chapter concludes: "Of all these men, who were fifty-seven Portuguese in all, no-one became a Moor, except the Fleming [called Fernão de Burges] as we already said, who is still there, and is charged with muskets and damascene (*oficial de espingarda e tauxia*)."[96]

The text of the *Primor e Honra* arguably shares some common elements with the contemporary writings of Portuguese *arbitristas* or reformers, men like Francisco Rodrigues Silveira or even Diogo do Couto (in a certain incarnation).[97] It wishes to improve the morale and behavior of the Portuguese soldiery, and is in a sense concerned with an idea of decadence. But it is above all a moral work, a form of collective hagiography that is rooted in ideas of soldierly martyrdom and filled with instances of miracles where soldiers die "good deaths." The best of the deaths in this understanding is the one that consists of resisting the temptations of Islam, and underlying these tales is a deeper realization: namely, that many Portuguese had indeed converted and entered the services of Muslim rulers across the width of Asia. To the author(s) of the *Primor e Honra*, such dishonorable behavior might come from a native of Bruges, but it was not to be accepted from a proper Portuguese.[98]

This, then, was the larger reality that also defined the urge behind Erédia's work. In such works, the moments of martyrdom are largely undermotivated, and we are never allowed to understand why (beyond the fact that they are "tyrants") various sultans are so determined to orchestrate gory and spectacular deaths for Portuguese soldiers. What we are meant to understand is the difference between the ordered and lawful life of the *Estado da Índia* (at least in its ideal version) and the noisy if opulent tyrannies that confronted it, whether in Gujarat or in Aceh.

It is ironic that the mode of martyrdom used here was one that was deployed about two centuries later for quite different moral purposes. In the aftermath of the Great Indian Rebellion of 1857–58, we are informed of the repeated use of a "frightful punishment, much favored by British commanders for its supreme deterrent value, of being 'blown from the cannon's mouth'."[99]

The text we have examined in detail here was also a deterrent of a sort, but one that was intended to deter Portuguese from having too much truck with the other side. For all that he was a *mestiço*, Erédia had to let his reader know that his faith was unwavering, as much as that of his hero Luís Monteiro Coutinho. Death by basilisk was for him surely part *topos* and part nightmare; above all, it was a measure of the fact that martyrdom was not simply a relic of the distant past, but a pressing reality when the lines between the cultures—even the courtly cultures—of Muslims and Christians became too blurred for comfort.

3

Courtly Representations

You hold the Glass, but turn the Perspective;
And farther off the lessen'd Object drive.
You bid me fear: in that your change I know:
You would prepare me for the coming blow.

— John Dryden, *Aureng-Zebe* (1675)

In this chapter, we turn in a more purposeful manner to questions of long-distance cultural circulation between courts and the closing of a rather wide circle. We have looked at courtly exchanges and encounters in the context of the Deccan, and then with the Portuguese in the world of the Indian Ocean, extending into Southeast Asia. More generally, the sixteenth and seventeenth centuries witnessed a considerable quickening in intercontinental trade and the circulation of humans, animals, plants, ships, commodities from bullion, guns, and pepper as well as porcelain and furs, and even (some would say especially) microbes.[1] In some instances, the situations in 1500 and 1700 were so radically apart that one can qualify the change as truly revolutionary; this is the case with the massive restructuring and even outright destruction of the fabric of pre-Columbian societies on the American continents over that period. In other cases, the pace of change was less dramatic but still appreciable. China and India had already been connected to the western Mediterranean in the fourteenth and fifteenth centuries, but the connection was a feeble one, probably comprising a few dozen direct traders and travelers each year, while practically no ships made it from the Mediterranean or the seas west thereof to the Indian Ocean. By 1700, the extent of connection was far more considerable, and even Japan— reputedly in its "restricted" (*kaikin* or *sakoku*) phase—continued to maintain contact with western Europe through the Dutch trading factory in Deshima.[2] It is still our habit when we recount this history to present it essentially as one of a growing European presence in and influence on Asia (the so-called expansion-and-reaction paradigm), with relatively little attention to the closing of the circle. One can see why such a habit of thought persists; in comparison with the rather large number of Europeans in Asian waters, relatively few Asians made it to, say, Portugal or the Netherlands between 1500 and 1700. Fewer still lived to tell the tale, though we may have underestimated the numbers of those who did. One half of the circle is thus drawn perforce in far stronger traits than the other. This is, however, not a reason to ignore the many and interesting ways in which the circle was indeed closed. One of these ways was arguably through art and visual representation at the courtly level.

To further the analysis, a central notion that we can return to here is that of "incommensurability," which we have already adverted to in our earlier discussion of Kuhn, Feyerabend, and their latter-day heirs. We have seen that Kuhn hesitated between an argument on the "indeterminacy of translation" and the idea that incommensurability was a failure of exact translation.[3] From the latter position arose the development of the idea of "cultural incommensurability," favoring a view in which cultures were seen as complexes that were both coherent in and of themselves and largely impermeable to others. Indeed, if they were permeated, the view was that this could only lead to forms of corruption or cultural degradation.[4] Now, as it happens, the implications of ideas such as these for the study of early modern visual encounters and interactions in an interimperial context have largely remained unexplored. In particular, the tension between ideas of commensurability and agency would merit further investigation, but this would surely require us to focus on well-defined actors and particular actions and processes rather than paint cultural interaction itself, as it were, in broad brushstrokes.

Receiving the Franks

Let us begin with the first half of our notional circle, that which takes us from Europe to India. In the course of about a half-century, between the arrival of the first Jesuit mission in Fatehpur Sikri in 1580 and the death of the emperor Nur-ud-Din Muhammad Jahangir in late October 1627, extant literature tells us that a substantial change took place in the artistic relationship between Europeans (*firangīs* or Franks) and the painters of the Mughal and other Indian royal and aristocratic ateliers. To state this is by now to state a commonplace. Hundreds, if not thousands, of pages have been devoted to the transformation of Mughal art under European (and in particular Catholic) influence: the brilliant and often startling paintings on Biblical themes by Keshav (Kesu) Das and others; the effect on the iconography and self-presentation of the emperors themselves— from depicting themselves with halos to surrounding themselves with cherubs and angels; the use of the symbolism of the globe to literalize the power of the rulers as "world-seizers"; and the use of set pieces of perspectivized urban and rural landscapes to provide the backdrop even to scenes where the content was not noticeably Christian. In the beginning, if conventional historiography may be credited, lay the fascination exercised by the printed books with their woodcuts and engravings that the Jesuits brought along as part of their portable libraries. Among these, pride of place is taken by the celebrated if unwieldy multivolume polyglot Bible, or *Biblia Regia*. It was printed at Antwerp in 1,200 copies and large folio format between 1568 and 1573 by the Flemish printer Christoffel Plantijn (or

Christophe Plantin), in collaboration with other scholars and under the supervision of the Spanish theologian Benito Arias Montano. This Bible, patronized and heavily subsidized by Philip II, contained text in Latin, Hebrew, Greek, and Syriac as well as several impressive engravings. Along with this work, the first Jesuits in Sikri—Fathers Acquaviva, Monserrate, and Henriques—also carried another major object produced by an associate of Plantijn, namely Abraham Ortelius's atlas entitled *Theatrum Orbis Terrarum*. By the end of his reign, it has been claimed, the emperor Akbar had "amassed an astounding collection of Renaissance visual and literary artifacts," and these included "a vast number of engravings of the work of artists ranging from Michelangelo, Raphael, and Taddeo Zuccaro to Dürer and Martin de Vos; oil paintings donated by the great aristocratic families of Rome; and even a Portuguese painter [unnamed]."[5]

The Mughals thus felt the effects of not only the Renaissance but also the Counter-Reformation at its height. To be sure, Plantijn and his larger circle (the so-called Family of Love, which was more or less a Nicodemite group) represented a rather moderate view of what Christianity might be in relation to other religions or beliefs; the same could not always be said of the Jesuits who carried the works printed by his press to India.

At any rate, there is little doubt that the polyglot Bible was given a suitably pomp-filled reception in the Mughal court on its arrival. Here is how that reception was described by an eyewitness, the Catalan Jesuit Antonio Monserrate:

> On the 3rd of March they [the Jesuits] took to the audience chamber a copy of the Holy Bible, written in four languages and bound in seven volumes; this they showed to the King. In the presence of his great nobles and religious leaders Zelaldinus [Jalal-ud-Din Akbar] thereupon most devoutly not only kissed the Bible, but placed it on his head. He then asked in which volume the Gospel was to be found. When he was shown the

right volume, he showed yet more marked reverence to it. Then he told the priests to come with their Bible into his own private room, where he opened the volumes once again with great reverence and joy. He shut them up again very carefully, and deposited them in a beautiful bookcase, worthy of such sacred volumes, which stood in the same private room, where he spent a great deal of his spare time.[6]

This attractive, well-plotted version of what seems to be the first Mughal exposure to the European book is not entirely convincing.

Surprisingly little attention has been paid to the presence of European books, whether printed or manuscript, in Asia in the years before the episode described by Monserrate. From a scanty bibliography, one learns of how a printing press was sent from Portugal to Ethiopia, but it wound up in Goa, where it was first put to use by the Jesuits from late 1556 to produce texts such as the *Conclusões de lógica e philosophia* (1556) and the *Doutrina cristãa* (1557), both unfortunately now lost to us.[7] This was somewhat after the first printing press had become operational in Mexico but preceded the one in Lima. The first printers in Goa were apparently the Spaniards Juan Bustamante (also known as João Rodrigues) and Juan González. In April 1563, the name of obscure German printer Johannes von Emden appears on a very celebrated work from the same city, the *Colóquios dos simples e drogas e cousas medicinais da Índia* by Doutor Garcia da Orta. By the late decades of the century, experiments had been made in printing text in Tamil (and even to a limited extent Nagari script, for Konkani); the more successful Tamil texts were printed from the late 1570s onward under the impetus of the energetic Jesuit Henrique Henriques in Cochin and Kollam for use on the Fishery Coast of southern Tamilnadu.[8] None of these works attained the sophistication or product quality of the polyglot Bible, yet they cannot entirely be neglected, even though they did not contain elaborate images.

Nor can we lay aside the issue of the circulation of manuscript European books, some undoubtedly with images on them. We have to assume that the crew and priests on the early fleets of Gama, Cabral, and João da Nova must have carried such books, usually Christian in character and content, with them. By 1509, when the Portuguese under Dom Francisco de Almeida were fighting a Mamluk fleet off Diu in Gujarat, they claimed to have encountered among the spoils of war "some books in Latin, and in Italian, some for praying and others of history, and even a prayer-book *(livro de orações)* in the Portuguese language."[9] A few years later, the governor Albuquerque noted that he had at his disposition in Cochin a good number of instructional religious pamphlets that could be used to instruct novices and young converts *(huma arca de cartinhas por omde imysnam os meninos).*[10]

By the time Goa came to be the focal point and center of Portuguese operations by about 1530, it is reasonable to suspect that certain small manuscript collections and even private libraries would have been available in that city. Nor can we rule out the possibility of individual Portuguese carrying books around in their wanderings. A somewhat neglected passage from the chronicle of Diogo do Couto provides us with a view of the Mughal encounter with Christian European imagery that considerably precedes the Jesuit presence in the court of Akbar. It appears in a chapter of the chronicle dealing with the situation in the late 1530s and early 1540s: "Of what happened to Hamau Paxa [Humayun Padshah], king of the Magores after he was defeated by Xirxa [Sher Shah]; and how with the favor of Xa Ismael [Shah Ismaʻil, *sic*: for Shah Tahmasp of Iran, r. 1524–76], king of Persia, he came back to conquer his kingdoms." Couto informs us that Humayun, when on his way into exile in Iran, was a protagonist in the following rather curious incident:

On this voyage *(jornada)*, there was a Portuguese by name Cosmo Correa, a settler *(cazado)* from Chaul with a wife and children (who is still alive) who, since he had assaulted a [Crown]

Factor fled to Cambay and from there passed to the court of the
Magor, who used to give a good account of this voyage, because
he was a well-informed man and on that account the Magor
was well-inclined towards him. And he used to recount many
things about him [Humayun], amongst which he used to say
that when he was talking with him one day, he [Humayun]
asked him to show the book using which he prayed and that he
[Correa] brought him the [Book of] Hours of Our Lady (which
had a binding illuminated in the old style in quarto), and on
opening it the King fell at once on the beginning of the seven
Psalms, where there was an illumination of the story of David
and Bathsheba.[11] And the king looking at it carefully, said to
Cosmo Correa: "What will you give me if I guess [the content
of] these stories?" Cosmo Correa responded to him: what did he
possess to give to such a great monarch? "Give me your lance,"
said the Magor (for it was one from Portugal), "and if [I do] not
[guess it] I will give you the head of a wild boar which I will kill
in front of you." And with that, he recounted the story to him
just as we have it in the Scriptures. And handing the book back
to him, he [Humayun] asked that he show him the four men
who had written the Law of the Christians, and Cosmo Correa
showed him the Evangelists [Matthew, Mark, Luke, and John]
who were illuminated in the beginning of the four Passions,
which the King looked at carefully and said: "Now, you should
know something, which is that on many occasions I heard my
father Babur Paxa say that if the Law of Muhammad were to
suffer a decline, that I should receive no other than that which
has been written by four men." And thus this barbarian was so
fond of Christians that whenever he saw them, he gave them
great honors and grants.[12]

Several aspects of this story are worthy of note. In the first place,
we can independently identify the existence of Cosmo Correa from

Chaul from state documents of the period.[13] Second, the account of the discussion around the image is in fact plausible, even though the last section appears to be a characteristic exaggeration. Muslim and Gentile rulers in Asia, if we are to believe the Portuguese, were forever on the verge of becoming Christian. In reality, very few freely did, and a large proportion of those who did apostatized. There is no reason to believe that either Babur or Humayun, however ambiguous their relationship might have been between Sunnism and Shi'ism, ever really thought of Christianity as an option. Rather, what the anecdote does bring out was the existence of a complex relationship between the books of the Christians and the culture of Muslims like the Timurids. Humayun obviously liked and patronized painting—though only a few paintings from his atelier such as his "garden party" have survived—and he had no aversion at all to the painted image, even the human one.[14] The stories of the Old Testament and its kings and prophets, such as that of David, were a part of a familiar repertory for him. There is thus every reason to believe that in a dull moment during a long and difficult voyage, he might have taken some delight in leafing through a book in an unfamiliar script but with intelligible (and in this instance somewhat erotic) images. The text in question was, as Couto notes, a Book of Hours of Our Lady, or in Latin the *Horæ beate marie virginis*. It is unclear whether the book was manuscript or printed; if printed, it must almost certainly have come from a source external to Portugal, such as the busy printing presses of Paris.[15]

This is a first and important point to note, and it is something of a paradox. Christian-oriented imagery in sixteenth-century India was far more of a success than Christianity itself. There were only two broad areas where conversion to Catholicism produced substantial results. The first was Goa, in particular after the mid-century, when temples were destroyed on some scale and a mixture of carrot and stick was employed to bring the "Gentiles" within the fold of Christianity.[16] It is possible that, in this process, the visual medium played a significant role because some of the churches that were built in the course of the century had ambitious pictorial programs, such as the scenes from the *Vida e Martírios de Santa Catarina* painted in Lisbon by Garcia Fernandes for the See church in Goa.[17] The second area was the far south of the peninsula, already referred to as the Fishery Coast. Here, the language of communication was Tamil, and the target community was largely restricted to a single low-status caste, the Paravas. The Jesuits in this context devised and printed books in a colloquial register of Tamil, but they are also known to have had paintings on Old and New Testament themes made in Goa and transported to the churches of the Fishery Coast for didactic ends. Far less is known about how the paintings were received and what, if any, effect they had on painting and visual expression in the region itself.

The case is quite different with the Mughals. After 1580, it has been noted by Gauvin Bailey, "Akbar ordered his artists to paint hundreds of iconic portraits of Jesus, Mary, and a panoply of Christian saints in the styles of the late Renaissance to adorn books, albums, jewelry, and even treaties." Bailey is at some pains, however, to insist that "Catholic devotional art was produced and received [by the Mughals] in a profoundly different manner than in Europe and many of its colonies," and he suggests several possible reasons for the paths taken by the Mughals. The first of these, in his view, lay in the "common Neoplatonic heritage" shared by Sunni Islam as practiced in Mughal India and Counter-Reformation Christianity. Less plausibly, he claims that "it is quite possible that the Mughals chose Catholic imagery because Islam itself did not provide an iconographic tradition capable of combating the visually potent pantheon of Hindu deities." In other words, Catholic devotional art could build bridges because it was somehow "culturally neutral"; indeed, the even stronger claim is made that "its realism and immediacy were believed to be universal and allowed it to transcend cultural and ethnic boundaries and embrace the whole of humanity."[18] Believed by whom to be universal?, one is entitled to ask.

A discussion reported by François Bernier with Brahmins in Benares in the 1660s is relevant here. Bernier had chosen to mock the Brahmins on their bathing rituals, stating that "in the cold countries it would be impossible to observe their law [on bathing] during the winter, which was a sign that it was a pure human invention." He reports that they responded as follows: "that they did not claim that their law was universal; that God had made it for them and it was for that reason that they could not receive a foreigner into their religion; that for the rest, they did not claim at all that our [religion] was false; and that it might well be that it was good for us and that God had created different paths to go to heaven, but that they did not wish to accept that our [religion] being valid for all of the earth, theirs was nothing more than a fable and pure invention."[19] The idea that what was Catholic was obviously universal, embraced all of humanity, and transcended cultural and ethnic boundaries was thus a perfectly Catholic idea but was not shared by anyone else. The Brahmins, for their part, seem to have been relative relativists, in a Latourian mode.

Fortunately, in the case of the Mughals and Jesuits, we are not obliged to rest our case on inference and speculation alone. The Mughal court has left behind a corpus of documents and narrative materials regarding its perception of the Jesuits and the materials they submitted to the imperial gaze. These do not appear for the most part in the great imperial chronicles in Persian, which barely deign to mention the Jesuit presence at the court on a handful of occasions. Rather, they appear mainly in the dispersed writings of 'Abdus Sattar ibn Qasim Lahauri, whom Edward Maclagan refers to as "a prominent literary man of the day," and who was in many ways the chief intermediary figure between the Jesuits and the Mughal court in the late sixteenth and early seventeenth centuries. Sattar had initially been close to the Jesuit Jerónimo Xavier, but later had a substantial falling out with the Jesuits over issues of religion. The Jesuits for their part saw him as ungrateful; they claimed that he had been "as poor as Irus" when they first knew him and had only received an official rank through the intervention of Xavier.[20] Sattar was certainly a key participant in debates that took place on Christianity in the early years of the rule of Jahangir, while the emperor was in Agra. By this time, a considerable corpus of Christian texts had been translated into Persian, largely through the collaboration of Xavier and Sattar. The context for the debates is described as follows by Xavier in one of his letters:

> As the king was resting in Agra, one night his librarian on his orders brought him a great mass of books *(grande multidão de registros)* concerning our saints and other things (which in the previous years he had collected), in order to pass sections of the night looking at them, and through these images we managed this year to do what we had wanted for many years, which is to have a public dispute with the principal people of the king in front of him, regarding matters of our Holy Law and that of the Moors, and these exchanges and disputes went on for a month almost every night, and in order to do this he used to call us close to him *(junto de si)* where usually only the sons of the king and some of his confidants were, and the others were [standing] a bit further off. And since I trust that our dearest brothers would like to hear about this, I will recount in some detail some of the things that happened on some of these nights.[21]

Xavier's description then contents itself with describing the challenges that the Muslim *'ulamā'* of the court put to the Jesuits, and suggests that on each occasion that a challenge was presented, superior Jesuit rhetorical and logical skills prevailed.

The optimistic vision of a Mughal court where Christianity is on the verge of making a major breakthrough is preserved in these writings, as it was in the compendia made of them and presented to a larger audience in Europe. This is not at all the image that one receives from Sattar, in particular in his account of the nocturnal meetings of Jahangir's courtiers. The identity of the author supports the credibility in his account: 'Abdus Sattar was the author of *Samrat ul-Falāsifa* ("The Fruits of Philosophers"), also known as the *Ahwāl-i Firangistān*, a text based on his knowledge of Latin, which he had acquired through Jerónimo Xavier. He also collaborated with Xavier on a number of other works such as a life of Jesus entitled the *Mirāt ul-Quds* (or *Dāstān-i Masīh*, completed in A.H. 1011) and the *Dāstān-i Ahwāl-i Hawāriyān* or *Waqāʾiʿ-i Hawāriyān-i Duāzdagāna* (Account of the Twelve Companions), which was completed in A.H. 1014.[22] However, with the passage of time, Sattar grew increasingly disgruntled with the Jesuits in particular and with Christians in general. His position increasingly came to be that while Jesus was indeed a prophet, the work that the Christians claimed was the Gospel *(injīl)* was in fact a fabrication. These views, which were propounded by him in the court with detailed examples taken from his reading of texts in Latin, seemed to have been supported by many influential courtiers such as Mirza 'Aziz Koka.

One may take a single discussion in Jahangir's court as recounted by 'Abdus Sattar to gain a flavor of the status of Christianity there at the time, which is quite at odds with the Jesuit version. We focus not on the Jesuit participation in the debate or their attacks on Islam (of which there were several) but on the Mughal side of the argument and their critique of the Christians. The episode took place in around June 1610, when Jahangir had just received a gift from the Portuguese of the port of Goa accompanied by some new Jesuits *(dānāyān-i Farang)*, including one—probably the Florentine Francesco Corsi—who Sattar states was noted for his harsh speech, bigotry *(taʿassub)*, and sharp temper. On arriving at the courtly meeting, this Jesuit apparently began to praise his own faith and denigrate Islam, despite attempts by several courtiers to lighten the occasion. Eventually, when he stated that anyone with intelligence would not accept the Muhammadan faith *(dīn-i muhammadī)*, the emperor lost his patience a little and asked Sattar to intervene in view of his knowledge of matters Christian. A debate now began with the Jesuit, somewhat contemptuously termed a mere cross-worshipper (salīb-parast) here. When the Jesuit was asked whether he did not believe in prophethood as such (which would make him a kāfir-i mutlaq, an unqualified denier) or in the prophethood of Muhammad, he responded that his view was simply that Muhammad was no prophet (paighamabar). He himself was a Christian ('Isawī) and believed in the religion of the Gospel (dīn-i injīl). Sattar responded that he did not believe that the Frank's religion was the religion of Jesus or indeed that his book was the Gospel. He thus felt that he had turned the tables on him.

The debate resumed after a gap, with Sattar attacking the Christians most vigorously, declaring that he found their faith the most false (bātil-tarīn), the most impure (najis-tarīn), and the dirtiest (gandatarīn). He stated that he found even the faith of Hindus (dīn-i hunūd) better than Christianity. The emperor was shocked at this, however, and declared it unreasonable. Sattar responded that after all even the Hindus did not claim that their God had been crucified. Jahangir replied that they might not say that, but the Hindus did have a god who had sported with 12,000 women on a single day and impregnated them all! Sattar retreated from his position and said he was willing to concede that if the emperor felt that way then it must be true. But he still could not withdraw his objections to the God of the Christians, who had been crucified naked, received 5,000 lashes, had his face spat upon, worn a crown of thorns, and been mocked by people. Further, Sattar noted that he was not making this up but deriving his knowledge from the scriptures of the Christians.

The emperor asked the Jesuit padre for a response. The padre said that, in their view, God had not been killed, that this was a false accusation. Rather, he asserted the simultaneous humanity and divinity of Jesus. Sattar responded that he felt that the padre was simply wasting time. Could he deny what had been said regarding the crucifixion of Christ, the thousands of lashes, the crown of thorns, and the spitting? When the other agreed this was all true, Sattar asked bluntly: Was Jesus then God, and was God Jesus? The padre responded that he was. Sattar turned to the emperor and said that it was hence clear that their God had been crucified and had been humiliated. To sum up, Sattar pointed out that the Frankish wise men *(dānāyān)* claimed that Jesus was both God and man, just as something can have elements of both white and black. Yet, when it suited them, they denied that it was their God who was humiliated, crucified, and killed.[23]

We are not obliged to believe the account by 'Abdus Sattar any more than the letters of the Jesuits. However, several aspects of this narrative sequence, as well as other sections concerning the Jesuits in Sattar's work, are worthy of attention, though the anti-Christian objections raised in the debate are quite banal. First, we see that opposition to and skepticism concerning the Jesuits and their messages was certainly not confined to orthodox *'ulamā'*. Rather many high courtiers, historians, and intellectuals partook of it and outright rejected both the divinity (as opposed to the prophethood) of Jesus and the veracity of the Christian Gospel. Further, it is clear that this was not based on a lack of exposure to Christian materials but on a progressive exposure to them, as the debates between faiths proceeded apace in a courtly context. Sattar knew the Christian texts, and he knew them well; he was able to quote them and raised minute and even hair-splitting issues. For these reasons, it becomes increasingly difficult to accept the view that Christianity was somehow seen as a distant, neutral, and universal language of communication between different faiths. Rather, it raises a distinct other possibility, namely, that it was not the narrative content (Christian) of the images that the Jesuits brought with them that accounted for their success but their formal innovation. Bailey is indeed right to state that the Mughals and their artists "did not necessarily perceive the imagery as Christian," but he possibly does not draw the appropriate conclusions from there.[24]

What is of significance for our purposes is that the Mughal consumption, appropriation, and transformation of European visual representation were not limited to religious (or Christian) themes. It has long been known that geographical representations, both atlases and the globe, were not merely present in the Mughal court but also actively incorporated into Mughal painting. Akbar himself on one occasion is reported by Monserrate in the course of a discussion to have "an atlas brought [to see] . . . where Portugal was, and where his own kingdom."[25] A close analysis of the paintings made to illustrate Nizami Ganjawi's *Khamsa* from the early 1590s (in Akbar's court) by Gregory Minissale is thus premised on the need "to examine the adoption of the European techniques of *sfumato*, modeling and stereoscopic perspective in the *Khamsa* illustrations and then to trace the European sources for the motifs of some the key miniatures," and the author adds that "in this regard, it is necessary also to look at the use of motifs taken from European maps for Mughal background landscapes, which is a subject that has not been [adequately] dealt with in Mughal art history."[26] Equally, in a recent essay by Sumathi Ramaswamy, it has been noted that while "the terrestrial globe as an object and as representation was only introduced into India in the later years of the sixteenth century . . . it was incorporated within a few decades into the visual productions of the Mughal workshop to generate an aura of grandeur and singularity for the Mughal patrons."[27]

It would moreover be an error to look constantly for religious roots in Mughal art, as if only in the context of a clichéd axis between Sultan and Sufi, or in the alleged ascendance of the spiritual over the temporal, can the production of the imperial or subimperial ateliers be understood. This is precisely where the Jesuit-dominated literature misleads us, as in the case of the celebrated episode reported by Fernão Guerreiro, where the presence of a picture of the Virgin "which was of the height of a man," copied from that of Santa Maria del Popolo in Rome *(uma imagem da Virgem Nossa Senhora, retratada pela de Roma que se chama de Pópulo)*, is claimed to have created a tumult in the town. As was reported of one "great captain" among the Mughals, "as soon as he saw the picture [he] stood as one in a trance, so overcome was he with admiration," while another high *mansabdār* "gazed on it for a long time in silent wonder [until] presently, tears filled his eyes and began, one by one, to roll down his cheeks." Eventually, we are told, the Mughal court painters attempted to copy it: "but although the painters put forth their utmost skills, they were fain at last to lay down their implements, acknowledging that such perfection of portraiture was beyond their skill, and that they were unable to compete with the Portuguese in this art *(nem nesta arte se podiam igualar com os portugueses)*."[28]

The issue, however, is the presentation of the episode in the language of the miraculous and hagiographical, which makes it almost impossible to extricate from the Christian religious sphere. If indeed the painting had been a copy of Annibale Carracci's recently completed *Assumption of the Virgin* (rather than the Virgin above the altar of the Popolo), we could have placed a rather more mundane construction on the alleged difficulties faced by the artists from the Mughal atelier in reproducing an extremely dense structure replete with human forms and the play of light and shade. But it seems that the painting was instead a copy of the rather archaizing Madonna icon from the same church (brought there by Pope Gregory IX in the thirteenth century, and attributed to St. Luke), and the reaction described by the Jesuits can only be deemed somewhat improbable, especially once we have read 'Abdus Sattar's counter-narrative, where the very Mughal nobles who were apparently transfixed by this image (like 'Aziz Koka) consistently made disparaging remarks about Christians.

What lends credibility to the hypothesis that the Christian content of the visual materials was secondary to their interesting and innovative visual language from the perspective of their Mughal appropriators is an accumulation of episodes from the seventeenth century involving European art that did not come directly from the contexts of the Renaissance and Counter-Reformation. The first incident, which is relatively well known, concerns a Dutch artist from Haarlem, Cornelis Claesz de Heda. After spending time in a Mannerist context at Prague with Rudolf II, Heda found himself in Goa and then in Bijapur under Sultan Ibrahim 'Adil Shah II, where he later died around 1622. Heda, who arrived in Bijapur around 1610, left behind letters dating to about 1619; their contents make it clear that he was treated well at the court and his art much appreciated.[29] (The travel narrative of Heinrich von Poser from 1622 notes that when he arrived in Bijapur, Heda had just died, leaving behind a beautiful mansion in Nauraspur that was sufficiently magnificent to be eventually given over to the use of the Safavid envoy.[30]) To the extent that Heda speaks of his experiences as an artist, he notes that the Bijapur ruler's taste ran to classical European painting involving themes such as Venus, Bacchus, and Cupid. Although none of Heda's paintings have survived, this is evidence that this sultan had no apparent interest in patronizing art by Heda with an explicitly Christian content.[31]

The same is true from the few cases we can identify of other Dutch artists in south and southwest Asia in the seventeenth century. Their presence in the Mughal court often has proved elusive to trace, but we can be certain that they existed and that their "naturalism" and "minutely-observed nature studies and psychological portraiture" continued to be incorporated into the painterly vocabulary of the court of Jahangir and Shahjahan.[32] Much work needs to be done to track down individual artists in circulation, since we are still dependent to a fair extent on the pioneering research of P. A. Leupe in the 1870s.[33] In the mid-1620s, we find Jan Lucasz van Hasselt, who Dutch Company sources in Iran reported had at that time "already served the King [Shah 'Abbas I] for some years as a painter," and whose paintings in which human figures (*menschelijke figuren*) were depicted were sent by him to Surat.[34] In the same period, one of the

Dutch factors in Agra, Hendrik Arentsz Vapoer (d. 1632), is reputed to have been a more-than-competent painter; he appears frequently in the records of the Agra and Surat establishments of the time in association also with the well-known Francisco Pelsaert, who served as a source for the humanist Johannes de Laet in his account of the Mughal Empire, *De imperio magni mogolis*.[35] Also of note is the Mughal request from late in Jahangir's reign in 1626 that they be allowed to send a court painter to Europe on a Dutch ship (with a retinue of five or six others) to buy "curiosities"; in this case, Mughal curiosity was defeated by Dutch obduracy.[36] However, Dutch painters and their production clearly continued to be in demand in the Mughal domains. A slightly later intriguing instance is that of Isaac Koedijck, who in 1651 was apparently recruited as a court painter by the Mughals but (despite the fact that he might have served as a key informant) was not permitted to travel from Surat to Delhi by the Dutch Company's director, who found it scandalous that a Christian—accompanied moreover by his wife and children—would wish to live in a Muslim court. Koedijck eventually joined the Company, and rose to a position of prominence in the Gujarat establishment in the 1650s, though some other factors complained that he was "more interested in painting than in trade *(niet in de negotie, maar in de schilderkunst)*."[37] Whether his paintings reached the hands of Mughal consumers we do not know, and we can only speculate whether he for his part was interested in the artistic production of western or northern India. Late in Shahjahan's reign, in January 1657, two other Dutch artists were somewhat reluctantly sent by the Surat establishment of the Company to his court; one of these painters, Jorephas Vos (or Vosch), left soon after and could be found serving the VOC as a commander in Trincomalee and Jaffna in the 1660s; the other—Abraham Emanuelsz van Weteren (from Leiden)—seems to have remained at the court longer and with greater success.[38]

We are on stronger ground with some other artists, some of whom circulated between the Safavid and Mughal domains. An interesting episode is reported by the French jeweler and traveler Jean-Baptiste Tavernier, while visiting the Safavid court of Shah ʿAbbas II (r. 1642–66). He writes:

> His Majesty, knowing that I was on the point of departing for India, sent for me to give me several drawings (desseins), of which some were from his own hand. For the King had learnt to draw very well from two Dutch painters, one called Angel and the other Lokar, who had been sent to him by the Dutch Company. He had then had wooden models made from all these drawings, of which some were for drinking cups, some for types of plates, and there was one for a dagger. All of this was meant eventually to make enameled gold-work (orfèvrerie émaillé) set with stones, and the king had all these models placed in my hands.[39]

The idea apparently was that Tavernier would have the jeweled objects made, but he eventually and tactfully refused, fearing that it might cost him over 200,000 écus, which the Shah might refuse to pay if his mood or tastes changed. But the two painters in question are clearly identifiable. The second of them was Hendrick Boudewijn van Lockhorst, who was at Isfahan from 1644 to 1647 and was noted there for his high living (luxurieus ongeboden leven). The first, rather more celebrated, artist was Philip (or Philips) Angel, who despite financial difficulties with the Dutch East India Company (on account of his financial misdemeanors and private trade) was nevertheless an important figure of the mid-seventeenth century.

Angel was born and trained in Leiden, where he first gained attention for a text that he presented in public, which was published in 1642 as Lof der Schilder-Konst ("In Praise of the Painter's Art").[40] A few years later, in about 1645, he seems to have left for Asia under straitened financial circumstances as a Dutch Company employee, and spent time in Batavia and Sri Lanka. In 1651, he eventually found his way to Iran as part of a Dutch embassy sent to the Safavid court under Johan Cunaeus, and he remained there for several years, first as a Dutch Company employee, and then from 1653 as a painter in the court of Isfahan.[41] Here, Angel apparently painted but also taught the young Shah and other members of the court artistic skills; he then returned to Batavia, where he spent several more years and eventually managed to clear himself of the charges mounted against him and served in a variety of employments. He also produced (or perhaps copied) a text on the ten *avatāras* of Vishnu, which he dedicated to the Governor-General of the Dutch Indies Carel Hartsinck, whose son he tutored for a time. This text comes accompanied by very curious illustrations, at least some of which seem to be in Angel's hand and to which we shall return briefly later.

By the mid-seventeenth century, the reception and incorporation of elements of representational techniques of a European provenance into Mughal painting can be taken as a given. In one direction at least, there seems to have been little problem with the issue of commensurability. While we may find nothing that is identifiable in quite the same way as the *farangi sāz* of Safavid Iran, it takes no more than a cursory examination of a magnificent work like the Windsor Castle *Pādshāh Nāma*, produced for Shahjahan, to see innumerable elements from Europe that had been taken in, adapted, and transformed. Thus the painting that depicts the Mughal siege of Hughli in 1632 is quite striking for its portrayal of a European enclave, manifestly derived from a European engraving of a cityscape (perhaps in the Flemish tradition), that seems to exist somewhat autonomously of the scene in the foreground involving Mughal boats and cannon.[42]

The purpose of the first section of this chapter has not been simply to belabor the obvious point of the reception of European elements, techniques, and forms (including those used to depict the Europeans themselves), but to point to how the context for such a reception should not necessarily be seen as religious. It is also evident that what emerged was not domination by the European structures; the use of perspective remained limited and almost sequestered within certain sections of Mughal painting, and no great effort was necessarily made to reconcile the landscapes or cityscapes taken from a Dutch engraving with the other compositional features of the painting. In this sense, while European visual representation was received, and even well received, within an Indian and Mughal context, it did not enter as a conquering and all-powerful visual and painterly vocabulary. Rather, as Ebba Koch sums up the matter, "an artist like Payag could adopt an eclectic approach, which drew upon the whole range of Netherlandish illusionism, from fifteenth-century microscopic naturalism in the manner of Jan van Eyck to the freer techniques of seventeenth-century landscape painting."[43]

Bring the Mughals Back Home

We may now wish to close the circle and look to see how Indian visual representation was received in sixteenth- and seventeenth-century Europe. This seemingly simple task is in reality a difficult one. We must look at the formation of the early European collections of Mughal and related art, and at the practices of painters and engravers in Europe of the time. A first step in this direction was taken three decades ago by the Indian art historian Partha Mitter, who examined European reactions to Indian art.[44] It would appear that, in the course of the sixteenth century, no European really thought to collect visual representations in India, whether from the world of the Mughals or farther south. Thus, the ivory casket sent by the king of Kotte in Sri Lanka to Portugal in about 1540 cannot be thought properly to fall into this category, and was in any event unsolicited.[45] The great Iberian armchair scholars such as João de Barros may have been interested in a limited fashion in Indian textual traditions, but their curiosity did not extend to the world of the visual. Let us recall in this context that the official work of Barros, like the parallel and unofficial work of Fernão Lopes de Castanheda, in fact did not contain any visual materials regarding Asia. The same was true of the *Décadas* of Diogo do Couto, who lived a good part of his life in Asia and even claimed (with whatever veracity) to have had access to Mughal texts.[46] During the first three quarters of the sixteenth century, and practically until the publication of Jan Huyghen van Linschoten's *Itinerario*, the only major European account of Asia that contained visual representations of South Asia was the travel narrative of the Bolognese voyager Ludovico di Varthema, which notoriously attempted—in the popular German version illustrated by the Augsburg artist Jörg Breu—to continue the tradition of monstrous and devilish stereotypes deriving from the European medieval tradition.

To be sure the mid-sixteenth century brought some innovations, but these remained almost exclusively in the manuscript sphere. A prominent example, dating from the 1540s or 1550s, is the so-called *Casanatense Codex,* a puzzling collection of mixed paintings in an album that may have involved the participation of some painters from western India. The paintings are composed broadly of two types: one set is ethnographic and depicts typical couples from different parts of Asia between the Cape of Good Hope and China, while the other is focused very largely on scenes of daily life in the Deccan and western India. Some of these paintings also present scenes relating to Indian temples, festivals, and religious activities.[47] The codex and its paintings do not seem to have enjoyed wide circulation, and they may in fact have been meant—though this is a speculation—as a manual for the edification of novice Catholic priests before they left Rome for India. In style, they are sparse though colorful, and they can scarcely be compared to the "high art" of Europe of the mid-sixteenth century. At the same time, they do not compare easily to the courtly painting one finds in western or northern India in the same period. Obviously intended to be instructive, they stand quite apart from many of the other visual representations we shall survey. They were never commented upon in the sixteenth century, and they had to be "rediscovered" by Jesuit scholars in the twentieth century and brought to the attention of modern writers.

They also stand strongly apart from the greater body of visual representations that we associate with the government of the great intellectual Dom João de Castro. Castro was a fair artist himself, and has left us cityscapes of Goa and Diu, as well as rutters and maritime maps. His time in Asia in the 1540s involved major conflicts with regional sultanates as well as with the Ottomans, and some of these are visually represented in both rich tapestries and watercolor paintings in a classicizing style, where the Ottomans and their allies (such as Khwaja Safar-us-Salmani of Surat) are portrayed much as one might depict Pontius Pilate or the pagan figures of classical antiquity.[48] Here, we are clearly dealing with the work of European painters who had never been to India or Asia but simply made use of those exotic landscapes as occasions to set out their wares. This process thus did not in any way involve how Deccani or fledgling Mughal artists might have portrayed scenes; it did not imagine that the "etic" vocabulary of European depiction had anything to gain or learn from the "emic" vocabulary employed by local painters and artists themselves.

Besides, it is true that while Arabic manuscripts were being collected episodically in Europe by the likes of Guillaume Postel in the sixteenth century, it does not appear that Persian manuscripts from Mughal India found takers in Europe at the time, and they do not appear in the catalogues of the great universities such as Oxford until somewhat later.[49] To be sure, some traveling savants such as the *marrano* Pedro Teixeira had begun to take an interest in translating excerpts of texts such as Mirkhwand's *Rauzat al-Safā'*, but they seem to have been on the intellectual margins in Europe.[50] But matters had changed from the early years of the seventeenth century, when the first collections of Persian manuscripts begin to appear in Europe. One of these is associated with the Scottish Jesuit George Strachan, who traveled extensively in the Arabic-speaking lands as well as Iran but does not seem ever to have attained the Mughal domains. Strachan's collections eventually came to find a rest in Rome.[51]

More adventurous still were the Vecchietti brothers, whose activities have been studied in recent years by Francis Richard. Richard notes that the two brothers, Giambattista (1552–1618) and Gerolamo (1557–c.1640), were extensive diplomatic travelers on behalf of the papacy; the older of the two had visited Qazwin, Hurmuz, and Goa in the 1580s. In the early seventeenth century, toward the end of the reign of Akbar, the brothers both visited Agra and made contact with Jerónimo Xavier and the other Jesuits there. Although one of the principal foci of the Vecchietti appears to have been texts on eastern Christianity, they also were particularly interested in materials in Judeo-Persian. Besides these areas, they also collected manuscripts, including texts by Khwandamir as well as a good variety of works by classical Persian poets such as Nizami, Anwari, Hatifi, 'Umar Khayyam, Shams-i Tabrizi, Jami, and 'Iraqi, some of whose texts seem to have been copied for them in India, others prepared in Iran, and still others obtained from the available market for manuscripts.[52] So far as we know, none of these appear to have contained paintings in the Mughal style. After the Vecchiettis in the 1620s, the aristocratic Roman traveler Pietro della Valle also showed a great deal of interest in Ottoman and Persian literature and came to travel in western India; he, too, put together a collection of rather interesting manuscripts but did not show any particular interest in the issue of illustration or in the visual vocabulary of Indian artists of the time.[53]

As a consequence, one of the earliest collections of Mughal miniatures in Europe may be found in the Vatican's "Barberini Album," which possibly dates from the 1630s.[54] It typifies what were to become seventeenth-century European collections of Mughal Indian art in that it focuses largely on individual portraits and seems to have been in the collection of the Florentine Pope Urban VIII (born Maffeo Barberini, who died in 1644). The album essentially contains sketches, some drafts, and a few complete paintings, including one in the form of a genealogical tree with Jahangir at its heart. This tree appears to have been completed sometime in the late 1610s, and Otto Kurz speculated that the original version (to which some features were added) came from "the first months, let us say January–March 1616." A second genealogical tree, with a youngish and still black-bearded Shahjahan at its center, was begun but left incomplete, which suggests that the album was put together in the early part of his reign, perhaps around 1630. Most of the remaining materials are individual portraits, including a sketch of Shah 'Abbas that Kurz was inclined to attribute to Bishan Das, as well as an accomplished portrait of an anonymous young lady whose rich dress and jewelry suggested to the art historian that "she must belong to the imperial harem." The question remains of how the album came to make its way to Italy; Kurz's speculation seems sound, that such an album would normally never have reached the hands of a collector, being "for the most part sketches, miniatures which were left unfinished, or, in one case, a tracing which has been pricked for transfer." He also suggested, once again plausibly, that "one of the [imperial] painters was persuaded to sell to a European visitor a small parcel of sketches and discarded or unfinished miniatures which no longer served any useful purpose in the imperial studios." We must disagree with him then on only one point, when he claims that painting was neglected at Shahjahan's court in favor of architecture.

However, there is an important further argument to be made. The curiously incomplete character of these drawings and miniatures makes it clear how difficult it was to simply procure such artifacts "on the market." Gurney, in his study of Della Valle, emphasized "the problem of purchasing books in the book-shops, their rarity, and the ignorance of those who sold them."[55] Ten years after the Roman traveler, matters would not have changed all that much, even if—as one strongly suspects—the hand that might have sent back the "Barberini Album" was that of a Catholic priest resident in Agra.[56] Although albums with paintings were often evaluated and a price set on them, these were no more than "shadow prices" or subjective evaluations for objects that circulated at this time essentially in the context of a gift and tribute economy.[57] This would begin to change as the seventeenth century drew to a close.

Thus, paradoxically, even as Mughal painters were eagerly laying hands on European engravings and putting them to creative use, European engravers of the late sixteenth and early seventeenth centuries did not seem to have had easy access to Mughal visual materials.[58] The solutions adopted are visible in a highly successful text (from a commercial viewpoint) such as Linschoten's *Itinerario*, where the author almost certainly advised the principal engraver, Jan van Doetechem. In depictions such as those of *banias* and Brahmins, the engraver has full recourse to a classicizing vocabulary, as if he were depicting a Biblical scene with muscular, full-bodied human figures, and a bare genuflection in the direction of exoticism through costume. The representation of the "horrible idols" of the temples (*scrickelicke beldenisse der Indiaesche affgoden*) lazily falls back on monstrous stereotypes.[59] This is quite similar as a strategy to that deployed by some of the tapestry makers of the sixteenth century or by other armchair illustrators and painters who imagined an India they had only seen depicted in words. It would take more than the "Barberini Album," sequestered as it was in a private collection, to change this.

The middle decades of the seventeenth century do see just such a sea change at work. At roughly the same time that the "Barberini Album" entered Italy, anonymous hands brought what appears to be the first collection of Indian paintings back to England and presented it to the Archbishop of Canterbury, William Laud, who in turn made a present of it to the Bodleian Library in 1640.[60] A certain amount of speculation surrounds this so-called Laud *rāgamāla*, a collection of thirty paintings of two types. Eighteen of the paintings represent various Indian musical modes, *rāgas* and *rāginīs*, here given human form and set in a scene. Thus, for example, one of the first paintings of the collection of Raga Megha Malhar shows the god Krishna embracing and dancing with a woman, while another standing woman plays a two-faced drum to accompany them. The painting is simple enough, and is one of several where this or other gods appear; in many others, solitary women are depicted. There are also twelve other paintings that do not conform to the Ragamala organization, and they include some portraits, paintings of birds, and perhaps most intriguingly a man holding a wine cup borne on a litter composed of women (on which more later). All of these display close attention to clothing and costume as well as gesture, which would have been valuable to any European engraver of the time. Unfortunately, none seem to have had access to it at the time. We cannot be certain where the paintings were produced or acquired; if we follow Karl Khandalavala, they would have been produced in the Deccan in about 1625. They must then have passed either through the English Company's factory in Surat or through its short-lived rival, Courteen's Association. Around the same time, in 1638, Shahjahan sent an illustrated manuscript of the *Gulistān* of Saʿdi produced in Agra in 1629 (with calligraphy by the hand of Hakim Rukn-ud-Din Masʿud) as a gift; the emperor wrote on the flyleaf that it was for "the glorious and exalted King of England."[61] The manuscript disappeared into the royal collection but was later to be presented by George IV in 1827 to the Qajar ruler of Iran.

From the 1640s forward, vastly greater numbers of Indian paintings began to arrive in Europe, mainly in the Netherlands. Unfortunately, none of these have been preserved as collections, and they have instead largely been dispersed or lost. The single most important indicator of their availability at the time comes from the atelier of Rembrandt, who diligently copied a good number of them—certainly at least twenty—probably in the years 1654–56, with pen and brush, usually on Japanese paper.[62] Of these, only one can be traced with confidence, namely, a collective portrayal of four elderly Sufi figures seated on a rug under a tree, which is today to be found in the *Millionenzimmer* of the Schönbrunn Palace in Vienna.[63] Regarding the others, there is some speculation but little certainty, and it is something of a puzzle as to why the great Dutch artist took such close interest in these paintings from a distant horizon. It is also not at all clear where he obtained the Mughal paintings in question. The obvious hypothesis suggests the Dutch Company's factory in Surat as a source; the Agra factory was a relatively short-lived affair, and the Dutch outposts in the Deccan such as Masulipatnam and Vengurla seem less likely to have had access to Mughal court painting in the years before 1650. It would seem, moreover, that what were purchased were often loose-leaf paintings or albums rather than illustrated manuscripts.

As regards Rembrandt's intentions, recent analysts have put forward a view that is nuanced and quite complex. It is noted by Nicola Courtright that while "Rembrandt was fascinated by foreign cultures, and certainly . . . often enlivened the copies with seemingly spontaneous handling, more naturalistic perspective, and greater spaciousness of setting, . . . despite these alterations it is striking how carefully Rembrandt sought to preserve and even enhance precisely what appears to Western eyes as the figural flatness, lack of contrappostal movement, angularity, and rigidity of the originals."[64] This refers mainly to the set of portraits, including a standing figure of Jahangir, several of Shahjahan, and courtly figures typically leaning on canes in a characteristic Mughal posture. However, if on such occasions "Rembrandt did not concern himself with exacting particulars" (in Courtright's words), on others it would seem that "his copies pay homage to the elaborate detail in the miniatures."[65] In other words, the painter was probably engaged in a complex inversion of the standard procedures of the engravers and painters of the sixteenth century, who—lacking direct visual ethnographic material to represent India—resorted to quoting from a classical and classicizing vocabulary. Indians in their work emerged looking either like Greeks and

Romans, swathed in a slightly modified equivalent of togas and tunics, or like figures from Biblical scenes, as we see with Jan van Doetechem's engravings to accompany Linschoten's work.

In contrast, Rembrandt attempted to draw on more or less contemporary paintings (or at any rate those from the seventeenth century) coming from Mughal India not to paint India itself but to paint classical scenes, even if, as has been noted, there are relatively few blatant "quotations" from the miniatures. The one major exception, art historians suggest, is provided by the Mughal painting (now in Vienna) of the four great Sufi masters, which clearly served as a proper compositional prototype for one of Rembrandt's etchings, entitled "Abraham Entertaining the Angels." We can thus conclude that at times the details of a headdress were taken directly from a costume book or miniature, and at other times the figures in Biblical scenes were made by Rembrandt (as his contemporary Philips Angel approvingly noted) to sit or recline "in the manner which is still in use in the lands of the Turks."[66] In sum, the miniatures were apparently intended to provide the master with both concrete material and minutiae as well as a broader access to an "archaic plain style [that] had in it a kind of authentic religiosity." In Courtright's terms, Rembrandt "may have regarded the contemporary Mughal illuminations as precious evidence about biblical antiquity that had survived to the present time."[67]

It is thus clear that Mughal India was seen in the seventeenth-century Netherlands as quite distinct from, say, Pernambuco in Brazil, where artists like Frans Post and Albert Eckhout had accompanied the expedition of Johan Maurits of Nassau in the 1630s and 1640s, and painted both nature and social life in a style that was eminently located within the norms of Dutch realism, even if the content was exotic and the purpose deeply exoticist.[68] Few paintings that are quite in the category of Post or Eckhout can be found for seventeenth-century Mughal India, despite the fact—as we have noted—that a good number of Dutch painters found their way there.

If such images had been produced, we can hardly see them quite serving the purposes that Rembrandt had in mind, namely, being "precious evidence" of any sort. The Mughal tradition of painting provided a vision from within Indian society of not only of what it was but of how—and employing what stylistic and other conventions—it was perceived by those who inhabited it. This was a quite different exercise than the two Dutch visions of Asia, which we can compare with Post and Eckhout.

The first of these is that of Hendrik van Schuylenburgh, who in the 1660s produced at least two large paintings of the Dutch factories in Bengal that were intended to hang in the Dutch Company's offices in the Netherlands.[69] Schuylenburgh probably had never visited India, but it is clear from his paintings that he had seen Mughal miniatures; from them, he drew the ethnographic information to surround the territory of the Dutch factory with an exotic landscape replete with details of widow burning, hook swinging, and the like. The other case is that of Andries Beeckman from Zutphen, who is best known for his panoramic oil painting of Batavia viewed from the river in the 1650s, but who also produced an important album of ethnographic watercolor paintings centering on Southeast Asia, as well as loose paintings on other parts of the world.[70]

In this context, it is worth returning to a daring experiment carried out by Rembrandt's younger contemporary, Willem Schellinks (1623–78), a rather enigmatic figure who has only recently begun to attract a good deal of attention. Besides being a painter, etcher, and draftsman, Schellinks was also a somewhat mediocre poet and an inveterate traveler, though he does not seem to have ever left Europe. Like Beeckman, mentioned earlier, Schellinks was associated with the figure of Laurens van der Hem, an Amsterdam-based bourgeois lawyer and collector, who put together a massive *Atlas* of fifty volumes that included many drawings by these and other painters.[71] The son of a tailor from Maasbree, Schellinks belonged to an extensive family, and we know that at least one of his brothers, Laurens, later would be employed as a surgeon and a draftsman in Asia by the Dutch Company and may even have left behind a diary of his voyages (which is, however, lost to us). His brother's travels were long after the period of Schellinks's life with which we are concerned, and which almost certainly preceded the painter's extensive travels to England, Italy, and elsewhere that he undertook with his wealthy patron Jaques Thierry and his son in the years 1661 to 1665.[72] The artist is particularly known for his English phase, which eventually provided the context for his best-known set of paintings, a series of imagined depictions of the Battle of Chatham (on the Medway River) in Kent, where an English fleet was attacked, burnt, and humiliated (with its flagship captured) by the Dutch under Admiral Michel de Ruyter in June 1667.

However, it would seem that in the 1640s and 1650s Schellinks circulated in the world of collectors and artists that included Rembrandt, and who had begun the process of acquiring Mughal paintings and drawings. This was a world that may have included Van der Hem, and which would later involve Nicolaas Witsen, another great traveler who was to become the burgomaster of Amsterdam. In 1671, the French doctor and antiquarian Charles Patin visited Amsterdam and came into contact with this milieu, which possessed (as he stated) "divers Paintings that we know, and others which are unknown to us; as also Indian and Chinese Pieces of an inestimable value." Patin noted that there were in particular "four Remarkable Repositories, in which are contain'd as many rarities as I ever saw elsewhere." The first of these, he noted, belonged to "M. de Witzen Recorder of the City," and he added somewhat sarcastically that "it seems as if his House were built less for an Habitation, than to delight the Eyes; nothing being to be found in any part of it but Magnificence and Symmetry; neither can it be distinguish'd whether the Repository serves as an Ornament to the House, or the House to the Repository." Besides Witsen, Patin also mentioned M. Gril (who possessed a collection of medals) and the lawyers Laurens van der Hem and Lucas Lucasz Occo as each having "their particular Museum" filled with both ancient objects and "a Multitude of new Rarities."[73]

Obviously immersed in these "new Rarities," Schellinks embarked on a series of ambitious oil paintings on Mughal themes, of which four have come down to us thus far. They can be divided for purposes of convenience into two pairs. The first of these is what is in general known as the "Hawking Party" (Figure 9).[74] It shows Shahjahan and his four sons—Dara Shikoh, Shah Shuja', Aurangzeb, and

Figure 9. Willem Schellinks, "Hawking Party." No date, oil on canvas. Private collection, after Sotheby's, London, *Old Master Paintings*, December 5, 2007. Photograph: courtesy Sotheby's Picture Library, London.

Murad Bakhsh—on horseback, accompanied by servants and hunt-
ers. One of the servants is a young African boy. The four princes resemble each other strongly, with similar beards and noses, and the
individual characteristics of their faces are less clearly brought out
than those of their father, who rides a white horse and prominently
occupies the center of the scene. They are fundamentally distinguished by their costumes and their horses. One of the princes, possibly Dara, carries a hawk perched on his hand. To the left, a landscape rolls out toward distant and dramatic mountains; in the middle
ground, an elephant and a rhinoceros are seen fighting. To the right
are two flowering trees, on one of which sits an exotic, red, long-
tailed parakeet. All in all, the painting is an excellent example of a
form of pseudo-realism, in which the five royal figures (and their
entourage) have been placed in a landscape that the artist has almost
entirely imagined and constructed through an accumulation of
exotic but improbable details. The vegetation, with the exception
of some distant palms, does not seem Indian; and the palms were
hardly appropriate for an evocation of Hindustan.

It may well have been that Schellinks had seen other Mughal
hunting scenes and adapted them; one such painting can be found
today in the Millionenzimmer of the Schönbrunn Palace in Vienna
and can be said to bear a generic resemblance: the central figure of
Shahjahan on horseback, his four sons accompanying him (one with
a hawk seated on his hand), and a landscape that extends beyond.[75]
This is a younger, black-bearded Shahjahan, perhaps from the early
1630s, and his sons are beardless youths, unlike the white-bearded
emperor who was accompanied by adult sons in Schellinks's vision.
But the other differences are more striking still: the landscape of
the Mughal painting takes us eventually to the banks of a river with
a boat in its middle, while tiny human and animal figures splash
and run about on the distant other bank. The vegetation is carefully
rendered, hardly exotic. No strange birds can be seen, and though elephants and other domestic animals are rendered, oddly paired ani-

mals do not fight to provide a bizarre backdrop. The Mughal painting also renders Shahjahan with a proper royal halo or nimbus, which the realistic demands of Schellinks's painting obviously cannot accommodate.

This painting can be paired with a second Schellinks painting, the often mistitled "A Turkish Sultan and His Court" (Figure 10).[76] Here, Shahjahan sits on a low canopied platform to the right of the painting, accompanied by one of his sons (perhaps Dara) and an elderly figure, similar to one of the Sufis in the Millionenzimmer painting. A square building, half-hidden by vegetation, lies in the background. The emperor, the same white-bearded figure of the other painting, is again portrayed in profile (as in conventional Mughal painting) and looks out to the space before him, which is occupied by a set of musicians and dancers. One of these is an excellently rendered female *bīn* player, seated and playing a gourded string instrument. However, Schellinks once more introduces a strongly exotic note in the form of the principal female dancer, who is portrayed wearing a diaphanous dress through which her body is visible. By this means, the painting draws at one and the same time on the genre of the courtly scene (where the emperor is presented with musicians, dancers, and the like) and the erotic or "harem" scene. Palm trees complete the impression of an exotic and tropical landscape. This is once again within the genre of a form of Dutch pseudo-naturalism, not unlike that practiced by Post and Eckhout, with an important exception: rather than being based on travel and observation, it derives from an earlier set of paintings or visual sources. Freed of the need to respond to an actual Indian experience, Schellinks can give open rein to his imagination while playing with the elements provided to him by the received body of paintings he has inspected.

The two remaining paintings, however, diverge entirely from those we have discussed; in point of fact, they entirely abandon the realistic or pseudo-naturalistic register in favor of something unprecedented. They were both painted after 1658 and the war of succession between

Figure 10. Willem Schellinks, "A Turkish Sultan and His Court" (*sic*). No date, oil on canvas. Private collection, after Sotheby's, London, *Old Master Paintings*, July 4, 1984, no. 365. Photograph: courtesy Sotheby's Picture Library, London.

Shahjahan's sons, for they clearly know its outcome. We may begin with the better-studied of the two, that in the Musée Guimet in Paris (Figure 11).

This painting shows a scene ostensibly from the court of Shahjahan, but it is extremely complex in its compositional structure in relation to the two paintings we previously discussed. The scene is painted from an off-stage perspective. The artist's eye looks from behind at the emperor in part-profile as he surveys a scene.[77] Shahja-

Figure 11. Willem Schellinks, Mughal court scene with Shahjahan and his sons. No date, oil on canvas. Musée Guimet, Paris. Photograph by Thierry Ollivier, courtesy Musée Guimet.

han appears at the bottom right of the composition, his arms akimbo and his knees folded under him as he surveys the scene before him. And what a scene it is! From right to left, his sons parade before him, respectively, on a camel, an elephant, a horse, and a palanquin. A rich canopy hangs above the emperor, and from behind the parade, courtiers in semi-darkness peer across. The emperor is flanked to the right by a courtier in a striped costume with a fly-whisk, and to the left by his daughter (undoubtedly Jahanara rather than Roshanara), who is in the same kneeling pose and is delicately sniffing a flower. It is as if the emperor is located in a sunken pit, while the action takes place at a level slightly above his position. Other servants and lackeys (one of whom is again African) occupy this lower level, as do a variety of luxurious objects. But that is not all: two important features set this painting apart from any attempts at naturalism or realism. First, the transports (the *vāhanas*, if one will) of all the Mughal princes are really composite entities made up of women and a few musical instruments; the camel also includes animals and a fish (Figures 12 and 13).[78] It is likely that the princes are represented as follows: Aurangzeb (significantly carrying a bloodied dagger) on the camel, Dara on the elephant with a parasol, Murad on the horse, and Shuja' on the palanquin (the last two are only probable attributions).[79] As in the other painting, the artist does not distinguish their physiognomies well enough for precise identification. Schellinks here has gone a step deeper into Mughal conventions by his use of the composite animal made from women and other creatures, which breaks completely with any attempt at realism.

A second feature is also curious. To the top left of the painting, within a cloud, is an imagined scene where the emperor's father and grandfather—Jahangir and Akbar—are found kneeling in a conversational mode, presumably in the hereafter. They oversee, but do not glance at, the parade of princes passing below them (Figure 14). This, as Robert Skelton was the first to point out, is a direct copy of an "apotheosis" scene featuring Akbar and Jahangir that Rembrandt had copied as well, of which a version can now be found in another collection (Figure 15).[80]

Faced with the extremely curious composition of this scene, entirely at odds with the received wisdom regarding the thrust of Dutch "realism" in the seventeenth century, art historians have attempted convoluted explanations. Whatever this is, it is certainly not easy to fit into the supposed "art of describing." In 1958, Jean de Loewenstein attempted to draw the painting back into the field of a form of realism by use of a singular device.[81] He proposed that Shahjahan in

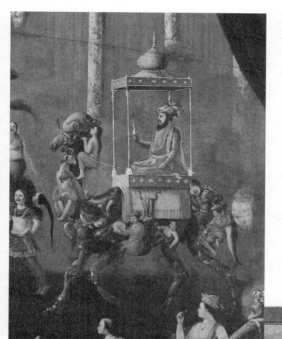

Figure 12. Detail of Aurangzeb on a composite camel (from Figure 11).

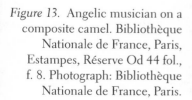

Figure 13. Angelic musician on a composite camel. Bibliothèque Nationale de France, Paris, Estampes, Réserve Od 44 fol., f. 8. Photograph: Bibliothèque Nationale de France, Paris.

Figure 14. Detail of Akbar and Jahangir in apotheosis (from Figure 11).

Figure 15. Seventeenth-century Mughal painting of Akbar and Jahangir in apotheosis. Bodleian Library, Oxford, Ms. Douce Or. a.1, f. 19a. Photograph: Bodleian Library, Oxford.

fact was not at all directly concerned with the parade of his sons in the first place. Rather, he argued, it was necessary to divide the painting into two parts, the first realist and the second illusory. The realist part, he argued, was the lower level of the scene, where the emperor, his daughter, and their entourage are found. The second, illusory part, is above that level and involves both the parade of the sons and the two deceased emperors in apotheosis. To explain the passage from the one to the other, Loewenstein proposed that the "key to the enigma" could be found in the figure of the short man holding a creature—a "black lamb" perhaps—in his arms, who appears in the center of the bottom section (Figure 16). This man—a dwarf *(nain)*, he suggested—was nothing short of a court magician and hypnotist, who thus produced the upper level of the scene as an illusion for Shahjahan's benefit. Loewenstein asserts, "It is clear that Schellinks has us attending a séance of hypnotism in which the dwarf is the principal actor." Shahjahan thus is entirely in the hands of this magician and imagines everything that he sees, be it the parade of his sons, or his father and grandfather in the sky. The tarnish on the "realism" of Schellinks could thus be rubbed off; all that he had done was to show us the hypnotized emperor imagining something. There was moreover a sort of smokescreen that covered the whole scene, which for its part was simply "the incense-smoke burnt by the magician's assistants; as we know, incense plays a central role in the Orient in religious cults and in magic."

This extremely ingenious explanation was perhaps credible in its time. However, a major difficulty is posed by the existence of a second painting of this type by Schellinks (in other words, the fourth in our series), which is to be found in the Victoria and Albert Museum in London (Figure 17).

In this second painting, Schellinks inverts the scene, somewhat as he would do later with the Battle of Chatham (where two of his paintings show the battle from above Sheerness and two others show it from the high ground to the north of Rochester Bridge). In this other

Figure 16. Detail of the "magician" figure (from Figure 11).

painting, the foreground is occupied by the parade of the princes, with the two deceased emperors suspended above them in apotheosis; the emperor, his daughter, and his companions (among whom the dwarf-magician is nowhere visible) are placed in the backdrop, while courtiers look on the scene from balconies above. Even more puzzling, the order of the princes and their vehicles remains the same: from right to left, Aurangzeb is on the camel, Dara on the elephant, Murad on the horse, and Shujaʿ on the palanquin. It is as though the artist has taken the parade as the central and stable item (save in details), reproduced the scene of the emperors in apotheosis, and then shifted the spectating eye from the foreground to the back-

Figure 17. Willem Schellinks, "Shahjahan Watching a Parade of His Sons on Composite Animals." No date, oil on canvas. Victoria and Albert Museum, London. Photograph: Victoria and Albert Museum, London.

ground. This allows us a presentation of the Mughal stage, for Shahjahan now appears with not one but two daughters. There is also a mysterious scene above his head that features an image of the sun behind a seated lion.

Whatever this is, it is neither a scene of hypnotism nor a scene requiring an immediate decoding in a neorealist language. Because the scene we are witnessing in the second painting is not from the emperor's point of view but from our own (a set of fringe curtains at the edges of the canvas makes it evident that it is a theater of some sort), we cannot easily fall back on such explanations. Rather, we are left to conclude that Schellinks has indeed descended into an unusual level of play. He had, so we may guess, been exposed to Mughal paintings of composite animals and was hence drawing on far more than the visual language provided to him by the likes of Arcimboldo.[82] Such paintings can in fact be found even in the Laud *Rāgamāla*, where we find a "man carried in a litter formed of women; he holds a wine cup."[83]

We are hence obliged to speculate that Schellinks adopted two modes, neither of which can be compared with the strategies of Rembrandt. The first of these was to rework Mughal miniatures into the vocabulary of Dutch naturalism of the seventeenth century, producing two vigorous—but essentially bogus—neorealist portraits, one with more erotic content than the other, but both deeply exoticist in their intent and execution. These paintings prefigure paintings by British artists in the later eighteenth and nineteenth centuries, and it is of some interest that they were created by a painter who had never set foot in India but was essentially working with the Mughal miniature paintings that were at his disposal in the 1640s and 1650s. This is effectively the content of the "hawking" and "harem" paintings, but the two other paintings are far more imaginative and risky. With the latter paintings, Schellinks enters into what he can comprehend of the vocabulary of the Mughal painters, creating composite animals, reproducing imaginary scenes of apotheosis, and accepting a set of compositional rules at some distance from his own. Nor are these paintings that can be understood as "allegorical" in any facile sense, as interpreters have sometimes been tempted to do with puzzling Mughal paintings. Rather, they are extremely playful—too playful perhaps to have found real acceptance in the context of seventeenth-century Amsterdam.[84] Schellinks himself, we know, turned in later years to painting naval battles and bucolic rural portraits of life in Italy.

The Problem of Print

Still another road to visual communication and the reception of Indian visual materials existed for Europe. It was provided by the printed book, whose images also drew at times on forms of representation produced in India. The earliest example we can find of an Indian painting used as the basis of an engraving is probably Renold Elstrack's "The true Pourtraicture of the Great and Most Potent Monarch, Padesha Shassallem, called the Great Mogoll of the Eastern India, King of forty[-five] Kingdoms," a free-standing picture that depicts Jahangir from waist up in profile.[85] Other printed portraits of Jahangir appeared in subsequent decades, including one in Samuel Purchas's version of the embassy account of Edward Terry, who had accompanied Sir Thomas Roe to India in the 1610s. This was a loose collective portrayal of three standing figures: "Sultan Corooan" (Khurram), "his woman slave," and on the right "Selim Shah the Great Mogull." The Persian inscription taken (as Purchas states) and approximately copied "out of the Indian Copies made by the Mogols painter," states that the original portrait "was painted by Manohar in the town of Mandu in 1026 Hijri [1616 C.E.] when I [Jahangir] was in my fiftieth year," and corresponds to the time of Roe's visit to the Mughal court.[86] These paintings, like the standing figure of Jahangir that appears on the frontispiece of de Laet's work on the Mughals (with a seated lion in a small panel next to him, as he rests his hand in a proprietorial gesture on the book's title cartouche), were part of an ongoing European interest not so much in ethnography but in physiognomy. It has been pointed out, for example, in relation to Venetian printed depictions of Ottoman subjects in the seventeenth century, that a vast number of these corresponded to the portraits of powerful political actors whose character was considered visible to be "read" from the portrayal.[87] To see the Mughal's visage, even if only in profile, was somehow to know him and his intentions, and thus to gauge him as a political personality.

We shall return to this question of portraiture later. Also of note were the printed works with an ethnographic vision of India that began to appear in the seventeenth century that attempted to reinforce or complement the printed word with the image. An excellent example of this can be found in the work of French aristocrat François le Gouz de la Boullaye, who traveled very extensively in Europe and Asia in the middle decades of the seventeenth century and eventually published in 1653 and then in 1657 an account of his experiences.[88] This account enjoyed considerable popularity for a brief time, until it was superseded by Bernier's writings and by Jean-Baptiste Tavernier's doubtful but lavishly illustrated travelogue.

In its original version, Bernier's text had no visual component. He apparently had made drawings of some of the Indian gods while visiting temples ("les figures de plusieurs de leurs dieux ou idoles"), but he had eventually decided not to use them after determining that better drawings were available in Europe by the Jesuit Heinrich Roth, who resided at the Mughal court and has served as a source for the celebrated work of Athanasius Kircher, *China Illustrata*.[89] As for Tavernier, the many illustrations found in his works do not seem to be based on any prior Indian representations; in all probability, they were concoctions of his engravers based on conversations with the traveler himself.[90]

The case of Boullaye proves more intriguing. Mitter had already remarked that some of the images in his work seemed to be "based on popular Indian religious paintings," though it had often been supposed that the traveler himself was something of an artist.[91] However, recent reexamination of a manuscript of his work in the Fondo Corsini at the library of the Accademia Nazionale des Lincei in Rome has considerably advanced our knowledge of the methods of illustration employed by Boullaye.[92] The manuscript contains forty-nine illustrations, as compared with the thirty-four found in the printed text, and that the manuscript illustrations are characterized by different styles. Michele Bernardini, who examined the text closely, has concluded that the weakest of the manuscript illustrations are probably by Boullaye himself. There are also traces of the work of a second, more "professional" European hand, notably in presenting drawings of Boullaye himself, such as one where he is shown dedicating the work to Cardinal Capponi. Of greatest interest, however, is the clear evidence from the manuscript of work by one or more Indian artists. These include drawings of Krishna and the *gopīs*, scenes from the life of Krishna, drawings of Indian divinities such as Rama, Sita, Hanuman, Mahadeva, Parvati, and Ganesha, and at least one drawing of a relatively minor figure, Shravana Kumar. Of the latter, Boullaye remarks:

> Seruan is honoured at Damaon [Daman] and the places around there, and he died in the kingdom of Guzerat. He is counted amongst the rank of the saints. Since his father and mother were very old, and were no longer able to walk, he took them out for strolls on a balance in the Indian style to keep them amused. This saint is the symbol of the honour and aid that children owe their parents for the trouble they have taken in their education.[93]

It is thus very likely that these drawings were made by artists in southern Gujarat (which Boullaye had visited), who had been exposed both to the tradition of the *Bhāgavata Purāna* and to other Indian paintings of Vaishnava, Saiva, and Jain figures. What is worth noting, however, is that the passage of the art from the Indian artist or artists to the eventual engravings resulted in considerable impoverishment of the figures: much of the subtlety and attention to detail in the costumes was lost, and certain misattributions also were introduced by the printer.

Another appropriation of images from western India that appeared in print, albeit through a more complex route, occurred in the work of Philips Angel, a figure we have already discussed. Angel, who in the 1640s and 1650s spent time in Batavia, Sri Lanka, India, and Iran, produced an interesting set of illustrations of the ten *avatāras* of Vishnu, which came to accompany a text on the same subject.[94] The authorship of the text, which exists in two copies, has been the subject of some controversy, and it has long been believed that Angel either translated it from an earlier Portuguese text originating in western India or appropriated an existing translation in Dutch. As for the images, they also present a puzzle. Those that appear with Angel's text are a hybrid: they appear to be based on a set of Indian originals (possibly in the Mughal style or a western Indian one), yet they also exhibit clear signs of adaptation to European narrative painting forms.[95] At the same time, they are not at all comparable to, say, Schellinks's reinscription of Mughal materials within the conventions of seventeenth-century Dutch realism or pseudo-realism. What is of interest for us is that Angel's paintings were then taken and presented without attribution in a work by the Dutch minister Philippus Baldaeus about the beliefs and gods of the heathens of India, which appeared to great public acclaim in 1672.[96] They thus became a part of the standard visual vocabulary for the presentation of the religious practices of India to a European audience, and they would be used time and again by other printers, engravers, and intellectuals.[97]

By the closing years of the seventeenth century, a close relationship and complicity existed in Europe between collectors, painters, and engravers in the presentation of the visual image of India. It was in the context of this complicity, we may say, that much of the reception of Indian (and especially Mughal) art came to be determined. This would mean that collectors such as Nicolaas Witsen would eventually be able to recover Indian and Persian materials from their traveling agents, some of whom were painters themselves, or from other personnel of the Dutch East India Company.[98] A great deal of this material remained in Amsterdam, but some of it made its way elsewhere in Europe.[99] One of the most remarkable European collections of Mughal painting at the close of the late seventeenth century was thus constituted in Italy by an aristocrat who had connections with Witsen and others in the Netherlands.

Conte Abate Giovanni Antonio Baldini (1654–1725) amassed a large collection of Oriental objects and paintings at his residence in Piacenza. Baldini had never traveled to India, but he had visited England, the Netherlands, France, and Austria, and he had also been the envoy of the Duke of Parma to Madrid. A diplomat and connoisseur with powerful friends in the Church, Baldini was equally able to deal with James II (in his French exile) and Newton. Baldini's collection was dispersed after his death, but fortunately a number of his contemporaries had already commented on it, and one of them—the celebrated savant Antonio Vallisnieri—produced a quite detailed description of its contents.[100] A clear sense may thus be gained of some of the principal items in the collection having to do with Mughal India. It also is clear that the bulk of them were groupings of individual portraits, often of the Mughal rulers. A standard series of these ran from Timur to Aurangzeb, extending as far as the emperor Farrukhsiyar in the mid-1710s. Related to these, but far more ambitious in its extent, was a series of 178 full-length figures, "tall, dressed in the oriental fashion, and representing the kings and queens of twenty-two families that are said to have ruled in the Indies for the space of 4,753 years, from Judister [Yudhishthira] the first King, until 1702, the year in which the book was painted." Of a more ethnographic nature were the eighteen paintings described as "representing various Fakirs, or penitent idolaters, who live continually in solitude and nakedness among the woods." Another lot of over a hundred miniatures contained many individual portraits of royalty, officials, and ministers, but also "public festivals, ceremonies, arms and customs of those peoples, with notes in explanation on the back, written by those who brought them to Europe."

Of all these albums, only one can currently be traced: the twenty-fourth item on Vallisnieri's list, described by him as "Kings of Mogol and other Indian princes . . . represented on parchment," which today resides in the Bibliothèque Nationale de France in Paris.[101] The manuscript carries some initial comments in Italian, apparently in the hand of Baldini, stating that "it contains forty-seven portraits in miniature *(ritratti in miniatura)* of the Princes of Mogol, which were collected on the voyage that was carried out in 1690 in Persia and India by Mr Claudio Le Brun, a Dutch painter. Vitzen [Witsen], the burgomaster of Amsterdam, had all the said portraits copied, and I saw the copies in his house in the year 1714" (Figure 18). The reference here is to Cornelis de Bruyn (c.1652–1727), a Dutch artist, traveler, and author of a travel account.[102] Baldini in his notes insists, as does Vallisnieri elsewhere, on the physiognomic significance of these portraits. Vallisnieri commented on three series of portraits of the Mughals that "the faces of the portraits . . . resemble each other so closely that it is quite evident they are not imaginary, but taken after the originals." To Baldini, the evaluation of another contemporary artist was equally precious: "Signore Carlo Cignani, having attentively considered the portraits of this book in the month of November 1716 said that almost all the heads could have been done by Titian or Tintoretto."[103]

During Baldini's lifetime, these works did not remain confined to his private museum but were more widely divulged. This was on account of Baldini's relationship with an important figure from the world of print, the engraver Bernard Picart.[104] Picart thus drew on Baldini's miniatures and his own expertise for his work on Henri Châtelain's *Atlas Historique*: in his introductory notes, Picart acknowledged his debt "to Mr le Comte Jean Anthoine Baldini, no less to be recommended for his excellent knowledge than for the particular care he has taken to collect such diverse, rare and curious pieces, the worthy fruits of his voyages."[105] These engravings are quite diverse, including at least four based on *rāgamāla* paintings

Figure 18. Late seventeenth-century portrayal of the Mughal emperor Akbar. Bibliothèque Nationale de France, Paris, Manuscrits, Smith-Lesouëf 233 rés., f. 25, portrait of the emperor Akbar, Golkonda, late seventeenth century. Photograph: Bibliothèque Nationale de France, Paris.

and several others of *faqīrs* and penitents (often misidentified by Baldini in a rather extreme fashion). Further, Picart also drew upon Baldini for a series of portraits of Mughal emperors, including Aurangzeb. However, there was a surprise among Picart's choices: he included two spectacular and elaborate paintings, one depicting the fort in Agra at the time of the emperor Jahangir, and the other the Battle of Samugarh in May 1658.[106] Here is how Vallisnieri describes these paintings:

- "A coloured drawing, folio size, of parchment, about two palms [44.5 cm] high, in which is represented the palace of Agra, where the Kings of Mogol reside, showing its plan, elevation and prospect, with more than a hundred persons standing inside and outside that regal structure, which consists of many courtyards. In the largest courtyard the King is shown, seated on his throne, with his wives also seated in front of him. This courtyard is dominated by the King's apartment, which is divided into three floors, one above the other; on the lowest floor are the rooms of the four principal Queens. In the courtyard before the palace the King is portrayed again on a high wooden platform watching a combat of two elephants. The custody of the interior of the palace is entrusted to Tartar women, armed with bows and arrows. By the principal gateway, which is opened only for the king, two of these women are shown standing and looking at each other, and two others stand in the same posture guarding a secret door. A eunuch stands there as a sentinel keeping an eye, though a little opening in the wall, on the room in which the royal treasure is kept." Picart adds for his part that this painting was "drawn exactly on the spot by a man of distinction (*un Homme de distinction*), who had done particular research on all sorts of remarkable singularities."

- "An Indian miniature, in which is represented the battle which Aurengzebe and Murad, sons of the King Shah Jehan, fought against their father in 1656 [*sic*]. The royal personages are seated on gilded thrones placed on the backs of elephants. In addition to the infantry and cavalry, several squadrons of soldiers who fight standing on elephants are seen in action; others stand on camels and carry swivel guns. Some of the above-mentioned soldiers bind the reins of their horses across their bodies in order to manage their swords more freely with their right hands, and their shields with their left."[107]

In order to transform these paintings into engravings, so Vallisnieri tells us, Picart first made pen drawings from the Mughal originals, and only then engraved them on copper. Paradoxically, from what one can see, these paintings, though spectacular, were not of the highest quality, a feature that also characterizes the surviving album collected by Cornelis de Bruyn.[108] De Bruyn, for his part, had a somewhat mediocre opinion of artistic talent in eastern lands, as we see from the following passage in his travel-account:

The greatest part of the Persians have pictures in their houses, and especially representations of horses, hunting-marches, and of all sorts of animals, birds and flowers, wherewith their walls are also filled, as hath already been said. They have even professed painters among them, the two best of which, in my time, were in the service of the King. I had the curiosity to pay a visit to one of them, and I found his works far above the idea I had conceived of the matter; they consisted only of birds in distemper, but extremely neat. Indeed I cannot say he knew any thing of lights and shades, and in this all the country are ignorant, whence it is that their paintings are very imperfect.[109]

This leads us to consider a final example, in itself a somewhat celebrated one. In the late seventeenth and early eighteenth centuries, the Venetian adventurer Nicolò Manuzzi, who had lived continuously in India since the 1650s, prepared an elaborate text on Mughal India. He used his own resources and a mixture of odd erudition and imagination, spiced with a dash of plagiarism. To further valorize this text, he had two sets of illustrations prepared, the first of which he claimed were made while he was in the service of the prince Shah 'Alam in the Deccan, through a friend called Mir Muhammad, also in that prince's service. These were royal portraits, roughly in the style of those possessed by Baldini, Witsen, and others, and of these Manuzzi had the following to say:

> Before leaving the kingdom of the Mogol, I had . . . all these portraits of kings and princes, from Tamerlane to Aurangzeb, and of the sons and nephews of the last. . . . No one, so far as I know, has presented these portraits to the [European] public, or if someone has done so, they bear no relation to mine, which are authentic, while the others can only be false. In fact, to have them I spared no expense and I had to give great gifts, and all that with a thousand difficulties and subterfuges, with the promise that I would never reveal that I possessed them.[110]

A second set of ethnographic depictions of scenes from daily life (not in the Mughal idiom) were sent by him later in 1705 to Europe, where they were delivered with other papers to Lorenzo Tiepolo, Venetian ambassador in Paris. Tiepolo wrote to the Venetian Senate in February 1706 describing the whole affair.[111] He even managed to persuade the Jesuits in Paris, who were at that time in possession of the first volume with copied Mughal paintings, to render them to him; he eventually announced to the Senate that he was sending them "all the papers of Manucci given to me by the said Capuchin— that is those of the History, the two books of drawings, and four-

teen pieces of bezoar stones." The package arrived in Venice two
weeks later.

Partly on account of the attractive character of the illustrations,
there seems to have been little doubt in Venice about the importance of the text and the need to have it published, but it was nevertheless deemed necessary to have the whole work examined by a
competent authority. It was thus handed over to the authoritative
university council, *Riformatori dello Studio di Padova*, in late July. In
late March 1707, a report was presented to the Senate confirming the
great significance of the work. Since the text was in a mixture of languages, a full translation into Italian was begun in 1708, and completed in 1712. But it eventually proved impossible to find a publisher
for the whole work. From 1706, the *Riformatori* had charged itself
with this task, but was unable to come to a satisfactory conclusion
with the Printer's Guild *(Stampatori)* in Venice, especially in view of
the costs involved in producing some 130 engravings of quality.

What is of interest, however, is that no one called the quality of
the images themselves into question. For Manuzzi's versions of the
portraits of the Mughals are, in fact, quaint but mediocre—the slap-
dash versions of a painter from a bazaar, not those of an artist trained
in the Mughal atelier. Like Witsen's collection from the Deccan or
Baldini's album of Safavid, Deccani, and Mughal portraits, it did not
meet the standards of the elite Mughal artist but rather was a sort of
ersatz Mughal painting. Ironically, from this point of view, Manuzzi's
second album—ethnographic depictions of scenes of daily life, rites
of passage, and the like, probably produced by textile painters in the
region of Madras—is the more interesting of the two collections of
visual representations of India that he produced.

Conclusion

The history that we have surveyed can be comprehended using
at least two distinct frameworks. The first of these is a model of

unequal or at least asymmetric exchange. In this version, over the course of a century and a half, the Europeans largely exported to Mughal India not original works of art but engravings and mass-produced images by means of the powerful technology of print, and yet they provoked a substantial reaction among Mughal artists, who deployed these materials creatively in a variety of ways and thus substantially reworked the canon of Mughal painting in the later sixteenth and seventeenth centuries. This is not to imply that European influences were all that counted in the dynamic of Mughal art, for that would be absurd, merely that they did count for something substantial.

In contrast, Mughal and related art when it arrived in Europe was usually in the form of the paintings themselves—in other words, they arrived in their original form, rather than as reproductions. To be sure, the flow was at first limited, but it seems to have increased considerably from the mid-seventeenth century onward. Yet the effect it had was limited, on a handful of artists, even if some of those artists were undoubtedly men of power and prestige. To the extent that Mughal art counted, it would be in terms either of its ethnographic impact (say, on the portrayal of the religious life of India) or its contribution to the political interest in physiognomy.

Typifying this model of asymmetric exchange is the analysis of Ebba Koch, which notes on the one hand that "the art of the democratic and bourgeois milieu of the Low Countries evoked a congenial response in an entirely different cultural and social context, at a court in Mughal India which was famed for its oriental absolutism and exotic splendour," but also remarks on the other hand that "Rembrandt and Schellincks's interest in Mughal miniatures seems to have been an isolated phenomenon."[112] If this is indeed our model, we might well deploy it, ironically enough, to contrast the Mughal artist's openness and creativity to the hidebound character of his European counterpart, even when—like Cornelis de Bruyn—he traveled far and wide.

A second framework, to which I must confess to being rather more sympathetic, would move away from a model based primarily on

concepts such as "influence" and "response" (however indispens-
able these may eventually turn out to be), to ideas of "connected
histories" based on the idea that the relations between cultures must
be mediated, and that this mediation involves among other things
the production (rather than the mere fact) of commensurability.[113]
Rather than posit that visual cultures were either commensurable or
incommensurable, we need to focus on the acts that produced commensurability. This in turn requires us to focus on the peculiar contexts of the actors as well as the concrete objects that were produced.
Because the contexts were usually interimperial ones, the processes
to which we refer were not innocent at all, but deeply political in their
nature. Herein lies the rub, and a suggestion as to why the repeated
encounters between the visual representations produced in western
Europe and those produced in Mughal India produced such a spec-
trum of outcomes over space and time. It may also help us to understand why things changed after 1760, when the British gained power
over the revenues and the material objects of the subcontinent.

In the loot that emerged after Plassey (in 1757) were many splendid
collections of Mughal paintings as well as illustrated manuscripts,
which came to grace the auction houses of London and eventually
would form the basis of most of the great collections of Mughal
paintings that we find today in Europe and beyond.[114] But these objects collected by Clive, Hastings, Johnson, and so many others entered a different market from that in which Baldini and Witsen had
not long before operated. These post-1760 paintings were for the most
part no longer needed as witnesses to a current Indian reality; for that
purpose, one had British and other European academic painters and
engravers, who embarked on ships to produce the authoritative vision
of the East India Company's new domains.[115]

There is thus an important transition marked between the confident and still playful output of an artist such as Mir Kalan Khan
and a later generation of artists in cities such as Lucknow who wholly
internalized the dominant conventions of European painting.[116]

Rather, those who held to the "Mughal style" were now just nostalgic witnesses to the past, producing archaic objects that could be
cherished as such. With the help of a political revolution or two, one
could indeed now "turn the Perspective / And farther off the lessen'd
Object drive."

Conclusion

Difficult Junctions

In the third book of Baldesar Castiglione's celebrated early sixteenth-century work *Il Libro del Cortegiano* ("The Book of the Courtier"), one of his characters—messer Federico—while initially reflecting on a comparison with courtly life in France and England, eventually casts his gaze even farther afield. "I thought too," he states, "if I had time enough, to speak not only of the diversity of customs that are in use at the courts of Christian princes in serving them, in merry-making, and in appearing at public shows, but also to say something of the Grand Turk's court, and much more particularly of the court of the Sofi king of Persia." For, in the final analysis, he has little difficulty in placing all of them on a single plane, "having heard, from merchants who have been long in that country, that the noblemen there are of great worth and gentle behavior, and that in their intercourse with one another, in their service to ladies and in all their actions, they practise much courtesy and much discretion."[1] All these courts, he appears to reason, have their common interest in "weapons, games and festivals" *(nell'arme, nei giochi e nelle feste)*. If Mark Twain's Connecticut Yankee could travel back many centuries in time to find the denizens of King Arthur's court "gracious and courtly," even if somewhat inclined to "telling lies of the stateliest pattern with a most gentle and winning naivety," the movement from Urbino to Istanbul or Tabriz seemed equally to present no real problems for Castiglione's imagined courtiers.[2]

It is common enough to accuse historians of projection, and thus of finding in the past what they wish to see in the present or immediate future. This is an accusation directed at both individuals and the tribe at large; somehow, whatever the mood of the moment or the pressing issues of the day, many historians—faithfully following a peculiar reading of Benedetto Croce's dictum that all history is contemporary history—seem to find its necessary antecedents in the past.[3] So it might be thought that my work addressing the issue of encounters between courtly cultures in the sixteenth and seventeenth centuries is motivated by some urge to find a genealogy for "multi-culturalism" or for "assimilation," or even as a plea for societies built on greater tolerance of difference. If I have indeed given such an impression, I must strive to disabuse the reader. Greater mutual tolerance in the complex societies of our day surely needs no historical examples to justify it. Further, if our collective past is often a chronicle of lesser and greater disasters, that need not set rigid limits on how we imagine future societies and their cultural politics.

Rather, my intention here was both to dismantle and to provide a historical context for the concept of the encounter, which has played such an important role in the historiography of the past half-century and more. To reiterate a point made before, societies do not encounter each other in their entirety; rather, they do so as fractions or even—in the extreme case—embodied in individuals. The nature of the fractions is, in turn, partly a function of morphology, for all societies that existed at the same moment were obviously not constituted in identical ways. But it is only partly the case, because encounters do not occur in a state of nature; they do not simply happen, but are necessarily made. Let us imagine a Portuguese traveler of the mid-sixteenth century, a hypothetical companion of Francis

Xavier, who—on a long voyage from Lisbon to Japan—touched on and described a series of polities, in each seeking out the equivalent of a set of categories he had in mind: a king and kingdom (*rei* and *reino*), a nobility (*nobreza* or *fidalguia*), a court (*corte*), temples (*templos*), merchants (*mercadores*), peasants (*lavradores*), and so on. Readers of such texts will be aware that they were usually not written by uncompromising relativists, and that their authors in most instances found the empirical equivalents of such categories, whether they were in West Africa, Iran, India, or the South China Sea. But occasionally they fell short, when no easy equivalence was to be found; this usually occurred with matters classified under "religion and customs" (*lei e costumes*). Thus Domingo Paes, writing about Vijayanagara around 1520, had no difficulty with referring baldly to kings, merchants, and even "captains" (for *nāyakas*), but he was brought up short at the term *bramines*. Here, he provided a long gloss, as if to explain why the word had to be retained in its original form.

> These *bramines* are like friars amongst us, and they are taken by them to be holy men, I mean to say the *bramines* [who are] sacerdotes and scribes of the *pagodes*, because though the king has many *bramines*, they are officials of the towns and cities and of his government, and other are merchants, and others live by their possessions and crops and fruits, which are [from] their inheritances; and these [others] who are in charge of the *pagodes* are men of letters (*letrados*), and don't eat any dead thing, neither meat nor flesh.[4]

Paes therefore does not simply translate and eliminate the word "Brahmin" by rendering it as "friar" or "sacerdote," just as he retains the hybrid term *pagode*—derived from the word *bhagavatī*—so as not to use the term "temple" without any further markers. Over the course of the sixteenth century, we may witness an accumulation of such terms into overseas Portuguese dialect, of African and Asian terms and institutions that were judged somehow "untranslatable," as we can also see with the Spaniards in America. By the end of the sixteenth century, as we have noted, the Jesuit Luís Fróis was thus even tempted to propose a systematic reflection on the "contradictions and differences in customs" *(contradições e diferenças de costumes)* between Europeans and Japanese, and this exercise could have been repeated a dozen or more times over at different sites. It was not until the very end of the seventeenth century that Europeans found themselves capable once more of asking systematically whether in fact there was some "conformity" between Chinese and Indian "customs" and "ceremonies" and those that they knew rather better, such as of the Mediterranean world in antiquity.[5]

While this was so with regard to customs in general, the courtly sphere was quite another matter. Here, an early writer like Paes or even Nunes found it relatively easy to translate both ideas and actions, resorting on only the rare occasion to words and concepts such as *sallema* (from the Persian *salām*, for salutation) or *cabaya* (from the Persian *qabā'*, for a robe of honor). By the mid-sixteenth century, Persian terms such as *saughāt* (for a magnificent courtly gift) had made their way into common Indo-Portuguese vocabulary as *sagoate*, as had some other terms that we continue to see in the Jesuit letters written from the Mughal court after 1580. What is crucial, however, is that it was very rare that a substantive argument hung on the use of these terms. For the most part—rightly or wrongly—there was a confident assumption that in the encounter between courtly cultures, whether through formal diplomacy or other means, most things passed easily precisely because of an implicit theory of broad congruence once inside this sphere. It is interesting to note, for example, how easily the Iberian term *valido* (used for a court favorite such as Olivares or Richelieu) was employed by Portuguese writers speaking of the sultanates of Bijapur or Golkonda in the same period.

To be sure, with the emergence in the later sixteenth and early seventeenth century of notions of oriental "despotism" to characterize a whole host of polities, this confidence was to an extent shaken. European envoys in a range of polities began to find the court ritual there far too oppressive, complaining—like the Dutch in mid-seventeenth-century Arakan—that their clothes were soiled from the incessant "crawling" at various stages during the royal audience. Insults and slights were both perceived and imagined by various parties. But whenever one court society imagined it had found another, exchange was facilitated and could be codified. No hastily improvised *pas de deux* was needed. This was not like late eighteenth-century Port Jackson, where a specialist of intercultural encounters tells us that "the Australians and the British began their relationship by dancing together."[6] It may have happened there perhaps precisely because two court cultures did not meet.

The same historian, Inga Clendinnen, is also the author of a well-known study of the encounter between Spaniards and Maya in Yucatan in the sixteenth century, an encounter that led to the subjugation and conquest of the latter group. Interestingly, we learn from her that the Spaniards struggled for an extended period "to discover any stable political groupings in the [Maya] country." At first, they thought the relevant political unit was the town and its chief, the *batab*; then they came to the view that there were indeed what they termed "provinces," headed by a single lord called the *halach uinic*.[7] But the substantive royal structure with its corresponding courtly apparatus that Hernán Cortés had found and dealt with so expeditiously in central Mexico failed in this case to reveal itself. Between Spaniard and Maya, then, no courtly encounters were feasible. But even where such encounters occurred, we must guard ourselves against the illusion that they were the only mode of contact between two distinct societies. Rather, they often represented the most ritualized and circumscribed of such encounters, despite their general neglect both by historians of well-known themes such as "court society" and "royal ritual."[8]

This means in turn that the materials we have presented here must be counterposed to others, where the outcomes were far more diverse. Two concluding examples may be cited to give a sense of this diversity.

In the early eighteenth century, Augustus II, Elector of Saxony and more briefly King of Poland, purchased a curious piece of work from his court jeweler, Johannes Melchior Dinglinger. Executed over some seven or eight years by Dinglinger, his two brothers, and many apprentices, and completed in 1708, the massive enameled and be-jeweled work entitled "The Court at Delhi on the Birthday of the Great Mogul Aureng-Zeb" is estimated to have cost between 55,000 and 60,000 *Reichsthalern*, more than some castles of the time.[9] The work is undoubtedly unique, not least of all because of the enormous labor expended on it. But despite Dinglinger's obvious investment in reading late seventeenth-century travel texts and compendia (such as that of Olfert Dapper), and his effort to identify Mughal personages or titles such as the *Khān-i Khānān* or the *Khān-i 'Ālam*, what be-comes apparent is his incapacity or lack of desire to separate the Mu-ghal court from that of Qing China, the Ottoman Empire, or even ancient Egypt. What appears to be Chinese script (or a pastiche thereof) features prominently even on the throne canopy, and many Mughal notables are depicted simply as mandarins on their sedan chairs or as turbaned Ottoman pashas. Only the bearded emperor and a few other figures represent a vague genuflection to the Mughals themselves. Dinglinger thus condensed an enormous geographical variety of courtly practice to produce a single, dense object. His mag-nificent and absurd "Court at Delhi" stands in short at the antipodes of the work of Schellinks in terms of its attention to and engagement with the actual materials and representational conventions of the Mughal court.[10]

A quarter century after the completion of Dinglinger's work, an-other piece of exotica appeared in Europe, this one a printed text from Lisbon concerning the Ottomans. Claiming to be the Portu-guese translation of an Italian work, it described the appearance of an amphibious monster off Istanbul on the night of October 14,

1732. The monster, it was noted, was "half man and half fish, who in the size of his body equaled the size of the Bosphorus."[11] The giant merman did not enter the city, finding its streets too narrow for his taste, and instead sent out an enigmatic message to the Ottoman court consisting of the vowels *AEIOU*. These fiery letters and the thunder of his voice, it is noted, were enough to ruin "palaces, mosques, towers and other proud edifices." The strange incident, it is reported, incited the Grand Vizier to call a meeting of the council, where some suggested abandoning the city entirely in favor of Edirne. But a great Muslim savant of the 'Ishraqi order, Vani Efendi, interpreted the enigma. The letters, he stated, stood for *"Acabará Este Império Othomano Vencedor"*—"This Victorious Ottoman Empire Will End"—and thus announced the emergence of a new universal empire, to which the Ottomans would have to submit. No doubt the author or authors also knew that the Austrian Habsburgs employed *AEIOU* as their device (for "Austriae Est Imperare Orbi Universo"). This work, together with others from the late 1720s and early 1730s, all described the emergence of various monstrous creatures that posed a threat to the Ottoman court and its capacity to rule. They suggested an altogether different mode of dealing with a rival court—albeit a court with which the Portuguese (and other Europeans) had by then had two or even three centuries of relations.[12] The immediate context was the troubled end of the reign of Sultan Ahmet III (r. 1703–30), and his eventual replacement by his nephew after a janissary revolt in September 1730. Already in 1727, another work, entitled *Emblema Vivente*, had appeared in Lisbon claiming that the Ottoman Empire was menaced by a peculiar monster, fifteen palms high, lacking sexual organs, with a crescent moon atop its head and a luminous cross on its chest.[13] Captured by the governor of Amasya and sent to the sultan's menagerie in Istanbul, the creature had managed to escape, killing huge numbers of soldiers and setting off a plague.

The author or authors of these texts (who included one Monterroio de Mascarenhas) were certainly aware that they could be read as mere "fables" (fábulas), especially given the heavy-handed symbolism of crescent and cross. But they tended instead to stress various other aspects: that these were not their own inventions but were taken from either Ottoman accounts or from letters by prisoners held there; that they formed a part of a set of reflections on the imminent end of the Ottoman Empire; and that they were "the presage of some inauspicious and unhappy outcome," which was also signaled by the resurgence of Iran after the fall of the Safavid dynasty. Still, had they fallen into the hands of someone like Yirmisekiz Çelebi Mehmed Efendi, who had been Ottoman envoy to the court of the young Louis XV in 1720–21, one wonders what he—who had so admired the French and their courtly sophistication—would have made of them.[14]

At any rate, these works concerning "political monstrosities" can be distinguished from common works of teratology, which did not always carry such political implications; but it is also important to separate the works concerned with familiar spaces from those that bear on notably exotic ones. A complex geography of gradients thus comes to be defined, such that these "virtual encounters"—whether those of Dinglinger or of the Lisbon pamphleteers—could rival, and at times even overwhelm, the more matter-of-fact engagements and the accounts they produced.

Ironically, the year 1721, when Mehmed Efendi concluded his visit, was also the year when Montesquieu published his Lettres persanes, in which two improbably named visitors from Safavid Iran— Usbek and Rica—were used by him to present a falsely naïve critique of France and its polity. Montesquieu, as we know, was an assiduous reader of French travelers to Asia such as Jean Chardin and Jean-Baptiste Tavernier, whose writings he cleverly used to give a local flavor to his text. His principal "Persian" characters were somewhat subtly constructed, in that they were both contrasted to each other and (particularly in the case of Usbek) somewhat unstable in themselves. However, his choice of characters is interesting not merely for their geographical origin but also for their social class: these men were clearly a part of what would have been the Persian *umarā'*, with extensive households and harems—in short, very much a part of the courtly society of Isfahan. The *Lettres persanes* are thus meant not quite to parody ambassadorial and consular reports from Istanbul and Aleppo, for they contain too much that is personal for that; rather, they are meant to be a *jeu de miroir*, a back-and-forth play with mirrors between two courtly societies. They are both about difference and the use of difference to produce a critique, and are based on a profound conceit that in the final analysis such differences were really not insuperable.

We know that there were profound flaws of perspective in any such attempt at ventriloquism, whether executed by Montesquieu or later in the same century by Voltaire. The deepest of these flaws was the navel-gazer's view that one had to produce such critiques oneself, since no one else's criticism was, in the final analysis, worth taking into consideration. But the central premise of the *Lettres persanes* nevertheless remains a challenging one. What were the critical and creative external voices that the elite in a given society of the sixteenth or seventeenth century could hear and absorb, but which it was at the same time incapable of producing itself? Who were its authors, and why were they heard—or at times first heard and then violently dismissed? There are surely no simple answers to these questions. My own response in these pages has been to turn to the manner in which courtly societies dealt with one another, not only in terms of their projections and imaginations, and not only as sociological abstractions and idealizations, but as day-to-day realities. The preceding pages have thus taken us far deeper into the history of events than the imperious play makers of history might have imagined a half-century ago. But it is eventually in these events, in the narrative texts and images that bring them to us, and in our capacity to make sense of them that we may yet find a good part of our answers.

Notes

Introduction

1. See Anonymous, *The Negotiations of Sir Thomas Roe, in His Embassy to the Ottoman Porte from the Year 1621 to 1628 Inclusive* (London: Samuel Richardson, 1740), p. 30.

2. Gregory Benford, "Aliens and Knowability: A Scientist's Perspective," in George E. Slusser, George R. Guffey, and Mark Rose, eds., *Bridges to Science Fiction* (Carbondale: Southern Illinois University Press, 1980), pp. 53–63. Benford distinguishes between what he terms "anthropocentric" and "unknowable" aliens, but it is clear that the former continue to dominate. For a useful survey (which at times fails however to appreciate the irony and playfulness of some science-fiction authors), see Carl D. Malmgren, "Self and Other in SF: Alien Encounters," *Science Fiction Studies* 20, no. 1 (1993): 15–33.

3. See David N. Livingstone, "The Preadamite Theory and the Marriage of Science and Religion," *Transactions of the American Philosophical Society*, n.s., 82, no. 3 (1992): 1–78, as well as the more general considerations in Giuliano Gliozzi, *Adamo e il nuovo mondo: La nascita dell'antropologia come ideologia coloniale; Dalle genealogie bibliche alle teorie razziali (1500–1700)* (Florence: La Nuova Italia, 1977).

4. Muḥammad Qāsim Hindushāh Astarabadi, *Tārīkh-i Firishta*, ed. Muḥammad Reza Nasiri, 2 vols. (Tehran: Anjuman-i Asar wa Mafakhir-i Farhangi, 2009–11), 1:28–30.

5. For other reactions from the same times, see Mohamad Tavakoli-Targhi, "Contested Memories of Pre-Islamic Iran," *Medieval History Journal* 2, no. 2 (1999): 245–75.

6. For instance, see Peter C. Perdue, *China Marches West: The Qing Conquest of Central Eurasia* (Cambridge, Mass.: Belknap Press of Harvard University Press, 2005); Laura Hostetler, *Qing Colonial Enterprise: Ethnography and Cartography in Early Modern China* (Chicago: University of Chicago Press, 2001); and Jane Burbank, Mark von Hagen, and Anatolyi Remnev, eds., *Russian Empire: Space, People, Power, 1700–1930* (Bloomington: Indiana University Press, 2007).

7. Tsvetan Todorov, "Cortés et Moctezuma: De la communication," *L'Ethnographie* 76, nos. 1–2 (1980): 69–83, further developed in Tzvetan Todorov, *The Conquest of America: Perceiving the Other*, trans. Richard Howard (New York: Harper and Row, 1984). Also see Greg Dening, *Islands and Beaches: Discourse on a Silent Land, Marquesas, 1774–1880* (Carlton, Victoria, Australia: Melbourne University Press, 1980).

8. It is nevertheless useful to distinguish the bulk of Kuhn's reflection in this sphere from the far more simplistic Sapir-Whorf hypothesis, which posits a strong form of language-based relativism.

9. See Howard Sankey, "Kuhn's Changing Concept of Incommensurability," *British Journal for the Philosophy of Science* 44, no. 4 (1993): 759–74. Also see the reflections (from an anthropological viewpoint) in Elizabeth A. Povinelli, "Radical Worlds: The Anthropology of Incommensurability and Inconceivability," *Annual Review of Anthropology* 30 (2001): 319–34.

10. See the interesting reflections in Daniel Carey, "Questioning Incommensurability in Early Modern Cultural Exchange," *Common Knowledge* 6, no. 3 (1997): 32–50.

11. I return here to my earlier discussion in Sanjay Subrahmanyam, "Par-delà l'incommensurabilité: Pour une histoire connectée des empires aux temps modernes," *Revue d'histoire moderne et contemporaine* 54, no. 5 (2007): 34–53.

12. Anthony Pagden, *European Encounters with the New World: From Renaissance to Romanticism* (New Haven, Conn.: Yale University Press, 1993), p. 180.

13. Johann Gottfried Herder, *Reflections on the Philosophy of the History of Mankind*, abridged, intro. Frank E. Manuel (Chicago: University of Chicago Press, 1968), p. 130.

14. See the broad perspective in Francis Robinson, "Ottomans-Safavids-Mughals: Shared Knowledge and Connective Systems," *Journal of Islamic Studies* 8, no. 2 (1997): 151–84.

15. For a brief account of this personage in the Basra context, see the remarks in Devin Stewart, "The Humor of the Scholars: The Autobiography of Niʿmat Allāh al-Jazāʾirī (d. 1112/1701)," *Iranian Studies* 22, no. 4 (1989): 47–81.

16. Shahnawaz Khan, *Maʾasir-ul-Umara, Being Biographies of the Muhammadan and Hindu Officers of the Timurid Sovereigns of India from 1500 to about 1780* A.D., trans. H. Beveridge and Baini Prashad, 3 vols. (Calcutta: Asiatic Society of Bengal, 1911–52), 1:698–701, for the Persian text of which see Nawwab Samsam al-Daula Shahnawaz Khan, *Maʾāsir al-Umarāʾ*, ed. Maulavi ʿAbdur Rahim and Maulavi Mirza Ashraf ʿAli, 2 vols. (Calcutta: Asiatic Society of Bengal, 1888–90), 1:241–47.

17. By way of example, see Jamsheed K. Choksy and M. Usman Hasan, "An Emissary from Akbar to ʿAbbās I: Inscriptions, Texts and the Career of Amīr Muhammad Maʿsūm al-Bhakkarī," *Journal of the Royal Asiatic Society*, 3rd ser., 1, no. 1 (1991): 19–29; and Z. A. Desai, "A Foreign Dignitary's Ceremonial Visit to Akbar's Tomb: A First-Hand Account," in Iqtidar Alam Khan, ed., *Akbar and His Age* (New Delhi: Northern Book Centre, 1999), pp. 188–97.

18. Ernst Schulin, "Rankes erstes Buch," *Historische Zeitschrift* 203, no. 3 (1966): 581–609; Lucette Valensi, *The Birth of the Despot: Venice and the Sublime Porte*, trans. Arthur Denner (Ithaca, N.Y.: Cornell University Press, 1993).

19. J. E. Heeres and F. W. Stapel, eds., *Corpus Diplomaticum Neerlando-Indicum: Verzameling van politieke contracten en verdere verdragen door de Nederlanders in het Oosten gesloten*, 6 vols. (The Hague: Martinus Nijhoff, 1907–55); preceded by Júlio Firmino Júdice Biker, ed., *Colecção de tratados e concertos de pazes que o Estado da Índia Portugueza fez com os Reis e Senhores com quem teve relações nas partes da Ásia e África Oriental*, 14 vols. (Lisbon: Imprensa Nacional, 1881–87).

20. For a recent schematic consideration of the Portuguese, see Zoltán Biedermann, "Portuguese Diplomacy in Asia in the Sixteenth Century: A Preliminary Overview," *Itinerario* 29, no. 2 (2005): 13–37. An important comparative consideration is John E. Wills Jr., *Embassies and Illusions: Dutch and Portuguese Envoys to K'ang-hsi, 1666–1687* (Cambridge, Mass.: Harvard Council on East Asian Studies, 1984).

21. K. W. Goonewardena, *The Foundation of Dutch Power in Ceylon, 1638–1658* (Amsterdam: Djambatan, 1958).

22. A classic account is C. H. Alexandrowicz, *An Introduction to the History of the Law of Nations in the East Indies: (16th, 17th and 18th Centuries)* (Oxford: Clarendon Press, 1967). A recent and less convincing attempt at such an analysis without adequate regard for the issue of "conventions" is Jean-Michel Sallmann, *Géopolitique du XVIe siècle, 1490–1618* (Paris: Seuil, 2003).

23. António Pinto Pereira, *História da Índia no tempo em que a governou o visorey D. Luís de Ataíde*, intro. Manuel Marques Duarte (Lisbon: Imprensa Nacional, 1987), pp. 333–34.

24. The mention of another ambassador, "a Persian captain called Coração Cão" (Pereira, *História*, p. 347), is confusing; manifestly, the name is unlikely to have been Khorasan Khan.

25. Muzaffar Alam and Sanjay Subrahmanyam, *Writing the Mughal World: Studies in Political Culture* (Ranikhet: Permanent Black, 2011), pp. 33–87.

26. Jean Aubin, "Les documents arabes, persans, et turcs de la Torre do Tombo," in Jean Aubin, *Le Latin et l'Astrolabe: Recherches sur le Portugal de la Renaissance, son expansion en Aie et les relations internationales*, vol. 2, ed. Françoise Aubin (Paris: Centre Culturel Calouste Gulbenkian, 2000), pp. 417–52. The essay first appeared in *Mare Luso-Indicum* 2 (1973).

27. "O estilo com o seu colorido oriental prova que o autor não era português," writes the Jesuit historian, in Georg Schurhammer, "O Tesoiro do Asad Khan: Relação inédita do intérprete António Fernandes (1545)," in Schurhammer, *Gesammelte Studien: Varia*, vol. 1, ed. László Szilas (Rome: IHSI, 1965), pp. 31–45.

28. Luís Filipe F. R. Thomaz, "As cartas malaias de Abu Hayat, Sultão de Ternate, a El-Rei de Portugal, e os primórdios da presença portuguesa em Maluco," *Anais de História de Além-Mar* 4 (2003): 381–446.

29. I do not know of any archival version of this document. But it appears in Leonardo Nunes, *Crónica de Dom João de Castro*, ed. J. D. M. Ford (Cambridge, Mass.: Harvard University Press, 1936), pp. 63–65, as "Resposta d'el Rey do Patane ao guovernador."

30. Arquivo Nacional da Torre do Tombo, Lisbon, Corpo Cronólogico, III-14-44, letter from Hadim Süleyman Pasha to the *wazīr* Ulugh Khan, or "Olucão Gozil" (the lost original is dated December 10, 1538, and the Portuguese translation May 7, 1539).

31. Sanjay Subrahmanyam, "Sobre uma carta de Vira Narasimha Raya, rei de Vijayanagara (1505–1509), a Dom Manuel I de Portugal (1495–1521)," in Isabel de Riquer, Elena Losada, and Helena González, eds., *Professor Basilio Losada: Ensinar a pensar con liberdade e risco* (Barcelona: Universitat de Barcelona, 2000), pp. 677–83.

32. Felicia J. Hecker, "A Fifteenth-Century Chinese Diplomat in Herat," *Journal of the Royal Asiatic Society*, 3rd ser., 3, no. 1 (1993): 86–98; also the earlier essay by Morris Rossabi, "Two Ming Envoys to Central Asia," *T'oung Pao*, 2nd ser., 62, nos. 1–3 (1976): 1–34.

33. The narrative of this set of events may be found in C. R. Boxer, *O Grande Navio de Amacau*, trans. Manuel Vilarinho (Macao: Fundação Oriente, 1989), 142–46.

34. Jurgis Elisonas, "Christianity and the Daimyo," in John Whitney Hall and James L. McClain, eds., *The Cambridge History of Japan*, vol. 4: *Early Modern Japan* (Cambridge: Cambridge University Press, 1991), pp. 301–72.

35. Hecker, "A Fifteenth-Century Chinese Diplomat."

36. David Ayalon, *Gunpowder and Firearms in the Mamluk Kingdom: A Challenge to a Mediaeval Society* (London: Vallentine and Mitchell, 1956). This view was generalized by Jean-Claude Garcin, "The Mamlūk Military System and the Blocking of Medieval Moslem Society," in Jean Baechler, John A. Hall, and Michael Mann, eds., *Europe and the Rise of Capitalism* (Oxford: Basil Blackwell, 1988), pp. 113–30. In contrast, for an analysis of Mamluk-Ottoman relations and commonalities, see E. Cihan Muslu,

"Ottoman-Mamluk Relations: Diplomacy and Perceptions" (PhD diss., Harvard University, 2007).

37. The remark is placed in Alba's mouth in Luis Vélez de Guevara, *La Mayor Desgracia de Carlos V*, ed. William R. Manson and C. George Peale (Newark, N.J.: Juan de la Cuesta, 2002), vv. 1501–8. Guevara draws on the chronicle of Fray Prudencio de Sandoval, *Segunda parte de la vida y hechos del emperador Carlos V* (Valladolid, Spain: Sebastian de Cañas, 1606), book 25, 367: "no le [Cortés] quisieron oyr, y aun dizen que huvo algunos que hizieron burla del." Sandoval in turn seems to embroider on accounts of the combat of 1541 in the works of the chronicler Gómara, who was himself present in Algiers. See Francisco López de Gómara, *Guerras de mar del Emperador Carlos V*, ed. Miguel Angel de Bunes Ibarra and Nora Edith Jiménez (Madrid: Sociedad Estatal para la Conmemoración de los Centenarios de Felipe II-Carlos V, 2000), pp. 221–22. For the Algiers expedition in general, see the valuable reconsideration (with extensive documentation) in Daniel Nordman, *Tempête sur Alger: L'expédition de Charles Quint en 1541* (Saint-Denis, France: Bouchène, 2011).

38. António Real to Dom Manuel, letter of December 15, 1512, in Inácio Guerreiro and Vítor Luís Gaspar Rodrigues, "O 'grupo de Cochim' e a oposição a Afonso de Albuquerque," *Studia*, no. 51 (1992): 119–44 (citation on 133).

39. For a broader discussion, see Giancarlo Casale, *The Ottoman Age of Exploration* (New York: Oxford University Press, 2010), 56–63.

40. Geoffrey Parker, *The Military Revolution: Military Innovation and the Rise of the West, 1500–1800* (Cambridge: Cambridge University Press, 1987), pp. 115–45. Most critiques of this important work have focused on its European component. Another version of the argument appears as Geoffrey Parker, "Europe and the Wider World, 1500–1700: The Military Balance," in James D. Tracy, ed., *The Political Economy of Merchant Empires: State Power and World Trade, 1350–1750* (New York: Cambridge University Press, 1991), pp. 161–95. For another look at some of its central themes, see Geoffrey Parker and Sanjay Subrahmanyam, "Arms and the Asian: Revisiting European Firearms and Their Place in Early Modern Asia," *Revista de Cultura* [Macau], no. 26 (2008): 12–42.

41. Parker, *The Military Revolution*.

42. Rhoads Murphey, *Ottoman Warfare, 1500–1700* (New Brunswick, N.J.: Rutgers University Press, 1999).

43. See the extensive discussion in Velcheru Narayana Rao, David Shulman, and Sanjay Subrahmanyam, *Textures of Time: Writing History in South India, 1600–1800* (New York: Other Books, 2003), pp. 73–75.

44. Robert Orme, *A History of the Military Transactions of the British Nation in Indostan from the Year MDCCXLV*, 3rd ed., vol. 2 (London: John Nourse, 1780), pp. 259–60.

45. Jos Gommans, *Mughal Warfare: Indian Frontiers and High Roads to Empire, 1500–1700* (London: Routledge, 2002), pp. 205–6.

46. Jos Gommans, "Indian Warfare and Afghan Innovation during the Eighteenth Century," in Jos J. L. Gommans and Dirk H. A. Kolff, eds., *Warfare and Weaponry in South Asia, 1000–1800* (Delhi: Oxford University Press, 2001), pp. 365–86.

47. Darius Cooper, "The White Man's Burdens and Whims of the Chess-Besotted Aristocrats: Colonialism in Satyajit Ray's *The Chess Players*," *Journal of South Asian Literature* 28, nos. 1–2 (1993): 205–25.

48. Gerald M. Berg, "The Sacred Musket: Tactics, Technology and Power in Eighteenth-Century Madagascar," *Comparative Studies in Society and History* 27, no. 2 (1985): 261–79.

49. Melville J. Herskovits, *Acculturation: The Study of Culture Contact* (New York: J. J. Augustin, 1938). But also see the earlier brief statement by Robert Redfield, Ralph Linton, and Melville J. Herskovits, "Memorandum for the Study of Acculturation," *American Anthropologist* 38, no. 1 (1936): 149–52.

50. Nathan Wachtel, "L'acculturation," in Jacques Le Goff and Pierre Nora, eds., *Faire de l'histoire*, vol. 1 (Paris: Gallimard, 1974), pp. 126–33.

51. Bill Ashcroft, Gareth Griffiths, and Helen Tiffin, *Post-Colonial Studies: The Key Concepts* (London: Routledge, 2000), p. 118; compare Serge Gruzinski, "Images and Cultural Mestizaje in Colonial Mexico," *Poetics Today* 16, no. 1 (1995): 53–77. Gruzinski's work has been criticized by some representatives of the so-called New Philology for being much the same as Lévi-Straussian structuralism, but this seems rather a caricature;

compare Matthew Restall, "A History of the New Philology and the New Philology in History," *Latin American Research Review* 38, no. 1 (2003): 113–34.

52. Luís Fróis, *Tratado das Contradições e Diferenças de Costumes entre a Europa e o Japão*, ed. Rui Manuel Loureiro (Macao: Instituto Português do Oriente, 2001). Compare this to a curious work of ventriloquism: Duarte de Sande, *Diálogo sobre a missão dos emabaixadores japoneses à Cúria Romana*, trans. Américo da Costa Ramalho (Macao: Fundação Oriente, 1997).

53. See Serge Gruzinski, *The Mestizo Mind: The Intellectual Dynamics of Colonization and Globalization*, trans. Deke Dusinberre (London: Routledge, 2002).

54. Jurgis Elisonas [George Elison], "Introduction: Japan in the Sixteenth Century," in George Elison and Bardwell L. Smith, eds., *Warlords, Artists and Commoners: Japan in the Sixteenth Century* (Honolulu: University of Hawaii Press, 1981), pp. 4–5.

55. Ronald P. Toby, *State and Diplomacy in Early Modern Japan: Asia in the Development of the Tokugawa Bakufu* (Princeton, N.J.: Princeton University Press, 1984).

56. Sanjay Subrahmanyam, *Three Ways to Be Alien: Travails and Encounters in the Early Modern World* (Waltham, Mass.: Brandeis University Press, 2011), pp. 136–72. Though the full original text of Manuzzi has never been published, see the partial edition (with valuable illustrations) by Piero Falchetta, ed., *Storia del Mogol di Nicolò Manuzzi veneziano*, 2 vols. (Milan: Franco Maria Ricci, 1986).

57. Carlo Ginzburg, "Latitude, Slaves and the Bible: An Experiment in Microhistory," *Critical Inquiry* 31 (2005): 665–83.

58. See, for example, Gauvin Alexander Bailey, *Art on the Jesuit Missions in Asia and Latin America, 1542–1773* (Toronto: University of Toronto Press, 1999); Serge Gruzinski, *Les quatre parties du monde: Histoire d'une mondialisation* (Paris: La Martinière, 2004).

59. Milo Cleveland Beach and Ebba Koch, *King of the World: The Padshahnama, an Imperial Mughal Manuscript from the Royal Library, Windsor Castle* (London: Thames and Hudson, 1997), p. 180.

60. For a persuasive set of arguments on such materials, see Ebba Koch, *Mughal Art and Imperial Ideology: Collected Essays* (Delhi: Oxford University

Press, 2001); see also Sumathi Ramaswamy, "Conceit of the Globe in Mughal Visual Practice," *Comparative Studies in Society and History* 49, no. 4 (2007): 751–82.

61. These issues have also been explored by addressing the uses and limits of the idea of a "cultural paradigm"; compare Jorge Arditi, "Geertz, Kuhn and the Idea of a Cultural Paradigm," *British Journal of Sociology* 45, no. 4 (1994): 597–617.

62. Peter Galison, *Image and Logic: A Material Culture of Microphysics* (Chicago: University of Chicago Press, 1997); for the idea of "prejudgments" *(Vorurteil)* in the context of the Enlightenment and thereafter, see Hans-Georg Gadamer, *Truth and Method,* trans. W. Glen-Doepel, Joel Weinsheimer, and Donald G. Marshall (New York: Continuum, 2004), pp. 268–85.

63. Ian Hacking, *Historical Ontology* (Cambridge, Mass.: Harvard University Press, 2002), pp. 152–58.

64. See the important remarks in Roger Preston Hart, "Translating Worlds: Incommensurability and Problems of Existence in Seventeenth-Century China," *Positions* 7, no. 1 (1999): 95–128. Hart draws on the earlier work of the historian of science, Mario Biagioli, notably "The Anthropology of Incommensurability," *Studies in History and Philosophy of Science* 21, no. 2 (1990): 183–209, and Hart heavily criticizes the position on incommensurability of the Sinologists from an earlier generation such as Jacques Gernet, *China and the Christian Impact: A Conflict of Cultures,* trans. Janet Lloyd (Cambridge: Cambridge University Press, 1985). For a somewhat distinct attempt to approach the matter (while also participating in a critique of Kuhn, Feyerabend, and others), see Alessandro Zir, *Luso-Brazilian Encounters of the Sixteenth Century: A Styles of Thinking Approach* (Lanham, Md.: Rowman and Littlefield, 2011).

65. This is a trend that one still observes in works such as Joan-Pau Rubiés, *Travel and Ethnology in the Renaissance: South India through European Eyes, 1250–1625* (Cambridge: Cambridge University Press, 2000). Rubiés attempts to place a fig leaf over his European exceptionalist argument, but others of his intellectual ilk are less deft at this task; see John M. Headley, *The Europeanization of the World: On the Origins of Human Rights and Democracy* (Princeton, N.J.: Princeton University Press, 2008).

66. For an overview of trends in South and Southeast Asia in this period, see Claude Markovits and Sanjay Subrahmanyam, "Inde et Asie du Sud-Est: Lendemains des empires," in Patrick Boucheron, ed., *Histoire du monde au XVe siècle* (Paris: Librairie Arthème Fayard, 2009), pp. 232–48.

67. See the classic study by Denys Lombard, *Le Sultanat d'Atjéh au temps d'Iskandar Muda, 1607–1636* (Paris: École Française d'Extrême-Orient, 1967).

1. Courtly Insults

Epigraph: Gogulapati Kurmanatha Kavi, *Simhādri-Narasimha-śatakamu,* ed. Pantula Lakshminarayana Sastri (Simhachalam: Simhachalam Devasthanam, 1983), verse 41. This translation was done together with Velcheru Narayana Rao.

1. Letter from George Pigot and J. L. Smith at Vizagapatam, November 22, 1753, to Thomas Saunders, Governor, and Council of Fort St. George, in B. S. Baliga, ed., *Letters to Fort St. George 1752–53* (Madras, India: Government Press, 1941), pp. 209–10; also see M. S. R. Anjaneyulu, *Vizagapatam District, 1769–1834: A History of Relations between the Zamindars and the East India Company* (Vishakapatnam, India: Andhra University, 1982), pp. 17–19, for a brief discussion.

2. David Parkin, "The Creativity of Abuse," *Man,* n.s., 15, no. 1 (1980): 45–64. Compare Janet M. Green, "Queen Elizabeth I's Latin Reply to the Polish Ambassador," *Sixteenth-Century Journal* 31, no. 4 (2000): 987–1008.

3. For a recent attempt to reconsider the political and courtly culture of these sultanates, see Emma J. Flatt, "Courtly Culture in the Indo-Persian States of the Medieval Deccan, 1450–1600" (PhD diss., School of Oriental and African Studies, University of London, 2008).

4. Thus, see the well-known evocation of Vijayanagara (and Hampi) in V. S. Naipaul, *India: A Wounded Civilization* (New York: Vintage, 1976), pp. 4–8, and—albeit in a very different mode—in the serialized television work *Bhārat ek khoj* by Shyam Benegal (1988), especially episodes 28 to 30. This latter work drew direct inspiration from Jawaharlal Nehru, *The Discovery of India* (New York: John Day, 1946), which in turn draws largely on colonial authors for its views of Vijayanagara.

5. Pierre Berthier, *La bataille de l'Oued el-Makhâzen, dite bataille des Trois Rois (4 aout 1578)* (Paris: Editions du CNRS, 1985).

6. Lucette Valensi, *Fables de la mémoire: La glorieuse bataille des trois rois* (Paris: Seuil, 1992).

7. H. K. Sherwani, *History of the Qutb Shāhī Dynasty* (New Delhi: Munshiram Manoharlal, 1974), p. 137.

8. Thus, one of the earliest historians to wish to downplay or relativize the importance of 1565 did indeed point a finger at Sewell; see R. Satyanatha Aiyar, "The Climacteric of Talikota," *Journal of Indian History* 6, no. 1 (1927): 67–78.

9. For a sense of how the field had developed until the 1980s, see Sindigi Rajasekhara, "Vijayanagara Studies: A Bibliography," in Anna Libera Dallapiccola and Stephanie Zingel-Avé Lallemant, eds., *Vijayanagara— City and Empire: New Currents of Research*, 2 vols. (Wiesbaden, Germany: Franz Steiner Verlag, 1985), 2:9–65. For a synthesis of Vijayanagara politics and diplomacy between the 1540s and the 1560s, the standard account is that of Burton Stein, *Vijayanagara: The New Cambridge History of India*, vol. 1, pt. 2 (Cambridge: Cambridge University Press, 1989), pp. 113–20.

10. For the first two texts, see David Lopes, ed., *Chrónica dos Reis de Bisnaga: Manuscripto Inédito do século XVI* (Lisbon: Imprensa Nacional, 1897).

11. Robert Sewell, *A Forgotten Empire (Vijayanagar): A Contribution to the History of India* (London: S. Sonnenschein & Co., 1900; reprint, New York: Barnes and Noble, 1972), 1.

12. N. Venkataramanayya, *Studies in the Third Dynasty of Vijayanagara* (Madras, India: University of Madras, 1935); also Venkataramanayya, *Vijayanagara: The Origin of the City and the Empire* (Madras, India: University of Madras, 1933).

13. B. A. Saletore, *Social and Political Life in the Vijayanagara Empire (A.D. 1346–A.D. 1646)*, 2 vols. (Madras, India: B. G. Paul, 1934); Henry Heras, *The Aravidu Dynasty of Vijayanagara* (Madras, India: B. G. Paul, 1927).

14. K. A. Nilakantha Sastri and N. Venkataramanayya, *Further Sources of Vijayanagara History*, 3 vols. (Madras, India: University of Madras, 1946); as the title suggests, this followed on from S. Krishnaswami Ayyangar, *Sources of Vijayanagar History* (Madras, India: University of Madras, 1919).

15. Jonathan Scott, *An Historical and Political View of the Decan, south of the Kistnah; including a sketch of the extent and revenue of the Mysorean dominions, as possessed by Tippoo Sultaun, to the period of his latest acquisitions of territory, and commencement of the present war in 1790* (London: J. Debrett, 1791), pp. 2–3.

16. Colonel Colin Mackenzie, "View of the principal Political Events that occurred in the Carnatic, from the dissolution of the Ancient Hindoo Government in 1564 till the Mogul Government was established in 1687, on the Conquest of the Capitals of Beejapoor and Golconda; compiled from various Authentic Memoirs and Original MSS, collected chiefly within the last ten years, and referred to in the Notes at the bottom of each page," *Journal of the Asiatic Society of Bengal* 13, pts. 1 and 2 (1844): 421–68, 578–608.

17. Mackenzie, "View of the Principal Political Events," pp. 421–23. For Mackenzie's collection techniques and his relations with his collaborators, see Phillip B. Wagoner, "Precolonial Intellectuals and the Production of Colonial Knowledge," *Comparative Studies in Society in History* 45, no. 4 (2003): 783–814.

18. Mark Wilks, *Historical Sketches of the South of India, in an attempt to trace the History of Mysoor*, vol. 1 (London: Longman, Hurst, Rees and Orme, 1810; reprint, Madras: Higginbotham, 1869), 12.

19. Jonathan Scott, *Ferishta's History of Dekkan, from the First Mahummedan Conquests*, 2 vols. (London: John Stockdale, 1794).

20. Khwaja Nizam-ud-Din Ahmad Bakhshi, *The Tabaqāt-i-Akbarī of Khwājah Nizāmuddīn Ahmad: A History of India from the Early Musalman Invasions to the Thirty-Sixth Year of the Reign of Akbar*, trans. Brajendranath De, revised by Baini Prashad, 3 vols. (Calcutta: Asiatic Society, 1927–39).

21. Perhaps the best discussion of Firishta, however, is remarkably old now. This is Jules Mohl, "Tarikh-i-Ferishta," 3 pts., *Journal des Savants*, 1840: 212–26, 354–72, 392–403, an extended review article of John Briggs's translation and the two-volume lithographed edition of the text from 1831. Mohl himself was best known as a translator of Firdausi.

22. See the extensive discussion in Keelan Overton, "A Collector and His Portrait: Book Arts and Painting for Ibrahim 'Adil Shah II of Bijapur (r. 1580–1627)" (PhD diss., Department of Art History, University of California–Los Angeles, 2011).

23. For a recent account of the principal manuscripts, see the "Pesh-guftār," in Muhammad Qasim Hindu Shah Astarabadi, *Tārīkh-i Firishta*, ed. Mohammad Reza Nasiri, 2 vols. (Tehran: Anjuman-i Asar wa Ma-fakhir-i Farhangi, 2009–11), 1:xviii–xlii. The remaining two volumes are forthcoming.

24. Samuel Johnson, *The Works of the English Poets, from Chaucer to Cowper*, vol. 21 (London: J. Johnson et al., 1810), p. 730.

25. In the first of these instances, in 1604, he must have been in the same party as the well-known Asad Beg Qazwini.

26. Here I follow Muhammad Qasim Firishta, *History of the Rise of Mahomedan Power in India till the Year* A.D. *1612*, trans. John Briggs (with the assistance of Mir Khairat ʿAli Khan Akbarabadi "Mushtaq"), 4 vols. (London: Longman, Rees, Orme, Brown, and Green, 1829). The last two volumes of the modern edition (Nasiri, ed., *Tārīkh-i Firishta*) have not been available to me. Hence, where necessary, I have compared the text to the Urdu trans-lation: Muhammad Qasim Firishta, *Tārīkh-i Firishta*, 2 vols., trans. ʿAbdul Hayy Khwaja (Lahore, Pakistan: Ghulam ʿAli and Sons, 1962).

27. Firishta, *Rise of Mahomedan Power*, 3:74–75; *Tārīkh-i Firishta*, Urdu trans., 2:108–9.

28. The modern construction of various dams on the Krishna River has intervened to change the terrain near these fords considerably. In the nine-teenth century, James Campbell in the *Bijapur Gazetteer* (1884) still reported traces of the Vijayanagara defensive earthworks on the southern bank.

29. Here I have followed the account in *Tārīkh-i Firishta*, Urdu trans., 2:113–14. Compare Firishta, *Rise of Mahomedan Power*, 3:78–79.

30. In the earlier Bijapur-related passage, Firishta writes that "the artil-lery, fastened together by strong chains and ropes, was drawn up in front of the line" (Firishta, *Rise of Mahomedan Power*, 3:78).

31. Briggs's translation has Rumi Khan filling his cannon with "bags of copper money," but the Urdu translation does not support this.

32. Firishta, *Rise of Mahomedan Power*, 3:150–52; *Tārīkh-i Firishta*, Urdu trans., 2:268–70. Briggs again radically summarizes the text.

33. As if to emphasize the point, Nizam-ud-Din Ahmad, *The Tabaqāt-i-Akbarī*, 3:141–44, even has it that "a cannon ball, shot from the army of Nizām-ul-mulk, hit Rām Rāj and killed him."

34. For the consequences for an important west coast commercial center such as Bhatkal, see Crispin Branfoot and Anna L. Dallapiccola, "Temple Architecture in Bhatkal and the 'Rāmāyana' Tradition in Sixteenth-Century Coastal Karnataka," *Artibus Asiae* 65, no. 2 (2005): 253–308.

35. See Joan-Pau Rubiés, *Travel and Ethnology in the Renaissance: South India through European Eyes, 1250–1625* (Cambridge: Cambridge University Press, 2000), pp. 164–250. Rubiés's work—despite its erudite appearance—should be used with extreme caution, in view of the manifold ideological prejudices of its author. It repeats many tropes derived from colonial British authors and is in reality entirely innocent of any direct knowledge of Indo-Persian or Indian vernacular materials.

36. Letters from Tristão de Paiva to D. João de Castro from Vijayanagara, February 11 and 16, 1548, in Elaine Sanceau et al., *Colecção de São Lourenço,* vol. 3 (Lisbon: Instituto de Investigação Científica Tropical, 1983), pp. 432–38. A better reading may be found in Armando Cortesão and Luís de Albuquerque, eds., *Obras Completas de D. João de Castro,* vol. 3 (Coimbra: Junta de Investigações Científicas do Ultramar, 1976), pp. 513–15, 518–19. We still lack a proper study of highly placed Muslims in the Vijayanagara court. The brief study by Hermann Goetz, "Muslims in Vijayanagar, the Record of Monuments," in H. K. Sherwani, ed., *Studies in Indian Culture: Dr. Ghulam Yazdani Commemoration Volume* (Hyderabad, India: Maulana Azad Oriental Research Institute, 1966), pp. 66–70, is inevitably quite sketchy. Also see Catherine B. Asher, "Islamic Influence and the Architecture of Vijayanagara," in Dallapiccola and Lallemant, *Vijayanagara—City and Empire,* 1:188–95. A number of buildings with a clear Indo-Persian stylistic influence may still be found in the site of Hampi, such as the so-called elephants' stable, and sections of the Dandanayaka's Palace.

37. Diogo do Couto, *Da Ásia, Década Sétima* (Lisbon: Livraria Sam Carlos, 1974), pt. 2, pp. 53–60; Anonymous, *Primor e honra da vida soldadesca no Estado da Índia,* ed. Laura Monteiro Pereira, Maria Augusta Lima Cruz, and Maria do Rosário Laureano Santos (Ericeira, Portugal: Mar de Letras, 2003), pp. 205–9.

38. Arquivo Nacional da Torre do Tombo, Lisbon (hereafter ANTT), Corpo Cronológico (hereafter CC), I-107-38, in José Wicki, "Duas cartas

oficiais de Vice-Reis da Índia, escritas em 1561 e 1564," *Studia*, no. 3 (1959): 36–89, quotations on pp. 83–85.

39. See the echoes of this in António Pinto Pereira, *História da Índia no tempo que a governou o visorei Dom Luís de Ataíde*, ed. Manuel Marques Duarte (Lisbon: Imprensa Nacional, 1987), pp. 143–47. Also see the wide-ranging overview in Luís Filipe F. R. Thomaz, "A Crise de 1565–1575 na História do Estado da Índia," *Mare Liberum*, no. 9 (1995): 481–520.

40. On this figure, see Farhad Daftary, "Shah Tahir b. Radi al-Din Husayni," in Oliver Leamand, ed., *The Biographical Encyclopaedia of Islamic Philosophy* (London: Continuum International, 2006), pp. 209–11; also Colin Paul Mitchell, "Sister Shi'a States?: Safavid Iran and the Deccan in the 16th Century," *Deccan Studies* 2, no. 2 (2004): 44–72 (particularly pp. 59–65). Shah Tahir maintained a correspondence with the Portuguese in the 1540s regarding the horse trade and other matters; see the letters from António de Sousa at Chaul to D. João de Castro, dated June 22, July 19, and August 1, 1546, in Sanceau et al., *Colecção de São Lourenço*, 3:233–34, 250–52, 257–59.

41. The chief source for his biography is Mirza Ibrahim Zubairi, *Tārīkh-i Bījāpūr musammā bi-Basātīn us-Salātīn* (Hyderabad, India: Sayyidi, 1880), pp. 133–37. The forthcoming University of Chicago dissertation by Roy Fischel will discuss him further.

42. Riazul Islam, ed., *A Calendar of Documents on Indo-Persian Relations (1500–1700)*, vol. 2 (Karachi: Institute of Central and West Asian Studies, 1982), Dn. 297, pp. 128–29. The document may be found in Asiatic Society of Bengal, Kolkata, Ms. Ivanow 350, *Inshā'-i Qāsim Tabasī*, fls. 38b–39a.

43. Ibid., Dn. 298, p. 130.

44. Firishta, *Rise of Mahomedan Power*, 3:89–91; *Tārīkh-i Firishta*, Urdu trans., 2:134–35.

45. ANTT, CC, I-107-87, letter dated December 16, 1565, in Josef Wicki, "Dokumente und Briefe aus der Zeit des indischen Vizekönigs D. Antão de Noronha (1563–1568)," *Aufsätze zur portugiesischen Kulturgeschichte*, no. 1 (1960): 225–315, citation on p. 253.

46. ANTT, CC, I-108-15, Goa, December 17, 1566, in Wicki, "Dokumente und Briefe aus der Zeit des indischen Vizekönigs D. Antão de

Noronha (1563–1568)," citation on p. 274 (also see the further brief remark on p. 292).

47. See, for example, José Wicki, "Duas relações sobre a situação da Índia portuguesa nos anos 1568 e 1569," *Studia*, no. 8 (1961): 133–220.

48. Maria Augusta Lima Cruz, *Diogo do Couto e a Década 8ᵃ da Ásia*, 2 vols. (Lisbon: Imprensa Nacional, 1993), 1:180–89.

49. Couto has a last confusing phrase in the chapter relating apparently to the changing value of the gold pagoda, which has risen from 7 silver *tangas* to 13 *tangas*. In the process, he also blames a certain unnamed viceroy of turning a blind eye to the counterfeiting of coins in Goa.

50. Sassetti to Bernardo Davanzati, Cochin, January 22, 1586, in Vanni Bramanti, ed., *Lettere da Vari Paesi, 1570–1588, di Filippo Sassetti* (Milan: Longanesi, 1970), letter 116, pp. 492–93.

51. Olga Pinto, ed., *Viaggi di C. Federici e G. Balbi alle Indie Orientali* (Rome: Istituto Poligrafico dello Stato, 1962), pp. 15–16; *The Voyage and Travaile of M. Caesar Frederick, merchant of Venice, unto the East India, the Indies, and beyond the Indies*, trans. Thomas Hickock (London: Richard Jones and Edward White, 1588), pp. 8v–9r.

52. See the eccentric account in S. S. Kanbargimath, "A Study of the Battle of Talikote," *Quarterly Journal of the Mythic Society* 60, nos. 1–4 (1969): 47–55. This author also continues to hold to the view that the battle was fought to the north of the Krishna. Another recent author, Rubiés, *Travel and Ethnology*, p. 284, assumes that it is necessarily a sign of "bias" on the part of Indo-Persian chroniclers to "neglect . . . the *fact*, attested by the Venetian traveller Cesare Federici, that the Hindu army had been betrayed by its Muslim cavalry" (emphasis added). Modern tourist guides in Hampi-Vijayanagara often add that the two "traitorous" Muslim captains were Rama Raya's brothers-in-law, through his two "Muslim wives."

53. Gonçalo Rodrigues, S.J., to António de Quadros, Bijapur, April 7, 1561, in Josef Wicki, ed., *Documenta Indica*, vol. 5: *1561–1563* (Rome: Monumenta Missionum Societatis Iesu, 1958), pp. 143–46. Also see the letter from the viceroy D. Constantino de Bragança to the queen, Cochin, 1561, ANTT, Colecção Moreira, Caderno 1A, fls. 23r–39v, in António dos Santos Pereira, "A Índia a preto e branco: Uma carta oportuna, escrita em

Cochim, por D. Constantino de Bragança, à Rainha Dona Catarina," *Anais de História de Além-Mar* 4 (2003): 449–84 (on p. 475).

54. John Briggs, "Essay on the Life and Writings of Ferishta," *Transactions of the Royal Asiatic Society of Great Britain and Ireland* 2, no. 1 (1829): 341–61.

55. Rubiés, *Travel and Ethnology*, p. 280.

56. Sayyid ʿAli [bin ʿAzizullah] Tabataba, *Burhān-i Maʾāsir*, ed. Sayyid Hashmi Faridabadi (Delhi: Matbaʿ Jamiʿa, 1936); for summary English translations, see J. S. King, *The History of the Bahmanī Dynasty, founded on the 'Burhān-i Maʾāsir'* (London: Luzac, 1900), and T. Wolseley Haig, *The History of the Nizam Shahi Kings of Ahmadnagar* (Bombay: British India Press, 1923). Haig's translation contains many errors and oddities, and has been compared here with the original text.

57. Haig, *History of the Nizam Shahi Kings*, p. 96; Tabataba, *Burhān*, pp. 411–12.

58. Tabataba, *Burhān*, p. 424. The very close (indeed near-literal) translation of this passage here was done in collaboration with Muzaffar Alam. It may be compared with the radically reduced version in Haig, *History of the Nizam Shahi Kings*, p. 100.

59. A third version in Persian of Rama Raya's end is to be found in Ibrahim Zubairi's *Basātīn al-Salātīn*, and seems to be based in turn on the earlier work of Rafiʿ-ud-Din Shirazi, *Tazkirat al-mulūk*. In this version, there is a brief conversation between Husain Nizam Shah and Rama Raya, and the latter's killing is on the explicit advice of the physician Qasim Beg Tabrizi. See K. K. Basu, "The Battle of Tālikōta—Before and after (from Muslim Sources)," in D. P. Karmarkar, ed., *Vijayanagara Sexcentenary Commemoration Volume* (Dharwar, India: Vijayanagara Empire Sexcentenary Association, 1936), pp. 245–54.

60. Haig, *History of the Nizam Shahi Kings*, p. 71; Tabataba, *Burhān*, p. 328.

61. Sherwani, *Qutb Shāhī Dynasty*, p. 42. To be sure, one of the sources on which this is based is the later, anonymous, *Tārīkh-i Sultān Muhammad Qutb Shāh* from the 1610s.

62. For an analysis of other such figures, see Phillip B. Wagoner, "Fortuitous Convergences and Essential Ambiguities: Transcultural Political

Elites in the Medieval Deccan," *International Journal of Hindu Studies* 3, no. 3 (1999): 241–64.

63. E. Vasumati, "Ibrahim Qutb Shah and the Telugu Poets," in S. M. Qadri Zore, ed., *Qutb Shahi Sultans and Andhra Samskriti* (Hyderabad, India: Idara-e-Adabiyat-e-Urdu, 1962), pp. 28–42.

64. Anonymous, *Primor e honra da vida,* pp. 219–20.

65. Firishta, *Rise of Mahomedan Power,* 3:71; *Tārīkh-i Firishta,* Urdu trans., 2:104.

66. *Tārīkh-i Firishta,* ed. Nasiri, 2:270–80 (quotation on p. 280). We note that the Sultan's chief adviser, the wise Malik Saif-ud-Din Ghuri, is portrayed as having been set against his pride and obstinacy in the matter.

67. *Tārīkh-i Firishta,* Urdu trans., 2:107. Compare Firishta, *Rise of Mahomedan Power,* 3:74.

68. *Tārīkh-i Firishta,* Urdu trans., 2:260. Compare Firishta, *Rise of Mahomedan Power,* 3:147. For a comment on the episode (based on Briggs's translation), see Richard Eaton, "From Kalyana to Talikota: Culture, Politics and War in the Deccan 1542–1565," in Rajat Datta, ed., *Rethinking a Millennium: Perspectives on Indian History from the Eighth to the Eighteenth Century (Essays for Harbans Mukhia)* (Delhi: Aakar Books, 2008), pp. 95–105.

69. Richard M. Eaton, " 'Kiss My Foot,' said the King: Firearms, Diplomacy, and the Battle for Raichur, 1520," *Modern Asian Studies* 43, no. 1 (2009): 289–313.

70. See Sumit Guha, "Literary Tropes and Historical Settings: A Study from Southern India," in Datta, *Rethinking a Millennium,* pp. 106–20; also Sumit Guha, "The Frontiers of Memory: What the Marathas Remembered of Vijayanagara," *Modern Asian Studies* 43, no. 1 (2009): 269–88. Guha suggests that this work should date at least to the 1670s, and may be even later than that.

71. See Sastri and Venkataramanayya, *Further Sources,* 3:204–42; 2:263–285 (Kannada text). For a discussion, see Christopher Chekuri, "Between Family and Empire: Nayaka Strategies of Rule in Vijayanagara South India, 1400–1700 AD" (PhD diss., University of Wisconsin–Madison, 2005), pp. 154–60.

72. See *Dīwān-i Hasan Shauqī,* ed. Jamil Jalibi (Karachi: Anjuman-i Taraqqi-yi Urdu Pakistan, 1971). The work consists of an erudite introduction

by the editor (pp. 1–68), the *Fath Nāma-i Nizām Shāh* (pp. 71–118), the shorter *Mīzbānī Nāma* (pp. 121–35), and some thirty *ghazals* and other verses by the poet (pp. 139–177). Attention was first drawn to Hasan Shauqi by Maulavi ʿAbdul Haq in 1929, and further work was then done by the scholars Sakhawat Mirza and Husaini Shahid. Two manuscripts exist of the work, one dating to the 1680s. For a discussion of the poet, also see Mohammed Jamal Shareef, *Dakan mein urdū shāʿirī Wali se pahle*, ed. Mohammad Ali Asar (Hyderabad, India: Idarah-i Adabiyat-i Urdu, 2004), pp. 458–69.

73. ʿAbdul Dihlawi, *Ibrāhīmnāma*, ed. Masʿud Husain Khan (Aligarh, India: Aligarh Muslim University, 1969); Nusrati, *Masnawī ʿAlī Nāma*, ed. ʿAbdul Majid Siddiqi (Hyderabad, India: Salar Jang Museum, 1959).

74. Hasan Shauqi, *Fath Nāma-i Nizām Shāh*, p. 73: Sharaf mard ka hai chalant khūb khās / Jo phūlon ki khūbī so phūlon kī bās / Har yak mulk mein nek raftār hai / Har yak qaum mein nek guftār hai. All translations from this text were done in collaboration with Muzaffar Alam.

75. Ibid., p. 90: Na pīrān ko māne na mīrān ke tein / Mudabbir ko jāne dabīrān ke tein / So masjid ke tein pār vīrān kare / Muazzin ke tein mār hairān kare / Na māne kidhain kis namāzī ke tein / Diwānā kahe Fakhr Rāzī ke tein. The reference is to the Iranian philosopher and theologian Fakhr-ud-Din Razi (1149–1210).

76. Ibid., p. 110: Madad jyon fath āsamānī jo pāy / Pakar Rām kūn Shāh nazdīk lyāe / Nazar Shāh kī us ūpar jyūn parī / Kiyā qatl kā hukm so us gharī / Garajtī ʿadālat kiyā dīn so / Khulyā dī so us guhar dīn so/ Khudāyā ba barkat nabī hor walī / Ba sar ganj yo Shāh-i Mardān ʿAlī / Dī taufīq zafar muj gharī sāth men / Zafar kī kalī manj diyā hāt men / So zālim ki mundī so wem kāt kar / So tyaven so tisko bārā bāt kar / Ke yā Rabb dī munj is sabar kā jazā/ Jo bedīn ko men jo dityā sazā / Āyā hātif-i ghaib te yo jawāb/ ʿibādat qabūlyā duʿa mustajāb / Ke buniyād yo dīn Islām kī / terī kharak men thī marag Rām kī/ khalal thā kufr kā diyā jas Khudā / kiyā Rām ka sen tan te judā.

77. Ibid., pp. 114–15.

78. Firishta, *Rise of Mahomedan Power*, 3:48–51; *Tārīkh-i Firishta*, Urdu trans., 2:76–79, which recounts the problems of Rama Raya with "Bhoj Tirmal Ray," which is to say Salakaraju Tirumala.

79. Aftabi, *Tarif-i-Husain Shah Badshah Dakhan*, eds. and trans. G. T. Kulkarni and M. S. Mate (Pune, India: Bharata Itihasa Samshodhaka Mandala, 1987). An earlier edition may be found by M. 'Abdullah Chaghatai, "Fārsī kī ek qalamī masnawī," *Urdū* (Delhi), April 1943. To the extent I can discern, the first discussion of this text by a historian may be found in Heras, *Aravidu Dynasty*, pp. xvii–xix, 555–66.

80. In fact, they are also inferior to the only other contemporary portrait of Husain Nizam Shah (on horseback) we possess, in the collection of the Cincinnati Art Museum, John J. Emery Fund (1983.311). For details, see Navina Najat Haidar and Marika Sardar, eds., *Sultans of the South: Arts of India's Deccan Courts, 1323–1687* (New York: Metropolitan Museum of Art, 2011), p. 220.

81. We also find the suggestion that she was the daughter of a certain Miyan Jiu, and descended from the Qara-qoyunlu clan. See Sayyid Ahmadullah Qadri, *Memoirs of Chand Bibi, the Princess of Ahmadnagar* (Hyderabad, India: Osmania University, 1939), p. 48.

82. See Mark Zebrowski, *Deccani Painting* (Berkeley: University of California Press, 1983), pp. 17–19. Zebrowski—who assumes the paintings were produced in or about 1565—argues this was done after 1569, when Khunza Humayun effectively lost power.

83. In what follows, I have compared the text with the sometimes divergent translations in Aftabi, *Tarif-i-Husain Shah*, trans. Kulkarni and Mate; and in Heras, *Aravidu Dynasty*, pp. 555–66 (the latter authored by Mohamed Kazem Nemazi), in order to prepare a corrected translation.

84. Georges Duby, "Avant-propos," in *Le dimanche de Bouvines: 27 juillet 1214* (Paris: Gallimard, 1985), p. x. The passage does not appear in Georges Duby, *The Legend of Bouvines: War, Religion and Culture in the Middle Ages*, trans. Catherine Tihanyi (Berkeley: University of California Press, 1990).

85. Jacques de Coutre, *Andanzas asiáticas*, ed. Eddy Stols, B. Teensma, and J. Verberckmoes (Madrid: Historia 16, 1991), p. 246.

86. Niccolao Manucci, *Mogul India, 1653–1708, or Storia do Mogor*, trans. William Irvine, 4 vols. (London: J. Murray, 1907–8; reprint, Delhi: Low Price Publications, 1990), 3:93–94.

87. For an attempt to contextualize the events discussed in this chapter in historiographical terms, also see Richard M. Eaton, *A Social History of*

the Deccan, 1300–1761: Eight Indian Lives (New Cambridge History of India I.8), (Cambridge: Cambridge University Press, 2005), pp. 78–104.

88. Garcia da Orta, Colóquios dos simples e drogas da Índia, ed. Conde de Ficalho, 2 vols. (Lisbon: Imprensa Nacional, 1891).

89. Thus, the simple structural opposition between the sultanates as "open" cultures and Vijayanagara as a "closed" culture once made by Phillip Wagoner is manifestly unsatisfactory, and I must therefore distance myself from the claims in Phillip B. Wagoner, Tidings of the King: A Translation and Ethnohistorical Analysis of the "Rāyavācakamu" (Honolulu: University of Hawaii Press, 1993), pp. 60–69. However, Wagoner's own position has since happily evolved to an extent; see Wagoner, "'Sultan among Hindu Kings': Dress, Titles and the Islamicization of Hindu Culture at Vijayanagara," Journal of Asian Studies 55, no. 4 (1996): 851–80.

90. For a classic exploration in this vein, see Aziz Ahmad, Studies in Islamic Culture in the Indian Environment (Oxford: Clarendon Press, 1964), preceded by Tara Chand, Influence of Islam on Indian Culture (Allahabad: Indian Press, 1954).

2. Courtly Martyrdom

Epigraph: Anonymous, Primor e honra da vida soldadesca no Estado da Índia (Anónimo do séc. XVI), ed. Laura Monteiro Pereira, Maria Augusta Lima Cruz, and Maria do Rosário Laureana Santos (Ericeira, Portugal: Mar de Letras, 2003), p. 99.

1. Suraiya Faroqhi, Pilgrims and Sultans: The Hajj under the Ottomans, 1517–1683 (London: I. B. Tauris, 1994).

2. See Qutb-ud-Din al-Nahrawali al-Makki, Lightning over Yemen: A History of the Ottoman Campaign (1569–71), trans. Clive K. Smith (London: I. B. Tauris, 2002).

3. Qutb-ud-Din al-Nahrawali, Journey to the Sublime Porte: The Arabic Memoir of a Sharifian Agent's Diplomatic Mission to the Ottoman Imperial Court in the Era of Suleyman the Magnificent (Beirut: Ergon Verlag, 2005), p. xv.

4. On this significant personage, also known as Roxelana or Roxolana, see Galina I. Yermolenko, ed., *Roxolana in European Literature, History and Culture* (Farnham, U.K.: Ashgate, 2010).

5. Nahrawali, *Journey to the Sublime Porte*, pp. 208–9. I have altered the transliteration in order to be consistent.

6. On this important figure, see Marco Salati, "Ricerche sullo Sciismo nell'Impero Ottomano: Il viaggio di Zayn al-Dīn al-Šahīd al-Tānī a Istanbul al tempo di Solimano il Magnifico, 952/1545," *Oriente Moderno*, n.s., 9 (1990): 81–92; also Devin J. Stewart, "The Ottoman Execution of Zayn al-Dīn al-ʿĀmilī," *Die Welt des Islams*, no. 48 (2008): 289–347.

7. See Sajida S. Alvi, "Religion and State during the Reign of Mughal Emperor Jahangir (1605–27): Nonjuristical Perspectives," *Studia Islamica*, no. 69 (1989): 95–119; Wayne R. Husted, "Karbalāʾ Made Immediate: The Martyr as Model in Imāmī Shīʿism," *Muslim World* 83, nos. 3–4 (1993): 263–78.

8. Louis E. Fenech, "Martyrdom and the Sikh Tradition," *Journal of the American Oriental Society* 117, no. 4 (1997): 623–42 (especially pp. 626–29). For a seventeenth-century Persian account, see Mirza Zuʾlfiqar Azar Sasani, *The Dabistan, or School of Manners*, trans. David Shea and Anthony Troyer, 3 vols. (Paris: Oriental Translation Fund, 1843), 2:270–73.

9. British Library, London, Additional 9854, fls. 38–52, Jerónimo Xavier in Lahore, September 25, 1606, in António da Silva Rego, ed., *Documentação ultramarina portuguesa*, vol. 3 (Lisbon: Centro de Estudos Históricos Ultramarinos, 1963), pp. 62–91; on the case of Guru Arjan, see fls. 43v–44r, pp. 73–74.

10. On the Islamic tradition, see the useful outline in David Cook, *Martyrdom in Islam* (Cambridge: Cambridge University Press, 2007).

11. Frédéric Tinguely, ed., *Un libertin dans l'Inde moghole: Les voyages de François Bernier (1656–1669)* (Paris: Chandeigne, 2008), p. 318; and Mirza Zuʾlfiqar Azar Sasani, *The Dabistan*, 2:293–97. More recently, see Nathan Katz, "The Identity of a Mystic: The Case of Saʿid Sarmad, a Jewish-Yogi-Sufi Courtier of the Mughals," *Numen* 42, no. 2 (2000): 142–60.

12. Carl W. Ernst, "From Hagiography to Martyrology: Conflicting Testimonies to a Sufi Martyr of the Delhi Sultanate," *History of Religions* 24, no. 4 (1985): 308–27; Shahid Amin, "On Retelling the Muslim Conquest of

North India," in Partha Chatterjee and Anjan Ghosh, eds., *History and the Present* (New Delhi: Permanent Black, 2002), pp. 19–32.

13. I. Ross Bartlett, "John Foxe as Hagiographer: The Question Revisited," *Sixteenth-Century Journal* 26, no. 4 (1995): 771–89. For a recent, revisionist view of the Marian period and of Foxe's role, see Eamon Duffy, *Fires of Faith: Catholic England under Mary Tudor* (New Haven, Conn.: Yale University Press, 2009).

14. Thus, see David Loades, ed., *John Foxe at Home and Abroad* (Aldershot, U.K.: Ashgate, 2004).

15. See Jorge Santos Alves, ed., *Fernão Mendes Pinto and the Peregrinação*, 4 vols. (Lisbon: Fundação Oriente, 2010), 2:29: "estes meus trabalhos, & perigos da vida que passei no discurso de vinte & hum anos em que fuy treze vezes cativo, & dezasete vendido."

16. Fernão Mendes Pinto, *The Travels of Mendes Pinto*, trans. Rebecca D. Catz (Chicago: University of Chicago Press, 1989); also the earlier work by Catz, *A sátira social de Fernão Mendes Pinto: Análise crítica da Peregrinação*, trans. Manolo B. R. Santos (Lisbon: Prelo, 1978).

17. Joan-Pau Rubiés, "The Oriental Voices of Mendes Pinto, or the Traveller as Ethnologist in Portuguese Asia," *Portuguese Studies* 10 (1994): 24–43, citation on p. 43.

18. It would eventually be interesting to compare captivity narratives from different imperial contexts of the sixteenth and seventeenth centuries; see, for example, Osmân Agha de Temechvar, *Prisonnier des infidèles: Un soldat ottoman dans l'Empire des Habsbourg*, trans. Frédéric Hitzel (Paris: Actes Sud, 1998), for such a captivity narrative of the period 1688–99, completed in 1724.

19. See the acclaimed work by Linda Colley, *Captives: Britain, Empire and the World, 1600–1850* (London: Jonathan Cape, 2002); for an important critique, Miles Ogborn, "Gotcha!," *History Workshop Journal*, no. 56 (2003): 231–38. More recently, see the interesting literary analysis in Lisa Voigt, *Writing Captivity in the Early Modern Atlantic: Circulations of Knowledge and Authority in the Iberian and English Imperial Worlds* (Chapel Hill: University of North Carolina Press, 2009), which may be read together with Nabil Matar, *Turks, Moors, and Englishmen in the Age of Discovery* (New York: Columbia University Press, 1999), and Nabil Matar,

Britain and Barbary, 1589–1689 (Gainesville: University Press of Florida, 2005).

20. Bartolomé Bennassar and Lucile Bennassar, *Les chrétiens d'Allah: L'histoire extraordinaire des renégats, XVIe et XVIIe siècles* (Paris: Perrin, 1989).

21. See the collection of essays by Anthony Reid, *An Indonesian Frontier: Acehnese and Other Histories of Sumatra* (Singapore: Singapore University Press, 2005), which includes his earlier essays "The Turkish Connection," pp. 69–93, and "Trade and the Problem of Royal Power in Aceh: Three Stages, c. 1550–1700," pp. 94–111.

22. "Relazione dell'Impero Ottomano del clarissimo Daniele Barbarigo tornato bailo da Costantinopoli nel 1564," in Eugenio Albèri, ed., *Relazioni degli Ambasciatori veneti al Senato*, series 3, vol. 3 (Florence: Società Editrice Fiorentina, 1844), p. 12. For further aspects of the Portuguese-Acehnese rivalry in the same decade, see Pierre-Yves Manguin, "Of Fortresses and Galleys: The 1568 Acehnese Siege of Melaka, Following a Contemporary Bird's-Eye View," *Modern Asian Studies* 22, no. 3 (1988): 607–28, and John Villiers, "Aceh, Melaka and the *Hystoria dos cercos de Malaca* of Jorge de Lemos," *Portuguese Studies* 17, no. 1 (2001): 75–85.

23. C. R. Boxer, "A Note on Portuguese Reactions to the Revival of the Red Sea Spice Trade and the Rise of Atjeh, 1540–1600," *Journal of Southeast Asian History* 10, no. 3 (1969): 415–28.

24. Most significant amongst these is Jorge Manuel dos Santos Alves, *O domínio do norte de Samatra: A história dos sultanatos de Samudera-Pacém e de Achém, e das suas relações com os Portugueses, 1500–1580* (Lisbon: Sociedade Histórica da Independência de Portugal, 1999); but also see Giancarlo Casale, "His Majesty's Servant Lutfi: The Career of a Previously Unknown Sixteenth-Century Ottoman Envoy to Sumatra Based on an Account of His Travels from the Topkapı Palace Archives," *Turcica*, no. 37 (2005): 43–81.

25. Muzaffar Alam and Sanjay Subrahmanyam, *Writing the Mughal World: Studies in Political Culture* (Ranikhet: Permanent Black, 2011), pp. 88–122.

26. For a useful overview, see Ronnie Po-chia Hsia, *The World of Catholic Renewal, 1540–1770* (Cambridge: Cambridge University Press, 1998).

27. For the broad context, also see William Cummings, "Islam, Empire and Makassarese Historiography in the Reign of Sultan Ala'uddin (1593–1639)," *Journal of Southeast Asian Studies* 38, no. 2 (2007): 197–214.

28. Anthony Reid, "Islamization and Christianization in Southeast Asia: The Critical Phase, 1550–1650," in Anthony Reid, ed., *Southeast Asia in the Early Modern Era: Trade, Power, and Belief* (Ithaca, N.Y.: Cornell University Press, 1993), pp. 151–79, citation on p. 166.

29. Shaykh Zainuddin Makhdum, *Tuhfat al-Mujāhidīn: A Historical Epic of the Sixteenth Century*, trans. S. Muhammad Husayn Nainar (Kuala Lumpur: Islamic Book Trust, 2006). In some manuscripts, the word *ahwāl* is substituted in the title by *akhbār*.

30. Sanjay Subrahmanyam, "Palavras do Idalcão: Um encontro curioso em Bijapur no ano de 1561," *Cadernos do Noroeste* 15, nos. 1–2 (2001): 513–24.

31. Ibn Battuta, *Travels in Asia and Africa, 1325–1354*, trans. H. A. R. Gibb (London: Routledge and Kegan Paul, 1929; reprint, New Delhi: Manohar, 2001), 274.

32. The classic essay on this theme is that of Maria Augusta Lima Cruz, "Exiles and Renegades in Early Sixteenth Century Portuguese India," *Indian Economic and Social History Review* 23, no. 3 (1986): 249–62.

33. See the useful reflection on the North African case in Maria de Lurdes Rosa, "Velhos, novos e mutáveis sagrados . . . : Um olhar antropológico sobre formas 'religiosas' de percepção e interpretação da conquista africana (1415–1521)," *Lusitania Sacra* 18 (2006): 13–85, and also in Lurdes Rosa, "Vom Heiligen Grafen zum Morisken-Märtyrer: Funcktionem der Sakralität im Kontext der nordafrikanischen Kriege (1415–1521)," in *Novos Mundos- Neue Welten: Portugal und das Zeitalter der Entdeckungen* (Dresden: Sandstein Verlag, 2007), pp. 88–105.

34. The sections that follow are largely based on J. G. Everaert, "Manuel Godinho de Erédia: Humaniste ou aventurier?," in Manuel Godinho de Erédia, *Suma de Árvores e Plantas da Índia Intra Ganges*, ed. J. G. Everaert, J. E. Mendes Ferrão, and M. Cândida Liberato (Lisbon: Comissão Nacional para as Comemorações dos Descobrimentos Portugueses, 2001), pp. 23–82.

35. Luís Filipe Thomaz, "Prefácio," in Godinho de Erédia, *Suma de Árvores*, p. 12.

36. Susan Neild-Basu, "The Dubashes of Madras," *Modern Asian Studies* 18, no. 1 (1984): 1–31.

37. Achille Bédier and Joseph Cordier, *Statistiques de Pondichéry (1822–1824)*, ed. Jean Deloche (Pondicherry, India: Institut Français de Pondichéry, 1988), p. 58.

38. See Rui Carita, ed., *O "Lyvro de Plantaforma das Fortalezas da Índia" da Biblioteca da Fortaleza de São Julião da Barra* (Lisbon: Edições INAPA, 1999).

39. Manuel Godinho de Erédia, *Eredia's Description of Malaca, Meridional India, and Cathay*, trans. J. V. Mills, intro. Cheah Boon Kheng (Kuala Lumpur: Malaysian Branch of the Royal Asiatic Society, 1997). On the other texts, also see Jorge Flores, "Dois retratos portugueses da Índia de Jahangir: Jerónimo Xavier e Manuel Godinho de Erédia," in Jorge Flores and Nuno Vassallo e Silva, eds., *Goa e o Grão-Mogol* (Lisbon: Fundação Calouste Gulbenkian, 2004), pp. 44–66.

40. For a general consideration on these questions, see Luís Filipe F. R. Thomaz, "The Image of the Archipelago in Portuguese Cartography of the 16th and Early 17th Centuries," *Archipel*, no. 49 (1995): 79–124.

41. The unique manuscript of this work (hereafter cited as *HSMLMC*) is in the Biblioteca Nacional de Lisboa, Fundo Geral, Reservados, Codex 414. The work may be consulted online at http://purl.pt/1275. One of the few modern works to make extensive use of this text is Paulo Jorge de Sousa Pinto, *Portugueses e Malaios: Malaca e os Sultanatos de Johor e Achém, 1575–1619* (Lisbon: Sociedade Histórica da Independência de Portugal, 1997). Also see Jorge Manuel dos Santos Alves, "Os mártires do Achém nos séculos XVI e XVII: Islão *versus* Cristianismo?," in *Missionação Portuguesa e Encontro de Culturas—Congresso Internacional de História: Actas*, vol. 2: *África Oriental, Oriente e Brasil* (Braga: Universidade Católica Portuguesa, 1993), pp. 391–406, where the author mentions (p. 398, n.24) the text by Erédia and states: "preparamos para breve a sua edição comentada e anotada," though it has not to our knowledge yet appeared or been prepared.

42. On this important and controversial personage, see Carlos Alonso, *Alejo de Meneses, O.S.A. (1559–1617), Arzobispo de Goa (1595–1612): Estudio biográfico* (Valladolid, Spain: Estudio Agustiniano, 1992); also Sanjay Subrahmanyam, "Dom Frei Aleixo de Meneses (1559–1617) et l'échec des

tentatives d'indigénisation du christianisme en Inde," *Archives de Sciences Sociales des Religions*, no. 103 (1998): 21–42.

43. *HSMLMC*, fl. 3r.

44. On the basilisk, see for example John Vogt, "Saint Barbara's Legion: Portuguese Artillery in the Struggle for Morocco, 1415–1578," *Military Affairs* 41, no. 4 (1977): 176–82; and Leonid Tarassuk, "Model of a Basilisk by Petrus de Arena," *Metropolitan Museum Journal* 24 (1989): 189–97. Also see William Shakespeare, *Henry V*, act 5, scene 2: "Your eyes, which hitherto have borne in them / Against the French, that met them in their bent, / The fatal balls of murdering basilisks: / The venom of such looks, we fairly hope, / Have lost their quality, and that this day / Shall change all griefs and quarrels into love."

45. *HSMLMC*, fl. 4r.

46. See the discussion in Pinto, *Portugueses e Malaios*, pp. 253–62, "O Sultanato de Achém: Questões e problemas de genealogia."

47. Hoesein Djajadiningrat, "Critisch overzicht van de in maleische werken vervatte gegevens over de geschiedenis van het Soeltanaat van Atjeh," *Bijdragen tot de Taal-, Land- en Volkenkunde van Nederlandsch Indië* 65 (1911): 135–265 (especially pp. 159–62). On foreign *'ulamā'* in Aceh around 1600, see Paul Wormser, *Le Bustan al-Salatin de Nuruddin ar-Raniri: Réflexions sur le rôle culturel d'un étranger dans le monde malais au XVIIe siècle* (Paris: Editions de la Maison des Sciences de l'Homme, 2012).

48. Jorge de Lemos, *História dos cercos de Malaca (1585)* (facsimile ed., Lisbon: Biblioteca Nacional, 1982), pp. 58–64; for the larger context, see B. N. Teensma, "An Unknown Portuguese Text on Sumatra from 1582," *Bijdragen tot de Taal-, Land- en Volkenkunde* 145, nos. 2–3 (1989): 308–23.

49. Diogo do Couto, *Vida de D. Paulo de Lima Pereira, por Diogo do Couto (com uma descripção que de novo deixou feita o mesmo author desde a Terra dos Fumos até o Cabo das Correntes)* (Lisbon: Escriptório, 1903).

50. In this respect, another interesting comparison would be to the hagiographical texts produced around the "martyred" figure of Constantino de Sá de Noronha in seventeenth-century Sri Lanka; cf. Jorge Flores and Maria Augusta Lima Cruz, "A 'Tale of Two Cities', a 'Veteran Soldier', or the Struggle for Endangered Nobilities: The Two *Jornadas de Huva* (1633, 1635) Revisited," in Jorge Flores, ed., *Re-exploring the Links: History and*

Constructed Histories between Portugal and Sri Lanka (Wiesbaden, Germany: Harrassowitz Verlag, 2007), pp. 95–124. More generally, on the subject of martyrdom in Sri Lanka in the period, see Alan Strathern, *Kingship and Conversion in Sixteenth-Century Sri Lanka: Portuguese Imperialism in a Buddhist Land* (Cambridge: Cambridge University Press, 2007), pp. 218–19, passim.

51. Luís de Albuqerque and José Pereira da Costa, "Cartas de 'Serviços' da Índia (1500–1550)," *Mare Liberum*, no. 1 (1990): 309–96; Historical Archives, Panaji, Goa, Mss. 1043, "Consultas de Partes."

52. Jacques Le Goff, *Saint Louis* (Paris: Gallimard, 1996), pp. 192–93, in which Le Goff remarks: "Être fait prisonnier est le pire malheur qui puisse arriver à un roi. . . . Mais être fait prisonnier par des Infidèles est le pire malheur qui puisse arriver à un roi chrétien." More generally, see Robert I. Burns, "Christian-Islamic Confrontation in the West: The Thirteenth-Century Dream of Conversion," *American Historical Review* 76, no. 5 (1971): 1386–434.

53. *HSMLMC*, fl. 5r. For a general history of the town and its bishopric, see M. Gonçalves da Costa, *História do bispado e cidade de Lamego*, 6 vols. (Braga, Portugal: Barbosa & Xavier, 1977–92), in particular vol. 3 (Renascimento I).

54. *HSMLMC*, fl. 5r.

55. On the expedition see Malyn Newitt, *History of Mozambique* (London: Hurst, 1995), pp. 56–58.

56. On this siege, see R. O. W. Goertz, "Attack and Defense Techniques in the Siege of Chaul, 1570–1571," in Luís de Albuquerque and Inácio Guerreiro, eds., *Actas do II Seminário Internacional de História Indo-Portuguesa* (Lisbon: Instituto de Investigação Científica Tropical, 1985), pp. 265–87.

57. *HSMLMC*, fl. 5v.

58. António Pinto Pereira, *História da Índia no tempo em que a governou o visorey D. Luís de Ataíde*, introd. Manuel Marques Duarte (Lisbon: Imprensa Nacional, 1987), pp. 429, 522.

59. See Farhat Hasan, *State and Locality in Mughal India: Power Relations in Western India, c. 1572–1730* (Cambridge: Cambridge University Press, 2006), pp. 20–30.

60. *HSMLMC*, fl. 6r. If this account may be credited, Coutinho would have been in the Mughal court in late 1573, at least some years before the first proper Jesuit mission there. On early Portuguese-Mughal relations, also see Jorge Flores and António Vasconcelos de Saldanha, *Os Firangis na Chancelaria Mogol: Cópias Portuguesas de documentos de Akbar (1572–1604)* (New Delhi: Embaixada de Portugal, 2003). Godinho de Erédia had some contacts with the early Jesuit missions at the Mughal court, and these may have been his source of information. On António Teixeira Pinto, see the brief mention in Costa, *História do bispado e cidade de Lamego*, 3:376.

61. On the *espadas pretas* or *espada negras* used for fencing, see the mention in Miguel de Cervantes, *Don Quijote*, pt. 2, chap. 19, of "*dos espadas negras de esgrima, nuevas, y con sus zapatillas,*" usually translated as "new fencing-foils with buttons."

62. Diogo do Couto, *Da Ásia, Década Nona* (Lisbon: Regia officina typografica, 1778; reprint, Lisbon: Livraria Sam Carlos, 1974), pp. 103–10. The dates in Erédia's account are, as usual, problematic, and he writes that the transition in government took place on October 18, 1574 (*HSMLMC*, fl. 6v).

63. *HSMLMC*, fls. 7v–8r.

64. See Pinto, *Portugueses e Malaios*, pp. 237–52, "O Sultanato de Johor: Questões e problemas de genealogia."

65. Also see Antonella Vignati, ed., "Vida e Acções de Mathias de Albuquerque, Capitão e Viso-Rei do Estado da Índia," *Mare Liberum*, no. 15 (1998): 139–245; no. 17 (1999): 267–360. The text was probably written by Miguel de Lacerda. The combat with the Acehnese armada is described in pt. 1, pp. 173–75, and among the captains of the galliots we do find Manoel Monteiro.

66. Maria Augusta Lima Cruz, "O assassínio do rei de Maluco: Reabertura de um processo," in Artur Teodoro de Matos and Luís Filipe F. Reis Thomaz, eds., *As Relações entre a Índia Portuguesa, a Ásia do Sueste e o Extremo Oriente: Actas do VI Seminário Internacional de História Indo-Portuguesa* (Macau: Instituto Cultural de Macau, 1993), pp. 511–30.

67. For the Portuguese at Ambon in this period, see Hubert Jacobs, "The Portuguese Town of Ambon, 1567–1605," in Albuquerque and Guerreiro, *Actas do II Seminário Internacional*, pp. 601–14.

68. On Solor, see the wide-ranging essay by Robert H. Barnes, "Avarice and Iniquity at the Solor Fort," *Bijdragen tot de Taal-, Land- en Volkenkunde* 143, nos. 2–3 (1987): 208–36.

69. *HSMLMC*, fls. 14r–14v.

70. Ibid., fl. 17r.

71. See Charles Ralph Boxer, *The Great Ship from Amacon: Annals of Macao and the Old Japan Trade, 1555–1640* (Lisbon: Centro de Estudos Históricos Ultramarinos, 1959).

72. It has been suggested that Erédia's narrative, and even Coutinho's actions in a way, may have been influenced by narratives that circulated at the time regarding the Battle of Lepanto. For the naval tactics followed there, see Niccolò Capponi, *Victory of the West: The Story of the Battle of Lepanto* (London: Macmillan, 2006).

73. *HSMLMC*, fls. 18r–18v.

74. Ibid., fl. 21r.

75. Diogo do Couto, *Da Ásia, Década Décima*, pt. 1 (Lisbon: Regia officina typografica, 1778; reprint, Lisbon: Livraria Sam Carlos, 1974), pp. 280–81, book 3, chap. 3: "De como os Turcos, que hiam na Armada do Achem, ordenáram humas balsas de fogo pera queimarem as náos: e de como Nuno Monteiro [*sic*], que andava no estreito em huma Galeaça, foi socorrer a Malaca: e da aspera batalha que teve com a Armada do Achem: e de como por desastre tomou fogo, e se arrazou, e queimou."

76. Couto, *Da Ásia, Década Décima*, pt. 1, pp. 283–84.

77. *HSMLMC*, fl. 21r.

78. Ibid., fl. 24r. The distance between Aceh and Pidie (on the Sumatran east coast) being not inconsiderable, the episode must have occupied a certain amount of time, if indeed it really occurred.

79. For example, see Nicholas B. Dirks, "The Pasts of a *Pālaiyakārar:* The Ethnohistory of a South Indian Little King," *Journal of Asian Studies* 41, no. 4 (1982): 655–83, in particular pp. 675–77.

80. This is a view that continues to be reflected in modern historiography in such significant texts as Luís de Albuquerque, "Alguns aspectos da ameaça turca sobre a Índia por meados do século XVI," *Biblos: Revista da Faculdade de Letras* 54 (1978): 87–113.

81. Compare Ottoman attitudes to conversion as portrayed recently in Marc David Baer, *Honored by the Glory of Islam: Conversion and Conquest in Ottoman Europe* (New York: Oxford University Press, 2008), and in Tijana Krstić, *Contested Conversions to Islam: Narratives of Religious Change in the Early Modern Ottoman Empire* (Stanford, Calif.: Stanford University Press, 2011).

82. *HSMLMC*, fl. 27r.

83. Ibid., fls. 27r–27v. For the geography of Aceh at this time, see Jorge M. dos Santos Alves and Pierre-Yves Manguin, *O "Roteiro das Cousas do Achem" de D. João Ribeiro Gaio: Um olhar português sobre o Norte de Samatra em finais do século XVI* (Lisbon: Comissão Nacional para as Comemorações dos Descobrimentos Portugueses, 1997), and the curious map of Aceh in Biblioteca Nacional de Rio de Janeiro, CAM. 3.5, "Plantas de praças das conquistas de Portugal feytas por ordem de Ruy Lourenço de Távora, Vizo-Rey da Índia por Manuel Godinho de Eredia, cosmographo em 1610," fl. 18.

84. *HSMLMC*, fl. 27v.

85. Ibid., fl. 28r. These may have included men like the enigmatic Diogo Gil, but we also know of other Portuguese such as Tomás Pinto who were active in Aceh at that time. See Alves and Manguin, *O "Roteiro das Cousas do Achem,"* pp. 22–25.

86. *HSMLMC*, fls. 28r–28v.

87. All the illustrations are to be found reproduced in my earlier essay, Sanjay Subrahmanyam, "Pulverized in Aceh: On Luís Monteiro Coutinho and his 'Martyrdom'," *Archipel*, no. 78 (2009): 19–60.

88. Tomé de Jesus, *Trabalhos de Jesus: Compostos pelo veneravel Padre Fr. Thomé de Jesus da ordem dos eremitas de Santo Agostinho, da Provincia de Portugal, estando cativo em Berberia,* 2 vols. (Oporto, Portugal: Typographia Porto Médico, 1925). The work is often accompanied by a life of its author written by none other than Dom Frei Aleixo de Meneses. For an English translation, see Tomé de Jesus, *The Sufferings of Our Lord Jesus Christ, written originally in the Portuguese by Fr. Thomas of Jesus, of the Order of the Hermits of St. Augustin,* 3 vols. (London: J. Marmaduke, 1753).

89. Jesus, *Sufferings of Our Lord,* 1:3–4.

90. Francisco de Sousa, *Oriente conquistado a Jesus Cristo pelos padres da Companhia de Jesus da Província de Goa*, ed. Manuel Lopes de Almeida (Oporto, Portugal: Lello e Irmão, 1978), pp. 1112–14. The relevant section of the text may also be found in Jorge Manuel dos Santos Alves, ed., *Notícias de missionação e martírio na Índia e Insulíndia* (Lisbon: Publicações Alfa, 1989), pp. 181–84.

91. Was this cannon in fact one of Gujarati manufacture? See Claude Guillot and Ludvik Kalus, "Inscriptions islamiques sur des canons d'Insulinde du XVIe siècle," *Archipel*, no. 72 (2006): 69–94.

92. Another brief notice of the martyrdom of Monteiro Coutinho, lacking the detail of Sousa's version, may be found in George [Jorge] Cardoso, *Agiológio Lusitano dos Sanctos, e Varoens illustres em virtude do Reino de Portugal e suas conquistas*, vol. 2 (Lisbon: Officina Craesbeekiana, 1657), pp. 290–91.

93. On Mesquita, also see Dejanirah Couto, "L'itinéraire d'un marginal: La deuxième vie de Diogo de Mesquita," *Arquivos do Centro Cultural Calouste Gulbenkian* 39 (2000): 9–35.

94. Anonymous, *Primor e honra da vida soldadesca*, pp. 108–10. Also see the interesting discussion in Matar, *Turks, Moors, and Englishmen*, pp. 113–27, under the heading "Sodomy and Conquest," where the author concludes: "Sodomy served to legitimate Christian/European moral authority and to prepare for holy war."

95. On Marramaque's activities, see Maria Augusta Lima Cruz, "A viagem de Gonçalo Pereira Marramaque do Minho às Molucas—ou os itinerários da fidalguia portuguesa no Oriente," *Studia*, no. 49 (1989): 315–40.

96. Anonymous, *Primor e honra da vida soldadesca*, pp. 110–12. This account involving an Ottoman ambassador (perhaps the famous Lütfi) appears to be of the same incident described in a near-contemporary letter from the Jesuit Lourenço Peres in Melaka to Gomes Vaz in Goa, dated November 1566, published in Josef Wicki, ed., *Documenta Indica*, vol. 7: *1566–1569* (Rome: Monumenta Missionum Societatis Iesu, 1962), pp. 33–35. Peres notes that the only two who accepted conversion were "hum mestiço e hum framengo"; he also claims that one of the Portuguese merchants was crucified.

97. Francisco Rodrigues Silveira, *Reformação da milícia e governo do Estado da Índia Oriental*, ed. B. N. Teensma, Luís Filipe Barreto, and George D. Winius (Lisbon: Fundação Oriente, 1996); Diogo do Couto, *O Primeiro Soldado Prático*, ed. António Coimbra Martins (Lisbon: Comissão Nacional para as Comemorações dos Descobrimentos Portugueses, 2001).

98. Interestingly, one of the early Dutch accounts of Aceh (in about 1601) is that of Frederik de Houtman, who claims to have refused to convert to Islam despite severe threats from the reigning Sultan 'Ala-ud-Din Ri'ayat Syah Sayyid al-Mukammil; see "Cort Verhael van 't gene wedervaren is Frederik de Houtman tot Atchein," in Willem S. Unger, ed., *De oudste reizen van de Zeeuwen naar Oost-Indië, 1598–1604* (The Hague: Martinus Nijhoff, 1948), pp. 64–111, and the discussion in Reid, "Islamization and Christianization," pp. 173–74.

99. Christopher Herbert, *War of No Pity: The Indian Mutiny and Victorian Trauma* (Princeton, N.J.: Princeton University Press, 2007), p. 46.

3. Courtly Representations

Epigraph: For discussions of this play, see Michael W. Alssid, "The Design of Dryden's Aureng-Zebe," *Journal of English and Germanic Philology* 64, no. 3 (1965): 452–69, as well as Balachandra Rajan, *Under Western Eyes: India from Milton to Macaulay* (Durham, N.C.: Duke University Press, 1999), pp. 67–77.

1. This was the subject, most famously, of Alfred W. Crosby Jr., *The Columbian Exchange: Biological and Cultural Consequences of 1492* (Westport, Conn.: Greenwood, 1972).

2. For the implications of this, see for example, Timon Screech, *The Shogun's Painted Culture: Fear and Creativity in the Japanese States, 1760–1829* (London: Reaktion Books, 2000), and more generally, Robert I. Hellyer, *Defining Engagement: Japan and Global Contexts, 1640–1868* (Cambridge, Mass.: Harvard University Press, 2009).

3. See Howard Sankey, "Kuhn's Changing Concept of Incommensurability," *British Journal for the Philosophy of Science* 44, no. 4 (1993): 759–74.

4. For an oblique and highly ambiguous statement regarding this matter, see Clifford Geertz, "Art as a Cultural System," *Modern Language Notes* 91, no. 6 (1976): 1473–99. Compare Serge Gruzinski, *The Mestizo Mind: The Intellectual Dynamics of Colonization and Globalization*, trans. Deke Dusinberre (London: Routledge, 2002).

5. Gauvin Alexander Bailey, "The Indian Conquest of Catholic Art: The Mughals, the Jesuits, and Imperial Mural Painting," *Art Journal* 57, no. 1 (1998): 25.

6. S. N. Banerjee and John S. Hoyland, *The Commentary of Father Monserrate* (Madras, India: Oxford University Press, 1922), p. 37.

7. Charles R. Boxer, "A Tentative Check-List of Indo-Portuguese Imprints," *Arquivos do Centro Cultural Português* (Paris) 9 (1975): 567–99, which supersedes the earlier discussion by the same author in the *Boletim do Instituto Vasco da Gama*, no. 73 (1956): 1–23.

8. See Henrique Henriques (Antirikku Atikalar), *Flos Sanctorum enra atiyār varalāru*, ed. Ca. Iracamanikkam (Tutukkudi [Tuticorin], India: Tamil Ilakkiyak Kalakam, 1967); Ines G. Županov, *Missionary Tropics: The Catholic Frontier in India* (Ann Arbor: University of Michigan Press, 2005), pp. 253–57.

9. João de Barros, *Da Ásia, Década Segunda* (Lisbon: Livraria Sam Carlos, 1973), book 3, chap. 6, p. 309.

10. Albuquerque to the King, Cochin, April 1, 1512, in R. A. de Bulhão Pato, ed., *Cartas de Afonso de Albuquerque seguidas de documentos que as elucidam*, vol. 1 (Lisbon: Academia Real das Sciencias de Lisboa, 1884), pp. 44–45.

11. Also see, in this context, Clare L. Costley, "David, Bathsheba, and the Penitential Psalms," *Renaissance Quarterly* 57, no. 4 (2004): 1235–77.

12. Diogo do Couto, *Década Quinta da Ásia*, ed. Marcus de Jong (Coimbra: Imprensa da Universidade, 1937), livro 8, capítulo 8, pp. 525–33, citation on pp. 532–33.

13. Correa's signature appears on letters from the City of Chaul to Dom João de Castro, dated May 22, 1546, April 3, 1547, and November 25, 1547, in Elaine Sanceau, et al., *Colecção de São Lourenço*, vol. 3 (Lisbon: Instituto de Investigação Científica Tropical, 1983), pp. 205, 270, 295.

14. Chahryar Adle, "New Data on the Dawn of Mughal Painting and Calligraphy," in Muzaffar Alam, Françoise N. Delvoye, and Marc Gaborieau, eds., *The Making of Indo-Persian Culture: Indian and French Studies* (New Delhi: Manohar, 2000), especially pp. 192–216.

15. Paul Lacombe, *Livres d'heures imprimés au XVe et au XVIe siècle, conservés dans les bibliothèques publiques de Paris* (Paris: Imprimerie nationale, 1907). Compare Artur Anselmo, *Les origines de l'imprimerie au Portugal* (Paris: Jean Touzot, 1983).

16. Ângela Barreto Xavier, *A invenção de Goa: Poder imperial e conversões culturais nos séculos XVI e XVII* (Lisbon: Imprensa de Ciências Sociais, 2008).

17. Rafael Moreira and Alexandra Curvelo, "A circulação das formas: Artes portáteis, arquitetura e urbanismo," in Francisco Bethencourt and Kirti Chaudhuri, eds., *História da Expansão Portuguesa*, vol. 2: *Do Índico ao Atlântico (1570–1697)* (Lisbon: Círculo de Leitores, 1998), pp. 538–40.

18. Bailey, "Indian Conquest of Catholic Art," pp. 28–29. See also Gauvin Alexander Bailey, *The Jesuits and the Grand Mogul: Renaissance Art at the Imperial Court of India* (Washington, D.C.: Smithsonian Institution, 1998), pp. 37–38.

19. "Quand je leur disais sur cela que dans les pays froids il serait impossible d'observer leur loi pendant l'hiver, ce qui était un signe qu'elle n'était qu'une pure invention des hommes, ils me donnaient cette réponse assez plaisante: qu'ils ne prétendaient pas que leur loi fût universelle; que Dieu ne l'avait faite que pour eux et que c'était pour cela qu'ils ne pouvaient pas recevoir un étranger dans leur religion; qu'au reste ils ne prétendaient point que la nôtre fût fausse; qu'ils se pouvait faire qu'elle fût bonne pour nous et que Dieu pouvait avoir fait plusieurs chemins différents pour aller au ciel, mais ils ne veulent pas entendre que la nôtre, étant générale pour toute la terre, la leur ne peut être que fable et que pure invention"; see Frédéric Tinguely, ed., *Un libertin dans l'Inde moghole: Les voyages de François Bernier (1656–1669)* (Paris: Chandeigne, 2008), p. 327.

20. See Edward Maclagan, *The Jesuits and the Great Mogul* (New York: Octagon Books, 1972), pp. 204, 210, 217.

21. Also see the letter from Jerónimo Xavier at Agra to the Provincial of the Company in India, Agra, September 24, 1608, British Library, Additional 9854, fls. 64r–76v, in António da Silva Rego, ed., *Documentação Ultramarina Portuguesa*, vol. 3 (Lisbon: Centro de Estudos Históricos Ultramarinos, 1963), pp. 111–33.

22. Muhammad 'Abdullah Chaghatai, "Mirat ul-Quds: An illustrated Manuscript of Akbar's Period about Christ's Life," in *Lahore Museum Heritage*, ed. Anjum Rehmani (Lahore, Pakistan: Lahore Museum, 1994), pp. 179–88.

23. 'Abdus Sattar ibn Qasim Lahauri, *Majālis-i Jahāngīrī: Majlis-hā-yi shabāna-i darbār-i Nūr al-Dīn Jahāngīr az 24 Rajab 1017 tā 19 Ramazān 1020*, ed. 'Arif Naushahi and Mu'in Nizami (Tehran: Miras-i Maktub, 2006). Majlis 29, Rabi II, A.H. 1019, pp. 70–75. For a full discussion, see Muzaffar Alam and Sanjay Subrahmanyam, *Writing the Mughal World: Studies in Political Culture* (Ranikhet: Permanent Black, 2011), pp. 249–310.

24. Bailey, *Jesuits and the Grand Mogul*, p. 35. Bailey's claims that the Mughals identified the Virgin directly with their mythical female ancestor Alanqoa, and that Akbar and Jahangir strongly identified themselves with Jesus, have rightly been met with a lukewarm reception in Mughal historiography.

25. Banerjee and Hoyland, *Commentary of Father Monserrate*, p. 126.

26. See Gregory Minissale, "The Synthesis of European and Mughal Art in the Emperor Akbar's *Khamsa* of Nizāmī," *asianart.com*, 2000, www.asianart.com/articles/minissale.

27. Sumathi Ramaswamy, "Conceit of the Globe in Mughal Visual Practice," *Comparative Studies in Society and History* 49, no. 4 (2007): 751–82, quotation on p. 778.

28. Pierre du Jarric, *Akbar and the Jesuits*, trans. C. H. Payne (London: Harper & Brothers, 1926), pp. 160–69; Fernão Guerreiro, *Relação anual das coisas que fizeram os padres da Companhia de Jesus nas suas missões (. . .) tirada das cartas que os missionários de lá escreveram*, vol. 1, ed. Artur Viegas (Coimbra: Imprensa da Universidade, 1930), pp. 299–302.

29. On Heda, see A. van der Willigen, *Les artistes de Harlem: Notices historiques avec un Précis sur la Gilde de St. Luc* (Nieuwkoop: B. de Graaf,

1970), pp. 152–56, 367–71; and Deborah Hutton, *Art of the Court of Bijapur* (Bloomington: Indiana University Press, 2006). An important new reconsideration on Heda is also in preparation by Deborah Hutton and Rebecca Tucker.

30. Gita Dharampal, "Heinrich von Poser's Travelogue to the Deccan," *Quarterly Journal of the Mythic Society* 73, nos. 3–4 (1981): 108.

31. For the intriguing case of a minor artist, Robert Hughes (d. 1623), who was in Jahangir's court in the 1610s, see Susan Stronge, "'Far from the arte of painting': An English Amateur Artist at the Court of Jahangir," in Rosemary Crill, Susan Stronge, and Andrew Topsfield, eds., *Arts of Mughal India: Studies in Honour of Robert Skelton* (London: Victoria & Albert Museum, 2004), pp. 129–37.

32. Ebba Koch, "Netherlandish Naturalism in Imperial Mughal Painting," *Apollo*, no. 152 (November 2000): 29–37.

33. P. A. Leupe, "Nederlandsche schilders in Persië en Hindostan in de eerste helft der 17e eeuw," *De nederlandsche spectator*, no. 33, August 16, 1873, 260–63; no. 34, August 23, 1873, 165–66. Also useful is Willem M. Floor, "Dutch Painters in Iran during the First Half of the Seventeenth Century," *Persica*, no. 8 (1979): 145–61.

34. Leonard J. Slatkes, *Rembrandt and Persia* (New York: Abaris Books, 1983), pp. 40–41.

35. On Vapoer, or Vapour, see the numerous references in Om Prakash and V. B. Gupta, eds., *The Dutch Factories in India*, vol. 2: *1624–1627* (New Delhi: Manohar, 2007), pp. 107–8, 260–61, 342–43, passim. Governor-General Carpentier's letter to Pieter van den Broecke of August 9, 1624, notes his talent as a painter (p. 107).

36. Letter from Van den Broecke at Surat to Batavia, April 6, 1626, in Prakash and Gupta, *Dutch Factories*, 2:264.

37. Slatkes, *Rembrandt and Persia*, pp. 127–28; Cornelis Hofstede de Groot, "Isaac Koedijck," in *Festschrift für Max J. Friedländer* (Berlin: E. A. Seemann, 1927), pp. 181–90.

38. However, he is not mentioned in the context of the Dutch embassy of Van Adrichem to the Mughal court in 1662, for which see A. J. Bernet Kempers, ed., *Journaal van Dircq van Adrichem's Hofreis naar den Groot-Mogol Aurangzeb (1662)* (The Hague: Martinus Nijhoff, 1941).

39. Pascal Pia, ed., *Voyage en Perse et Description de ce Royaume par Jean-Baptiste Tavernier, marchand français* (Paris: Editions du Carrefour, 1930), p. 135.

40. See Hessel Miedema, "Philips Angels 'Lof der Schilder-Konst'," *Oud-Holland* 103, no. 4 (1989): 181–222.

41. On this embassy, see the account by Cornelis Speelman, *Journaal der reis van den gezant der O.I. Compagnie Joan Cunaeus naar Perzië in 1651–1652*, ed. A. Hotz (Amsterdam: J. Müller, 1908).

42. Milo Cleveland Beach and Ebba Koch, *King of the World: The Pad-shahnama, an Imperial Manuscript from the Royal Library, Windsor Castle* (London: Azimuth Editions, 1997), illustration 20, pp. 58–59, 180.

43. Koch, "Netherlandish Naturalism," p. 36.

44. Partha Mitter, *Much Maligned Monsters: A History of European Reactions to Indian Art* (Oxford: Clarendon Press, 1977), pp. 321–25. Also see the valuable survey by Francis Richard, "Les manuscrits persans d'origine indienne à la Bibliothèque nationale," *Revue de la Bibliothèque nationale*, no. 19 (1986): 30–46.

45. Robert Skelton, "Indian Art and Artefacts in Early European Collecting," in Oliver Impey and Arthur Macgregor, eds., *The Origins of Museums: The Cabinet of Curiosities in Sixteenth- and Seventeenth-Century Europe* (Oxford: Clarendon Press, 1985), pp. 274–80.

46. See the interesting account by Rui Manuel Loureiro, *A Biblioteca de Diogo do Couto* (Macau: Instituto Cultural de Macau, 1998).

47. Luís de Matos, ed., *Imagens do Oriente no século XVI: Reprodução do Códice Português da Biblioteca Casanatense* (Lisbon: Imprensa Nacional, 1985); and the discussion in Sanjay Subrahmanyam, "O gentio indiano visto pelos Portugueses no século XVI," *Oceanos*, nos. 19/20 (1994): 190–96.

48. Jerónimo Corte-Real, *Sucesso do segundo cerco de Diu: Códice Cadaval 31—ANTT*, ed. Martim de Albuquerque (Lisbon: Edições INAPA, 1991), reproduced with paintings by the author Corte-Real; also Francisco Faria Paulino, ed., *Tapeçarias de D. João de Castro* (Lisbon: Museu Nacional de Arte Antiga, 1995).

49. On Arabic in western Europe, see P. M. Holt, "The Study of Arabic Historians in Seventeenth Century England: The Background and the Work of Edward Pococke," *Bulletin of the School of Oriental and African*

Studies 19, no. 3 (1957): 444–55; and more recently, G. J. Toomer, *Eastern Wisedome and Learning: The Study of Arabic in Seventeenth-Century England* (Oxford: Clarendon Press, 1996).

50. *Relaciones de Pedro Teixeira d'el origen, descendencia, y succession de los reyes de Persia, y de Harmuz, y de un viage hecho por el mismo autor desde la India oriental hasta Italia por tierra* (Antwerp: H. Verdussen, 1610).

51. On this Jesuit scholar, see the charming account in Giorgio Levi Dellavida, *George Strachan: Memorials of a Wandering Scottish Scholar of the Seventeenth Century* (Aberdeen: Third Spalding Club, 1956).

52. Francis Richard, "Les manuscripts persans rapports par les frères Vecchietti et conserves aujourd'hui à la Bibliothèque Nationale," *Studia Iranica* 9, pt. 2 (1980): 291–300.

53. See John D. Gurney, "Pietro della Valle: The Limits of Perception," *Bulletin of the School of Oriental and African Studies* 49, no. 1 (1986): 103–16.

54. Otto Kurz, "A Volume of Indian Miniatures and Drawings," *Journal of the Warburg and Courtauld Institutes* 30 (1967): 251–71. The reference is to Biblioteca Apostolica Vaticana, Codex Barb. Or. 136, "Disegni e miniature indiane (del periodo dell'impero del gran Mogol)."

55. Gurney, "Pietro della Valle," p. 109.

56. It is possible that this was in fact the Jesuit Francesco Corsi (1573–1635), himself a Florentine like Barberini.

57. The important essay by John Seyller, "The Inspection and Valuation of Manuscripts in the Imperial Mughal Library," *Artibus Asiae* 57, nos. 3–4 (1997): 243–349, leaves this part of the question somewhat ambiguous.

58. On the issue of engravings, see the useful remarks in Yael Rice, "The Brush and the Burin: Mogul Encounters with European Engravings," in Jaynie Anderson, ed., *Crossing Cultures: Conflict, Migration and Convergence; The Proceedings of the 32nd International Congress of the History of Art* (Carlton, Victoria, Australia: The Miegunyah Press, 2009), pp. 305–10.

59. Mitter, *Much Maligned Monsters*, pp. 21–22; also, more recently, Ernst van den Boogaart, *Civil and Corrupt Asia: Image and Text in the "Itinerario" and the "Icones" of Jan Huygen van Linschoten* (Chicago: University of Chicago Press, 2003).

60. Bodleian Library, Oxford, Ms. Laud Or. 149; also see the discussion in Herbert J. Stooke and Karl Khandalavala, *The Laud Ragamala Miniatures: A Study in Indian Painting and Music* (Oxford: B. Cassirer, 1953), and more recently in John Seyller, *Workshop and Patron in Mughal India: The Freer Rāmāyana and Other Illustrated Manuscripts of 'Abd al-Rahīm* (Zurich: Artibus Asiae Publishers, 1999), pp. 257–63. On Laud and his relations to Charles I, see L. J. Reeve, *Charles I and the Road to Personal Rule* (Cambridge: Cambridge University Press, 1989).

61. On the manuscript, see J. V. S. Wilkinson, "An Indian Manuscript of the *Golestān* of the Shāh Jahān Period," *Ars Orientalis*, no. 2 (1957): 423–25; and Elaine Wright, et al., *Muraqqaʿ: Imperial Mughal Albums from the Chester Beatty Library, Dublin* (Alexandria, Va.: Art Services International, 2008), pp. 246–48; as well as the brief discussion in Milo Cleveland Beach, *Mughal and Rajput Painting: The New Cambridge History of India*, vol. 1, pt. 3 (Cambridge: Cambridge University Press, 1992), pp. 138–39, 236–37. However, there is no trace of the transaction in William Foster, ed., *The English Factories in India, 1637–1641* (Oxford: Clarendon Press, 1912).

62. Pauline Lunsingh Scheurleer, "Mogol-miniaturen door Rembrandt nagetekend," *De kroniek van het Rembrandthuis*, no. 1 (1980): 10–40. Also see the pioneering essay by Friedrich Sarre, "Rembrandt Zeichnungen nach indisch-islamisch Miniaturen," *Jahrbuch der Königlich Preuszischen Kunstsammlungen* 25 (1904): 143–56. For a set of convenient reproductions, see Otto Benesch (and Eva Benesch), *The Drawings of Rembrandt*, 6 vols. (London: Phaidon, 1973), vol. 5, figs. 1486–1506.

63. Ebba Koch, "The 'Moghuleries' of the Millionenzimmer, Schönbrunn Palace, Vienna," in Crill, Stronge, and Topsfield, *Arts of Mughal India*, pp. 152–67; also the earlier discussion in Dorothea Duda, "Die Kaiserin und der Grossmogul: Untersuchung zu den Miniaturen des Millionenzimmers im Schloss Schönbrunn," in Karin K. Troschke, ed., *Malerei auf Papier und Pergament in den Prunkräumen des Schlosses Schönbrunn* (Vienna: Schloss Schönbrunn Kultur- und Betriebsges, 1997).

64. Nicola Courtright, "Origins and Meanings of Rembrandt's Late Drawing Style," *Art Bulletin* 78, no. 3 (1996): 485–510, quotation on p. 502.

65. Marijn Schapelhouman, *Rembrandt and the Art of Drawing* (Amsterdam: Rijksmuseum, 2006), pp. 17–19.

66. Slatkes, *Rembrandt and Persia*, pp. 13–17.

67. Courtright, "Origins and Meanings," pp. 503–4, drawing extensively on Slatkes's earlier discussion. Also see similar arguments on the use of Arabic script in paintings from the fourteenth and fifteenth centuries in Rosamund Mack, *Bazaar to Piazza: Islamic Trade and Italian Art, 1300–1600* (Berkeley: University of California Press, 2001).

68. Rebecca Parker Brienen, "Albert Eckhout and Frans Post: Two Dutch Artists in Colonial Brazil," in Edward J. Sullivan, ed., *Brazil: Body and Soul* (New York: Guggenheim Museum, 2001), pp. 92–111; and more recently Brienen, *Visions of Savage Paradise: Albert Eckhout, Court Painter in Colonial Dutch Brazil* (Amsterdam: Amsterdam University Press, 2006), as also the highly skeptical view of Eckhout and Post in Peter Mason, *Infelicities: Representations of the Exotic* (Baltimore: Johns Hopkins University Press, 1998). There is obviously a tension between these Dutch "colonial" paintings and the broad interpretation provided in Svetlana Alpers, *The Art of Describing: Dutch Art in the Seventeenth Century* (Chicago: University of Chicago Press, 1983). On these issues, also see Benjamin Schmidt, *Innocence Abroad: The Dutch Imagination and the New World, 1570–1670* (New York: Cambridge University Press, 2001).

69. For the paintings by Hendrik van Schuylenburgh from 1665 of the Dutch factories at Hughli and Kasimbazar in Bengal, see Martine Gosselink, "Schilderijen van Bengaalse VOC-loges door Hendrik van Schuylenburgh," *Bulletin van het Rijksmuseum* 46 (1998): 390–409. The former painting, now in Amsterdam, itself carries a description: "Afbeeldinge van de Vereenighde Nederlantze Oostindische Comp[es] Logie, ofte Hooft Comptoir in Bengale, ter stede Oügelij, Anno 1665."

70. Marie-Odile Scalliet, "Une curiosité oubliée: le 'Livre de dessins faits dans un voyage aux Indes par un voyageur hollandais' du marquis de Paulmy," *Archipel*, no. 54 (1997): 35–62; further on this traveler, see Erlend de Groot, "The Earliest Eyewitness Depictions of Khoikhoi: Andries Beeckman in Africa," *Itinerario* 29, no. 1 (2005): 17–50.

71. Peter van der Krogt and Erlend de Groot, *The atlas Blaeu-van der Hem of the Austrian National Library*, 7 vols. ('t Goy-Houten: HES Publishers, 1996–2008).

72. Maurice Exwood and H. L. Lehmann, eds. and trans., *The Journal of William Schellinks' Travels in England, 1661–1663* (London: Royal Historical Society, 1993); also Willem Schellinkx, *Viaggio al Sud, 1664–1665,*

ed. Bernard Aikema, Hans Brand, Fransje Kuyvenhoven, Dulcia Meijers, and Pierre Mens (Rome: Edizioni dell'Elefante, 1983).

73. Charles Patin, *Travels thro' Germany, Swisserland, Bohemia, Holland; and other Parts of Europe describing the most considerable Citys and the palaces of Princes: Together with Historical Relations, and Critical Observations upon Ancient Medals and Inscriptions* (London: A. Swall and T. Child, 1696), pp. 204–5. For the context of these and other collections, also see Ellinoor Bergvelt and Reneé Kistemaker, eds., *De Wereld binnen handbereik: Nederlandse kunst- en rariteitenverzamelingen, 1585–1735* (Zwolle: Waanders, 1992), and Joy Kenseth, ed., *The Age of the Marvelous* (Chicago: University of Chicago Press, 1991).

74. This painting, like the next one, was part of an undisclosed private collection sold at Sotheby's, London, on December 5, 2007. I have hence consulted a photographic reproduction.

75. See Pauline Lunsingh Scheurleer, "De Moghul-miniaturen van Rembrandt," in *Waarom Sanskrit? Honderdvijfentwintig jaar Sanskrit in Nederland*, ed. Hanneke van den Muyzenberg and Thomas de Bruijn (Leiden: Kern Institute, 1991), pp. 95–115, especially, 110 and plate 10; also Josef Strzygowski and Heinrich Glück, *Die indischen Miniaturen im Schlosse Schönbrunn* (Vienna: Wiener Drucke, 1923).

76. This painting has been in a private collection since it was sold at Sotheby's, London, July 4, 1984, lot 365. I was initially able to consult it in a reproduction at the Getty Research Institute, Los Angeles, Photo Study Collection, Renaissance to Modern, ND 644, and subsequently through an image kindly sent to me by Sotheby's Picture Library, London.

77. The first extensive discussion of this painting is in J. Auboyer, "Un maître hollandais du XVIIe siècle s'inspirant des miniatures mogholes," *Arts Asiatiques* 2 (1955): 251–73.

78. The camel is based on a Mughal painting or drawing of which an almost exact copy can be found in the Bibliothèque Nationale de France, Paris, Estampes, Réserve Od 44 fol., f. 8, titled "Chameau magique portant une houri." In general, also see the comments in Robert J. Del Bonta, "Reinventing Nature: Mughal Composite Animal Painting," in Som Prakash Verma, ed., *Flora and Fauna in Mughal Art* (Bombay: Marg Publications, 1999), pp. 69–82, with brief remarks on Schellinks.

79. There is an octagonal descriptive cartouche to the bottom left of the painting that states from top to bottom "Achber / Janguer / Shajan / Shabe-gum / Darasheko / Soltansouja / Aurunzeve / Moratbex." The figure on the elephant with the fly-whisk is clearly the heir-apparent Dara, and the conclusive identification of Aurangzeb as the figure on the camel derives from the dagger (a point I owe to Whitney Cox). This also helps to place the picture after 1658. Further, we do not know if Schellinks had read Bernier's text, first published in 1670, or if he had some other unpublished or oral source for the end of Shahjahan's reign.

80. Skelton, "Indian Art and Artefacts," p. 279. The painting of Akbar and Jahangir corresponds to Bodleian Library, Oxford, Ms. Douce Or. a.1, fol. 19a, "Akbar and Jahangir in Apotheosis." For Rembrandt's copy, see Benesch, *Drawings of Rembrandt*, vol. 5, fig. 1488.

81. Jean de Lœwenstein, "A propos d'un tableau de W. Schellinks s'inspirant des miniatures mogholes," *Arts Asiatiques* 5, no. 4 (1958): 293–98.

82. Arcimboldo (1527–93) is of course celebrated for his "composite" paintings using fruits, vegetables, and other elements to make up what are often satirical human portraits. See Thomas DaCosta Kaufmann, *Arcimboldo: Visual Jokes, Natural History, and Still-Life Painting* (Chicago: University of Chicago Press, 2009). For some intriguing remarks regarding parallels with other forms of Mughal representational art, see Wolfgang Born, "Ivory Powder Flasks from the Mughal Period," *Ars Islamica*, no. 9 (1942): 93–111.

83. Bodleian Library, Oxford, Ms. Laud Or. 149, fol. 13b.

84. However, see Annemarie Schimmel, *The Empire of the Great Mughals: History, Art and Culture*, trans. Corinne Attwood (London: Reaktion Books, 2004), p. 283, where the author seemingly disdains these Schellinks paintings as "the very embodiments of European fantasies of the sensuous orient."

85. For this and other illustrations, see Sanjay Subrahmanyam, "A Roomful of Mirrors: The Artful Embrace of Mughals and Franks, 1550–1700," *Ars Orientalis* 39 (2010): 39–83.

86. William Foster, ed., *The Embassy of Sir Thomas Roe to the Court of the Great Mogul, 1615–1619*, 2 vols. (London: The Hakluyt Society, 1899), 1:facing 114.

87. Bronwen Wilson, *The World in Venice: Print, the City, and Early Modern Identity* (Toronto: University of Toronto Press, 2005), pp. 248–55.

88. François Le Gouz de la Boullaye, *Les Voyages et Observations du Sieur de la Boullaye-le-Gouz, gentil-homme angevin* (Paris: François Clousier, 1657).

89. On Kircher and Roth, see Paula Findlen, ed., *Athanasius Kircher: The Last Man Who Knew Everything* (New York: Routledge, 2004); Arnulf Camps and Jean-Claude Muller, eds., *The Sanskrit Grammar and Manuscripts of Father Heinrich Roth, S.J. (1620–1668): Facsimile Edition of Biblioteca Nazionale, Rome, Mss. Or. 171 and 172* (Leiden: E. J. Brill, 1988), pp. 5–9; and Gita Dharampal-Frick, *Indien im Spiegel deutscher Quellen der Frühen Neuzeit (1500–1750): Studien zu einer interkulturellen Konstellation* (Tübingen: Niemeyer, 1994), pp. 88–92.

90. The lack of a manuscript corpus for Tavernier's work is troubling, as is his enormous dependence on ghostwriters such as Samuel Chappuzeau. A full modern treatment of his text is still awaited. But see Jean-Baptiste Tavernier, *Les six voyages en Turquie et en Perse*, 2 vols., ed. Stéphane Yerasimos (Paris: F. Maspero, 1981); and V. Ball and W. Crooke, eds. and trans., *Travels in India by Jean-Baptiste Tavernier, Baron of Aubonne*, 2nd ed., 2 vols. (London: Oxford University Press, 1925).

91. Mitter, *Much Maligned Monsters*, p. 55.

92. Michele Bernardini, "The Illustrations of a Manuscript of the Travel Account of François de la Boullaye le Gouz in the Library of the Accademia Nazionale dei Lincei in Rome," *Muqarnas* 21 (2004): 55–72.

93. Le Gouz de la Boullaye, *Les Voyages et Observations*, p. 187.

94. Siegfried Kratzsch, ed., *Deex Autaer von Philip Angel: Eine niederländische Handschrift aus dem 17. Jahrhundert über die zehn Avataras des Visnu* (Halle: Verlag der Franckeschen Stiftungen, 2007).

95. Thus, we may contrast Angel's paintings with those from the *Rāmāyana* illustrations prepared for ʿAbdur Rahim Khan-i-Khanan in the late sixteenth century; for a sample, see Milo Cleveland Beach, *The Adventures of Rama* (Washington, D.C.: Freer Gallery of Art, 1983).

96. Albert Johannes de Jong, ed., *Afgoderye der Oost-Indische heydenen door Philippus Baldæus* (The Hague: Martinus Nijhoff, 1917). The best treatment to date of the relationship between the works and images of Angel and

Baldaeus may be found in Carolien Stolte, *Philip Angel's Deex-Autaers: Vaisnava Mythology from Manuscript to Book Market in the Context of the Dutch East India Company, ca. 1600–1672* (New Delhi: Manohar, 2012).

97. See the discussion in Paola von Wyss-Giacosa, *Religionsbilder der frühen Aufklärung: Bernard Picarts Tafeln für die 'Cérémonies et Coutumes religieuses de tous les Peuples du Monde'* (Bern: Benteli Verlag, 2006).

98. See the discussion in Pauline Lunsingh Scheurleer, "Het Witsenalbum: Zeventiende-eeuwse Indische portretten op bestelling," *Bulletin van het Rijksmuseum* 44 (1996): 167–254.

99. The best overall survey of the question to date remains the remarkable essay by Ronald W. Lightbown, "Oriental Art and the Orient in Late Renaissance and Baroque Italy," *Journal of the Warburg and Courtauld Institutes* 32 (1969): 228–79.

100. "Catalogo di alcune rarità, che il Sig. Abate Co. Giovannantonio Baldini ha riportate da' suoi viaggi, venute principalmente dall'Indie e dalla Cina; indiritto al P. D. Piercaterino Zeno C. R. S. dal Sig. Antonio Vallisnieri, pubblico primario Professore di medicina teorica nello studio di Padova, con lettera data di Padova il dì terzo di novembre, 1719," *Giornale de' Letterati d'Italia* 33, no. 2 (1722): 118–48; "Altra Lettera del Signor Antonio Vallisnieri al Padre D. Piercaterino Zeno, C. R. S. con cui mandagli il Catalogo de' Re del Mogol, i ritratti de' quali serbansi nel ricco museo del Co. Ab. Giovannantonio Baldini," *Supplementi al Giornale de' Letterati d'Italia*, no. 3 (1726): 337–76.

101. Bibliothèque Nationale de France, Paris, Smith-Lesouëf 233, described as "Recueil de portraits des rois et des ministres des royaumes musulmans de l'Inde, fin du 17e siècle."

102. Cornelius le Bruyn, *Travels into Muscovy, Persia, and part of the East-Indies, Containing, an accurate description of whatever is most remarkable in those countries, and embellished with above 320 copper plates*, 2 vols. (London: A. Bettesworth, 1737).

103. The reference is to the Bolognese Baroque painter Carlo Cignani (1628–1719), on whom see Beatrice Buscaroli Fabbri, *Carlo Cignani: Affreschi, dipinti, disegni* (Bologna: Nuova Alfa, 1991).

104. On Picart, see Margaret C. Jacob, "Bernard Picart and the Turn to Modernity," *De Achttiende Eeuw* 37 (2005): 1–16. I also draw here on Sanjay

Subrahmanyam, "Monsieur Picart and the Gentiles of India," in Lynn Hunt, Margaret Jacob, and Wijnand Mijnhardt, eds., *The First Global Vision of Religion: Bernard Picart's "Religious Ceremonies and Customs of All the Peoples of the World"* (Los Angeles: Getty Research Institute, 2010), pp. 197–214.

105. Henri Abraham Châtelain, *Atlas historique, ou Nouvelle introduction à l'histoire, à la chronologie & à la géographie ancienne & moderne*, 7 vols. (Amsterdam: Z. Châtelain, 1732–39): vol. 5, *L'Asie en général & en particulier.*

106. These are reproduced in Lightbown, "Oriental Art," pp. 264–65.

107. Ibid., pp. 274–75.

108. The Bibliothèque Nationale de France, Paris, Smith-Lesouëf 233, the portraits are thus characterized by Francis Richard in his remarks on them as "grossiers," especially in regard to the backgrounds, lower garments, and shoes, where the painters were clearly negligent.

109. Bruyn, *Travels into Muscovy*, p. 220.

110. For a more extended discussion, see Sanjay Subrahmanyam, *Three Ways to Be Alien: Travails and Encounters in the Early Modern World* (Waltham, Mass.: Brandeis University Press, 2011), pp. 133–72.

111. Archivio di Stato di Venezia, Senato, Dispacci, Francia, Reg. 203, fls. 271v–72v.

112. Koch, "Netherlandish Naturalism," pp. 29, 36. Certainly, there was no full counterpart to the flourishing field of European painting of Ottoman themes, for which see AA. VV., *Image of the Turks in the 17th Century Europe* (Istanbul: Sakıp Sabancı Museum, 2005), and Karin Ådahl, ed., *The Sultan's Procession: The Swedish Embassy to Sultan Mehmed IV in 1657–1658 and the Rålamb Paintings* (London: I. B. Tauris, 2006).

113. See Sanjay Subrahmanyam, "Par-delà l'incommensurabilité: Pour une histoire connectée des empires aux temps modernes," *Revue d'Histoire Moderne et Contemporaine* 54, no. 5 (2007): 34–53; also Harold J. Cook, *Matters of Exchange: Commerce, Medicine, and Science in the Dutch Golden Age* (New Haven, Conn.: Yale University Press, 2007).

114. Natasha Eaton, "Nostalgia for the Exotic: Creating an Imperial Art in London, 1750–1793," *Eighteenth-Century Studies* 39, no. 2 (2006): 227–50.

115. For example, see Robert L. Hardgrave Jr., *A Portrait of the Hindus: Balthazar Solvyns and the European Image of India, 1760–1824* (New York: Oxford University Press, 2004).

116. For the impressive array of Mir Kalan Khan's output, see Stephen Markel and Tushara Bindu Gude, eds., *India's Fabled City: The Art of Courtly Lucknow* (Los Angeles: Los Angeles County Museum of Art, 2010).

Conclusion

1. Baldesar Castiglione, *The Book of the Courtier*, trans. Leonard Eckstein Opdycke (New York: H. Liveright, 1929), p. 109; for the Italian text, see Baldesar Castiglione, *Il Libro del Cortegiano*, ed. Giulio Preti (Turin: Einaudi, 1965), p. 215. For a consideration of this important work and its circulation, see Peter Burke, *The Fortunes of the "Courtier": The European Reception of Castiglione's "Cortegiano"* (University Park: Pennsylvania State University Press, 1995). It is intriguing to compare such a work with other early modern texts from the Islamic world; see, for example, Aziz Ahmad, "The British Museum Mīrzānāma and the Seventeenth-Century Mīrzā in India," *Iran* 13 (1975): 99–110.

2. Mark Twain, *A Connecticut Yankee in King Arthur's Court* (New York: Harper, 1889), p. 18.

3. For the debates of the past decades around history, fiction, and presentism, see the useful synthesis in Roger Chartier, "History, Time, and Space," *Republics of Letters* 2, no. 2 (2011): 1–13.

4. Davis Lopes, *Chrónica dos Reis de Bisnaga: Manuscripto Inédito do século XVI* (Lisbon: Imprensa Nacional, 1897), pp. 87–88; a variant translation to mine may be found in Robert Sewell, *A Forgotten Empire (Vijayanagar): A Contribution to the History of India* (London: S. Sonnenschein & Co., 1900; reprint, New York: Barnes and Noble, 1972), 245.

5. The most significant of these works is by De la Créquinière, *Conformité des coutumes des Indiens Orientaux, avec celles des Juifs et des autres Peuples de l'Antiquité* (Brussels: G. de Backer, 1704). La Créquinière was in Pondicherry in 1700, as we see from his letter of October 1, 1700, in Archives Nationales, Paris, Colonies, C^2 65, fls. 100–101. Also see Anonymous,

Conformité des cérémonies chinoises avec l'idolatrie grecque et romaine (Cologne: Héritiers de Corneille d'Egmond, 1700).

6. Inga Clendinnen, *Dancing with Strangers: The True History of the Meeting of the British First Fleet and the Aboriginal Australians, 1788* (Edinburgh: Canongate Books, 2005), p. 5.

7. Inga Clendinnen, *Ambivalent Conquests: Maya and Spaniard in Yucatan, 1517–1570*, 2nd ed. (Cambridge: Cambridge University Press, 2003), pp. 24–26.

8. See the classic work (originally written in the 1930s) by Norbert Elias, *The Court Society*, trans. Edmund Jephcott (New York: Pantheon Books, 1983), which says all too little about courtly encounters; also David Cannadine and Simon Price, eds., *Rituals of Royalty: Power and Ceremonial in Traditional Societies* (Cambridge: Cambridge University Press, 1987), which is also largely silent on the subject. On India, see the wide-ranging study (drawing inspiration from Elias) of Daud Ali, *Courtly Culture and Political Life in Early Medieval India* (Cambridge: Cambridge University Press, 2004).

9. There is a considerable bibliography on this object. See Dirk Syndram, *Der Thron des Grossmoguls im Grünen Gewölbe zu Dresden* (Leipzig: E. A. Seemann, 2009); also the older account in Joachim Menzhausen, *At the Court of the Great Mogul: The Court at Delhi on the Birthday of the Great Mogul Aureng-Zeb; Museum Piece by Johann Melchior Dinglinger, Court Jeweller of the Elector of Saxony and King of Poland, August II, Called August the Strong*, trans. Michael Horovitz (Leipzig: Edition Leipzig, 1965).

10. I cannot at all agree here with Annemarie Schimmel, *The Empire of the Great Mughals: History, Art and Culture*, trans. Corinne Attwood (London: Reaktion Books, 2004), pp. 283, 299, which entirely and regrettably conflates the conceptions of Schellinks and Dinglinger.

11. Anonymous, *Onomatopeia Oannense, ou Annedotica do Monstro Amphibio que na memoravel noite de 14 para 15 de Outubro do prezente anno de 1732 appareceu no Mar Negro (. . .)* (Lisbon: Mauricio Vicente de Almeyda, 1732).

12. Palmira Fontes da Costa, ed., *O Corpo Insólito: Dissertações sobre Monstros no Portugal do século XVIII* (Oporto, Portugal: Porto Editora, 2005).

13. Ibid., pp. 33–44. For an analysis, also see Laura Lunger Knoppers and Joan B. Landes, "Introduction," in Knoppers and Landes, eds., *Monstrous Bodies/Political Monstrosities in Early Modern Europe* (Ithaca, N.Y.: Cornell University Press, 2004), pp. 1–22.

14. For his account, see Julien-Claude Galland, *Le Paradis des infidèles: Relation de Yirmisekiz Çelebi Mehmed efendi, ambassadeur ottoman en France sous la Régence*, ed. Gilles Veinstein (Paris: François Maspero, 1981).

Bibliography

AA. VV. *Image of the Turks in the 17th Century Europe*. Istanbul: Sakıp Sabancı Museum, 2005.

'Abdul Dihlawi. *Ibrāhīmnāma*. Ed. Mas'ud Husain Khan. Aligarh, India: Aligarh Muslim University, 1969.

'Abdus Sattar ibn Qasim Lahauri. *Majālis-i Jahāngīrī: Majlis-hā-yi shabāna-i darbār-i Nūr al-Dīn Jahāngīr az 24 Rajab 1017 tā 19 Ramazān 1020*. Ed. 'Arif Naushahi and Mu'in Nizami. Tehran: Miras-i Maktub, 2006.

Ådahl, Karin, ed. *The Sultan's Procession: The Swedish Embassy to Sultan Mehmed IV in 1657–1658 and the Rålamb Paintings*. London: I. B. Tauris, 2006.

Adle, Chahryar. "New Data on the Dawn of Mughal Painting and Calligraphy." In Muzaffar Alam, Françoise N. Delvoye, and Marc Gaborieau, eds., *The Making of Indo-Persian Culture: Indian and French Studies*. New Delhi: Manohar, 2000, pp. 167–222.

Aftabi. *Tarif-i-Husain Shah Badshah Dakhan*. Ed. and trans. G. T. Kulkarni and M. S. Mate. Pune, India: Bharata Itihasa Samshodhaka Mandala, 1987.

Ahmad, Aziz. "The British Museum *Mīrzānāma* and the Seventeenth-Century *Mīrzā* in India." *Iran* 13 (1975): 99–110.

———. *Studies in Islamic Culture in the Indian Environment.* Oxford: Clarendon Press, 1964.

Alam, Muzaffar, and Sanjay Subrahmanyam. *Writing the Mughal World: Studies in Political Culture.* Ranikhet: Permanent Black, 2011.

Albèri, Eugenio, ed. *Relazioni degli Ambasciatori veneti al Senato,* 3rd ser., vol. 3. Florence: Società Editrice Fiorentina, 1844.

Albuquerque, Luís de. "Alguns aspectos da ameaça turca sobre a Índia por meados do século XVI." *Biblos: Revista da Faculdade de Letras* 54 (1978): 87–113.

Albuquerque, Luís de, and José Pereira da Costa. "Cartas de 'Serviços' da Índia (1500–1550)." *Mare Liberum,* no. 1 (1990): 309–96.

Alexandrowicz, C. H. *An Introduction to the History of the Law of Nations in the East Indies: (16th, 17th and 18th Centuries).* Oxford: Clarendon Press, 1967.

Ali, Daud. *Courtly Culture and Political Life in Early Medieval India.* Cambridge: Cambridge University Press, 2004.

Alonso, Carlos. *Alejo de Meneses, O.S.A. (1559–1617), Arzobispo de Goa (1595–1612): Estudio biográfico.* Valladolid, Spain: Estudio Agustiniano, 1992.

Alpers, Svetlana. *The Art of Describing: Dutch Art in the Seventeenth Century.* Chicago: University of Chicago Press, 1983.

Alssid, Michael W. "The Design of Dryden's Aureng-Zebe." *Journal of English and Germanic Philology* 64, no. 3 (1965): 452–69.

Alves, Jorge Manuel dos Santos, ed. *Fernão Mendes Pinto and the Peregrinação.* 4 vols. Lisbon: Fundação Oriente, 2010.

———, ed. *Notícias de missionação e martírio na Índia e Insulíndia.* Lisbon: Publicações Alfa, 1989.

———. *O domínio do norte de Samatra: A história dos sultanatos de Samudera-Pacém e de Achém, e das suas relações com os Portugueses, 1500–1580.* Lisbon: Sociedade Histórica da Independência de Portugal, 1999.

———. "Os mártires do Achém nos séculos XVI e XVII: Islão *versus* Cristianismo?" In *Missionação Portuguesa e Encontro de Culturas— Congresso Internacional de História: Actas,* vol. 2: *África Oriental, Oriente e Brasil.* Braga, Portugal: Universidade Católica Portuguesa, 1993, pp. 391–406.

Alves, Jorge Manuel dos Santos, and Pierre-Yves Manguin. *O "Roteiro das Cousas do Achem" de D. João Ribeiro Gaio: Um olhar português sobre o Norte de Samatra em finais do século XVI.* Lisbon: Comissão Nacional para as Comemorações dos Descobrimentos Portugueses, 1997.

Alvi, Sajida S. "Religion and State during the Reign of Mughal Emperor Jahangir (1605–27): Nonjuristical Perspectives." *Studia Islamica*, no. 69 (1989): 95–119.

Amin, Shahid. "On Retelling the Muslim Conquest of North India." In Partha Chatterjee and Anjan Ghosh, eds., *History and the Present.* New Delhi: Permanent Black, 2002, pp. 19–32.

Anjaneyulu, M. S. R. *Vizagapatam District, 1769–1834: A History of Relations between the Zamindars and the East India Company.* Vishakapatnam, India: Andhra University, 1982.

Anonymous. "Altra Lettera del Signor Antonio Vallisnieri al Padre D. Piercaterino Zeno, C. R. S. con cui mandagli il Catalogo de' Re del Mogol, i ritratti de' quali serbansi nel ricco museo del Co. Ab. Giovannantonio Baldini." *Supplementi al Giornale de' Letterati d'Italia*, no. 3 (1726): 337–76.

———. "Catalogo di alcune rarità, che il Sig. Abate Co. Giovannantonio Baldini ha riportate da' suoi viaggi, venute principalmente dall'Indie e dalla Cina; indiritto al P. D. Piercaterino Zeno C. R. S. dal Sig. Antonio Vallisnieri, pubblico primario Professore di medicina teorica nello studio di Padova, con lettera data di Padova il dì terzo di novembre, 1719." *Giornale de' Letterati d'Italia* 33, no. 2 (1722): 118–48.

———. *Conformité des cérémonies chinoises avec l'idolatrie grecque et romaine.* Cologne: Héritiers de Corneille d'Egmond, 1700.

———. *The Negotiations of Sir Thomas Roe, in His Embassy to the Ottoman Porte from the Year 1621 to 1628 Inclusive.* London: Samuel Richardson, 1740.

———. *Onomatopeia Oannense, ou Annedotica do Monstro Amphibio que na memoravel noite de 14 para 15 de Outubro do prezente anno de 1732 appareceu no Mar Negro (. . .).* Lisbon: Mauricio Vicente de Almeyda, 1732.

———. *Primor e honra da vida soldadesca no Estado da Índia.* Ed. Laura Monteiro Pereira (with Maria Augusta Lima Cruz and Maria do Rosário Laureano Santos). Ericeira, Portugal: Mar de Letras, 2003.

Anselmo, Artur. *Les origines de l'imprimerie au Portugal*. Paris: Jean Tou-
    zot, 1983.
Arditi, Jorge. "Geertz, Kuhn and the Idea of a Cultural Paradigm." *British
    Journal of Sociology* 45, no. 4 (1994): 597–617.
Ashcroft, Bill, Gareth Griffiths, and Helen Tiffin. *Post-Colonial Studies:
    The Key Concepts*. London: Routledge, 2000.
Asher, Catherine B. "Islamic Influence and the Architecture of Vijayana-
    gara." In Anna Libera Dallapiccola and Stephanie Zingel-Avé Lallemant,
    eds., *Vijayanagara—City and Empire: New Currents of Research*, vol. 1.
    Wiesbaden, Germany: Franz Steiner Verlag, 1985, pp. 188–95.
Aubin, Jean. "Les documents arabes, persans, et turcs de la Torre do Tombo."
    In Jean Aubin, *Le Latin et l'Astrolabe: Recherches sur le Portugal de la
    Renaissance, son expansion en Aie et les relations internationales*, vol. 2,
    ed. Françoise Aubin. Paris: Centre Culturel Calouste Gulbenkian, 2000,
    pp. 417–52.
Auboyer, J. "Un maître hollandais du XVIIe siècle s'inspirant des minia-
    tures mogholes." *Arts Asiatiques* 2 (1955): 251–73.
Ayalon, David. *Gunpowder and Firearms in the Mamluk Kingdom: A Chal-
    lenge to a Mediaeval Society*. London: Vallentine and Mitchell, 1956.
Baer, Marc David. *Honored by the Glory of Islam: Conversion and Conquest
    in Ottoman Europe*. New York: Oxford University Press, 2008.
Bailey, Gauvin Alexander. *Art on the Jesuit Missions in Asia and Latin
    America, 1542–1773*. Toronto: University of Toronto Press, 1999.
———. "The Indian Conquest of Catholic Art: The Mughals, the Jesuits,
    and Imperial Mural Painting." *Art Journal* 57, no. 1 (1998): 24–30.
———. *The Jesuits and the Grand Mogul: Renaissance Art at the Imperial
    Court of India*. Washington, D.C.: Smithsonian Institution, 1998.
Baliga, B. S., ed. *Letters to Fort St. George 1752–53*. Madras, India: Govern-
    ment Press, 1941.
Banerjee, S. N., and John S. Hoyland. *The Commentary of Father Monser-
    rate*. Madras, India: Oxford University Press, 1922.
Barnes, Robert H. "Avarice and Iniquity at the Solor Fort." *Bijdragen tot de
    Taal-, Land- en Volkenkunde* 143, nos. 2–3 (1987): 208–36.
Barros, João de. *Da Ásia, Década Segunda*. Lisbon: Régia officina typo-
    graphica, 1777. Reprint, Lisbon: Livraria Sam Carlos, 1973.

Bartlett, I. Ross. "John Foxe as Hagiographer: The Question Revisited." *Sixteenth-Century Journal* 26, no. 4 (1995): 771–89.

Basu, K. K. "The Battle of Tālikōta—Before and After (from Muslim Sources)." In D. P. Karmarkar, ed., *Vijayanagara Sexcentenary Commemoration Volume*. Dharwar, India: Vijayanagara Empire Sexcentenary Association, 1936, pp. 245–54.

Beach, Milo Cleveland. *The Adventures of Rama*. Washington, D.C.: Freer Gallery of Art, 1983.

——. *Mughal and Rajput Painting: The New Cambridge History of India*, vol. 1, pt. 3. Cambridge: Cambridge University Press, 1992.

Beach, Milo Cleveland, and Ebba Koch. *King of the World: The Padshahnama, an Imperial Mughal Manuscript from the Royal Library, Windsor Castle*. London: Thames and Hudson, 1997.

Bédier, Achille, and Joseph Cordier. *Statistiques de Pondichéry (1822–1824)*. Ed. Jean Deloche. Pondicherry, India: Institut Français de Pondichéry, 1988.

Benesch, Otto, and Eva Benesch. *The Drawings of Rembrandt*. 6 vols. London: Phaidon, 1973.

Benford, Gregory. "Aliens and Knowability: A Scientist's Perspective." In George E. Slusser, George R. Guffey, and Mark Rose, eds., *Bridges to Science Fiction*. Carbondale: Southern Illinois University Press, 1980, pp. 53–63.

Bennassar, Bartolomé, and Lucile Bennassar. *Les chrétiens d'Allah: L'histoire extraordinaire des renégats, XVIe et XVIIe siècles*. Paris: Perrin, 1989.

Berg, Gerald M. "The Sacred Musket: Tactics, Technology and Power in Eighteenth-Century Madagascar." *Comparative Studies in Society and History* 27, no. 2 (1985): 261–79.

Bergvelt, Ellinoor, and Reneé Kistemaker, eds. *De Wereld binnen handbereik: Nederlandse kunst- en rariteitenverzamelingen, 1585–1735*. Zwolle, The Netherlands: Waanders, 1992.

Bernardini, Michele. "The Illustrations of a Manuscript of the Travel Account of François de la Boullaye le Gouz in the Library of the Accademia Nazionale dei Lincei in Rome." *Muqarnas* 21 (2004): 55–72.

Berthier, Pierre. *La bataille de l'Oued el-Makhâzen, dite bataille des Trois Rois (4 aout 1578)*. Paris: Editions du CNRS, 1985.

Biagioli, Mario. "The Anthropology of Incommensurability." *Studies in History and Philosophy of Science* 21, no. 2 (1990): 183–209.

Biedermann, Zoltán. "Portuguese Diplomacy in Asia in the Sixteenth Century: A Preliminary Overview." *Itinerario* 29, no. 2 (2005): 13–37.

Biker, Júlio Firmino Júdice, ed. *Colecção de tratados e concertos de pazes que o Estado da Índia Portugueza fez com os Reis e Senhores com quem teve relações nas partes da Ásia e África Oriental.* 14 vols. Lisbon: Imprensa Nacional, 1881–87.

Born, Wolfgang. "Ivory Powder Flasks from the Mughal Period." *Ars Islamica*, no. 9 (1942): 93–111.

Boxer, Charles Ralph. *The Great Ship from Amacon: Annals of Macao and the Old Japan Trade, 1555–1640.* Lisbon: Centro de Estudos Históricos Ultramarinos, 1959.

———. "A Note on Portuguese Reactions to the Revival of the Red Sea Spice Trade and the Rise of Atjeh, 1540–1600." *Journal of Southeast Asian History* 10, no. 3 (1969): 415–28.

———. *O Grande Navio de Amacau.* Trans. Manuel Vilarinho. Macao: Fundação Oriente, 1989.

———. "A Tentative Check-List of Indo-Portuguese Imprints." *Arquivos do Centro Cultural Português* (Paris) 9 (1975): 567–599.

Bramanti, Vanni, ed. *Lettere da Vari Paesi, 1570–1588, di Filippo Sassetti.* Milan: Longanesi, 1970.

Branfoot, Crispin, and Anna L. Dallapiccola. "Temple Architecture in Bhatkal and the 'Rāmāyana' Tradition in Sixteenth-Century Coastal Karnataka." *Artibus Asiae* 65, no. 2 (2005): 253–308.

Brienen, Rebecca Parker. "Albert Eckhout and Frans Post: Two Dutch Artists in Colonial Brazil." In Edward J. Sullivan, ed., *Brazil: Body and Soul.* New York: Guggenheim Museum, 2001, pp. 92–111.

———. *Visions of Savage Paradise: Albert Eckhout, Court Painter in Colonial Dutch Brazil.* Amsterdam: Amsterdam University Press, 2006.

Briggs, John. "Essay on the Life and Writings of Ferishta." *Transactions of the Royal Asiatic Society of Great Britain and Ireland* 2, no. 1 (1829): 341–61.

Burbank, Jane, Mark von Hagen, and Anatolyi Remnev, eds. *Russian Empire: Space, People, Power, 1700–1930.* Bloomington: Indiana University Press, 2007.

Burke, Peter. *The Fortunes of the "Courtier": The European Reception of Castiglione's "Cortegiano."* University Park: Pennslvania State University Press, 1995.

Burns, Robert I. "Christian-Islamic Confrontation in the West: The Thirteenth-Century Dream of Conversion." *American Historical Review* 76, no. 5 (1971): 1386–434.

Camps, Arnulf, and Jean-Claude Muller, eds. *The Sanskrit Grammar and Manuscripts of Father Heinrich Roth, S.J. (1620–1668): Facsimile Edition of Biblioteca Nazionale, Rome, Mss. Or. 171 and 172.* Leiden, The Netherlands: E. J. Brill, 1988.

Cannadine, David, and Simon Price, eds. *Rituals of Royalty: Power and Ceremonial in Traditional Societies.* Cambridge: Cambridge University Press, 1987.

Capponi, Niccolò. *Victory of the West: The Story of the Battle of Lepanto.* London: Macmillan, 2006.

Cardoso, George [Jorge]. *Agiológio Lusitano dos Sanctos, e Varoens illustres em virtude do Reino de Portugal e suas conquistas,* vol. 2. Lisbon: Officina Craesbeekiana, 1657.

Carey, Daniel. "Questioning Incommensurability in Early Modern Cultural Exchange." *Common Knowledge* 6, no. 3 (1997): 32–50.

Carita, Rui, ed. *O "Lyvro de Plantaforma das Fortalezas da Índia" da Biblioteca da Fortaleza de São Julião da Barra.* Lisbon: Edições INAPA, 1999.

Casale, Giancarlo. "His Majesty's Servant Lutfi: The Career of a Previously Unknown Sixteenth-Century Ottoman Envoy to Sumatra Based on an Account of His Travels from the Topkapı Palace Archives." *Turcica,* no. 37 (2005): 43–81.

———. *The Ottoman Age of Exploration.* New York: Oxford University Press, 2010.

Castiglione, Baldesar [Baldassarre]. *The Book of the Courtier.* Trans. Leonard Eckstein Opdycke. New York: H. Liveright, 1929.

———. *Il Libro del Cortegiano.* Ed. Giulio Preti. Turin: Einaudi, 1965.

Catz, Rebecca D. *A sátira social de Fernão Mendes Pinto: Análise crítica da Peregrinação.* Trans. Manolo B. R. Santos. Lisbon: Prelo, 1978.

Chaghatai, Muhammad 'Abdullah. "Fārsī kī ek qalamī masnawī." *Urdū* [Delhi], April 1943.

———. "Mirat ul-Quds: An illustrated Manuscript of Akbar's Period about Christ's Life." In *Lahore Museum Heritage*, ed. Anjum Rehmani. Lahore, Pakistan: Lahore Museum, 1994, pp. 179–88.

Chand, Tara. *Influence of Islam on Indian Culture*. Allahabad: The Indian Press, 1954.

Chartier, Roger. "History, Time, and Space." *Republics of Letters* 2, no. 2 (2011): 1–13.

Châtelain, Henri Abraham. *Atlas historique, ou Nouvelle introduction à l'histoire, à la chronologie & à la géographie ancienne & moderne*. 7 vols. Amsterdam: Z. Châtelain, 1732–39.

Chekuri, Christopher. "Between Family and Empire: Nayaka Strategies of Rule in Vijayanagara South India, 1400–1700 AD." Ph.D. diss., University of Wisconsin–Madison, 2005.

Choksy, Jamsheed K., and M. Usman Hasan. "An Emissary from Akbar to ʿAbbās I: Inscriptions, Texts and the Career of Amīr Muhammad Maʿsūm al-Bhakkarī." *Journal of the Royal Asiatic Society*, 3rd ser., 1, no. 1 (1991): 19–29.

Clendinnen, Inga. *Ambivalent Conquests: Maya and Spaniard in Yucatan, 1517–1570*. 2nd ed. Cambridge: Cambridge University Press, 2003.

———. *Dancing with Strangers: The True History of the Meeting of the British First Fleet and the Aboriginal Australians, 1788*. Edinburgh: Canongate Books, 2005.

Colley, Linda. *Captives: Britain, Empire and the World, 1600–1850*. London: Jonathan Cape, 2002.

Cook, David. *Martyrdom in Islam*. Cambridge: Cambridge University Press, 2007.

Cook, Harold J. *Matters of Exchange: Commerce, Medicine, and Science in the Dutch Golden Age*. New Haven, Conn.: Yale University Press, 2007.

Cooper, Darius. "The White Man's Burdens and Whims of the Chess-Besotted Aristocrats: Colonialism in Satyajit Ray's *The Chess Players*." *Journal of South Asian Literature* 28, nos. 1–2 (1993): 205–25.

Corte-Real, Jerónimo. *Sucesso do segundo cerco de Diu: Códice Cadaval 31—ANTT*. Ed. Martim de Albuquerque. Lisbon: Edições INAPA, 1991.

Cortesão, Amando, and Luís de Albuquerque, eds. *Obras Completas de D. João de Castro*, vol. 3. Coimbra, Portugal: Junta de Investigações Científicas do Ultramar, 1976.

Costa, M. Gonçalves da. *História do bispado e cidade de Lamego*. 6 vols. Braga, Portugal: Barbosa & Xavier, 1977–92.

Costa, Palmira Fontes da, ed. *O Corpo Insólito: Dissertações sobre Monstros no Portugal do século XVIII*. Oporto, Portugal: Porto Editora, 2005.

Costley, Clare L. "David, Bathsheba, and the Penitential Psalms." *Renaissance Quarterly* 57, no. 4 (2004): 1235–77.

Courtright, Nicola. "Origins and Meanings of Rembrandt's Late Drawing Style." *Art Bulletin* 78, no. 3 (1996): 485–510.

Couto, Dejanirah. "L'itinéraire d'un marginal: La deuxième vie de Diogo de Mesquita." *Arquivos do Centro Cultural Calouste Gulbenkian* 39 (2000): 9–35.

Couto, Diogo do. *Da Ásia, Décadas IV–XII*. Lisbon: Régia officina typografica, 1778. Reprint. Lisbon: Livraria Sam Carlos, 1974.

——. *Década Quinta da Ásia*. Ed. Marcus de Jong. Coimbra, Portugal: Imprensa da Universidade, 1937.

——. *O Primeiro Soldado Prático*. Ed. António Coimbra Martins. Lisbon: Comissão Nacional para as Comemorações dos Descobrimentos Portugueses, 2001.

——. *Vida de D. Paulo de Lima Pereira, por Diogo do Couto (com uma descripção que de novo deixou feita o mesmo author desde a Terra dos Fumos até o Cabo das Correntes)*. Lisbon: Escriptório, 1903.

Coutre, Jacques de. *Andanzas asiáticas*. Ed. Eddy Stols, B. Teensma, and J. Verberckmoes. Madrid: Historia 16, 1991.

Crosby, Alfred W., Jr. *The Columbian Exchange: Biological and Cultural Consequences of 1492*. Westport, Conn.: Greenwood, 1972.

Cruz, Maria Augusta Lima. "A viagem de Gonçalo Pereira Marramaque do Minho às Molucas—ou os itinerários da fidalguia portuguesa no Oriente." *Studia*, no. 49 (1989): 315–40.

——. *Diogo do Couto e a Década 8ª da Ásia*. 2 vols. Lisbon: Imprensa Nacional, 1993.

——. "Exiles and Renegades in Early Sixteenth Century Portuguese India." *Indian Economic and Social History Review* 23, no. 3 (1986): 249–62.

——. "O assassínio do rei de Maluco: Reabertura de um processo." In Artur Teodoro de Matos and Luís Filipe F. Reis Thomaz, eds., *As Relações entre a Índia Portuguesa, a Ásia do Sueste e o Extremo Oriente: Actas do*

VI Seminário Internacional de História Indo-Portuguesa. Macau: Instituto Cultural de Macau, 1993, pp. 511–30.

Cummings, William. "Islam, Empire and Makassarese Historiography in the reign of Sultan Ala'uddin (1593–1639)." *Journal of Southeast Asian Studies* 38, no. 2 (2007): 197–214.

Daftary, Farhad. "Shah Tahir b. Radi al-Din Husayni." In Oliver Leamand, ed., *The Biographical Encyclopaedia of Islamic Philosophy.* London: Continuum International, 2006, pp. 209–11.

Dallapiccola, Anna Libera, and Stephanie Zingel-Avé Lallemant, eds. *Vijayanagara—City and Empire: New Currents of Research.* 2 vols. Wiesbaden, Germany: Franz Steiner Verlag, 1985.

De Bruin, Cornelis [Cornelius le Bruyn]. *Travels into Muscovy, Persia, and part of the East-Indies, Containing, an accurate description of whatever is most remarkable in those countries, and embellished with above 320 copper plates.* 2 vols. London: A. Bettesworth, 1737.

De Groot, Cornelis Hofstede. "Isaac Koedijck." In *Festschrift für Max J. Friedländer.* Berlin: E. A. Seemann, 1927, pp. 181–90.

De Groot, Erlend. "The Earliest Eyewitness Depictions of Khoikhoi: Andries Beeckman in Africa." *Itinerario* 29, no. 1 (2005): 17–50.

De Jong, Albert Johannes, ed. *Afgoderye der Oost-Indische heydenen door Philippus Baldæus.* The Hague: Martinus Nijhoff, 1917.

De la Créquinière. *Conformité des coutumes des Indiens Orientaux, avec celles des Juifs et des autres Peuples de l'Antiquité.* Brussels: G. de Backer, 1704.

Del Bonta, Robert J. "Reinventing Nature: Mughal Composite Animal Painting." In Som Prakash Verma, ed., *Flora and Fauna in Mughal Art.* Bombay: Marg, 1999, pp. 69–82.

Dellavida, Giorgio Levi. *George Strachan: Memorials of a Wandering Scottish Scholar of the Seventeenth Century.* Aberdeen: Third Spalding Club, 1956.

Dening, Greg. *Islands and Beaches: Discourse on a Silent Land, Marquesas, 1774–1880.* Carlton, Victoria, Australia: Melbourne University Press, 1980.

Desai, Ziyauddin A. "A Foreign Dignitary's Ceremonial Visit to Akbar's Tomb: A First-Hand Account." In Iqtidar Alam Khan, ed., *Akbar and His Age.* New Delhi: Northern Book Centre, 1999, pp. 188–97.

Dharampal [Dharampal-Frick], Gita. "Heinrich von Poser's Travelogue to the Deccan." *Quarterly Journal of the Mythic Society* 73, nos. 3–4 (1981): 103–14.

———. *Indien im Spiegel deutscher Quellen der Frühen Neuzeit (1500–1750): Studien zu einer interkulturellen Konstellation.* Tübingen, Germany: Niemeyer, 1994.

Dirks, Nicholas B. "The Pasts of a *Pālaiyakārar*: The Ethnohistory of a South Indian Little King." *Journal of Asian Studies* 41, no. 4 (1982): 655–83.

Djajadiningrat, Hoesein. "Critisch overzicht van de in maleische werken vervatte gegevens over de geschiedenis van het Soeltanaat van Atjeh." *Bijdragen tot de Taal-, Land- en Volkenkunde van Nederlandsch Indië* 65 (1911): 135–265.

Duby, Georges. *Le dimanche de Bouvines: 27 juillet 1214.* Paris: Gallimard, 1985.

———. *The Legend of Bouvines: War, Religion and Culture in the Middle Ages.* Trans. Catherine Tihanyi. Berkeley: University of California Press, 1990.

Duda, Dorothea. "Die Kaiserin und der Grossmogul: Untersuchung zu den Miniaturen des Millionenzimmers im Schloss Schönbrunn." In Karin K. Troschke, ed., *Malerei auf Papier und Pergament in den Prunkräumen des Schlosses Schönbrunn.* Vienna: Schloss Schönbrunn Kultur- und Betriebsges, 1997.

Duffy, Eamon. *Fires of Faith: Catholic England under Mary Tudor.* New Haven, Conn.: Yale University Press, 2009.

Du Jarric, Pierre. *Akbar and the Jesuits.* Trans. C. H. Payne. London: Harper & Brothers, 1926.

Eaton, Natasha. "Nostalgia for the Exotic: Creating an Imperial Art in London, 1750–1793." *Eighteenth-Century Studies* 39, no. 2 (2006): 227–50.

Eaton, Richard Maxwell. "From Kalyana to Talikota: Culture, Politics and War in the Deccan 1542–1565." In Rajat Datta, ed., *Rethinking a Millennium: Perspectives on Indian History from the Eighth to the Eighteenth Century (Essays for Harbans Mukhia).* Delhi: Aakar Books, 2008, pp. 95–105.

———. "'Kiss my foot', said the King: Firearms, Diplomacy, and the Battle for Raichur, 1520." *Modern Asian Studies* 43, no. 1 (2009): 289–313.

————. *A Social History of the Deccan, 1300–1761: Eight Indian Lives*. Vol. 1, pt. 8 of *New Cambridge History of India*. Cambridge: Cambridge University Press, 2005.

Elias, Norbert. *The Court Society*. Trans. Edmund Jephcott. New York: Pantheon Books, 1983.

Elisonas, Jurgis [George Elison]. "Christianity and the Daimyo." In John Whitney Hall and James L. McClain, eds., *The Cambridge History of Japan*, vol. 4: *Early Modern Japan*. Cambridge: Cambridge University Press, 1991, pp. 301–72.

————. "Introduction: Japan in the Sixteenth Century." In George Elison and Bardwell L. Smith, eds., *Warlords, Artists and Commoners: Japan in the Sixteenth Century*. Honolulu: University of Hawaii Press, 1981, pp. 1–6.

Erédia, Manuel Godinho de. *Eredia's Description of Malaca, Meridional India, and Cathay*. Trans. J. V. Mills, intro. Cheah Boon Kheng. Kuala Lumpur: Malaysian Branch of the Royal Asiatic Society, 1997.

————. *História de serviços com martírio de Luís Monteiro Coutinho, ordenada por Manoel Godino de Erédia, mathemático, Anno 1615*, Mss. Biblioteca Nacional de Lisboa, Fundo Geral, Reservados, Codex 414.

Ernst, Carl W. "From Hagiography to Martyrology: Conflicting Testimonies to a Sufi Martyr of the Delhi Sultanate." *History of Religions* 24, no. 4 (1985): 308–27.

Everaert, J. G. "Manuel Godinho de Erédia: Humaniste ou aventurier?" In Manuel Godinho de Erédia, *Suma de Árvores e Plantas da Índia Intra Ganges*, ed. J. G. Everaert, J. E. Mendes Ferrão, and M. Cândida Liberato. Lisbon: Comissão Nacional para as Comemorações dos Descobrimentos Portugueses, 2001, pp. 23–82.

Exwood, Maurice, and H. L. Lehmann, eds. and trans. *The Journal of William Schellinks' Travels in England, 1661–1663*. London: Royal Historical Society, 1993.

Fabbri, Beatrice Buscaroli. *Carlo Cignani: Affreschi, dipinti, disegni*. Bologna: Nuova Alfa, 1991.

Falchetta, Piero, ed. *Storia del Mogol di Nicolò Manuzzi veneziano*. 2 vols. Milan: Franco Maria Ricci, 1986.

Faroqhi, Suraiya. *Pilgrims and Sultans: The Hajj under the Ottomans, 1517–1683*. London: I. B. Tauris, 1994.

Federici, Cesare. *The Voyage and Travaile of M. Caesar Frederick, Merchant of Venice, unto the East India, the Indies, and beyond the Indies.* Trans. Thomas Hickock. London: Richard Jones and Edward White, 1588.

Fenech, Louis E. "Martyrdom and the Sikh Tradition." *Journal of the American Oriental Society* 117, no. 4 (1997): 623–42.

Findlen, Paula, ed. *Athanasius Kircher: The Last Man Who Knew Everything.* New York: Routledge, 2004.

Firishta, Muhammad Qasim Hindushah Astarabadi. *History of the Rise of Mahomedan Power in India till the Year* A.D. *1612.* 4 vols. Trans. John Briggs and Mir Khairat ʿAli Khan Akbarabadi "Mushtaq." London: Longman, Rees, Orme, Brown, and Green, 1829.

———. *Tārīkh-i Firishta.* 2 vols. Urdu trans. ʿAbdul Hayy Khwaja. Lahore, Pakistan: Ghulam ʿAli and Sons, 1962.

———. *Tārīkh-i Firishta.* 2 vols. Ed. Mohammad Reza Nasiri. Tehran: Anjuman-i Asar wa Mafakhir-i Farhangi, 2009–11.

Flatt, Emma J. "Courtly Culture in the Indo-Persian States of the Medieval Deccan, 1450–1600." Ph.D. diss., School of Oriental and African Studies, University of London, 2008.

Floor, Willem M. "Dutch Painters in Iran during the First Half of the Seventeenth Century." *Persica*, no. 8 (1979): 145–61.

Flores, Jorge. "Dois retratos portugueses da Índia de Jahangir: Jerónimo Xavier e Manuel Godinho de Erédia." In Jorge Flores and Nuno Vassallo e Silva, eds., *Goa e o Grão-Mogol.* Lisbon: Fundação Calouste Gulbenkian, 2004, pp. 44–66.

Flores, Jorge, and Maria Augusta Lima Cruz. "A 'Tale of Two Cities', a 'Veteran Soldier', or the Struggle for Endangered Nobilities: The Two *Jornadas de Huva* (1633, 1635) Revisited." In Jorge Flores, ed., *Re-exploring the Links: History and Constructed Histories between Portugal and Sri Lanka.* Wiesbaden, Germany: Harrassowitz Verlag, 2007, pp. 95–124.

Flores, Jorge, and António Vasconcelos de Saldanha. *Os Firangis na Chancelaria Mogol: Cópias Portuguesas de documentos de Akbar (1572–1604).* New Delhi: Embaixada de Portugal, 2003.

Foster, William, ed. *The Embassy of Sir Thomas Roe to the Court of the Great Mogul, 1615–1619.* 2 vols. London: The Hakluyt Society, 1899.

——, ed. *The English Factories in India, 1637–1641*. Oxford: Clarendon Press, 1912.

Fróis, Luís. *Tratado das Contradições e Diferenças de Costumes entre a Europa e o Japão*. Ed. Rui Manuel Loureiro. Macao: Instituto Português do Oriente, 2001.

Gadamer, Hans-Georg. *Truth and Method*. Trans. W. Glen-Doepel, Joel Weinsheimer, and Donald G. Marshall. New York: Continuum, 2004.

Galison, Peter. *Image and Logic: A Material Culture of Microphysics*. Chicago: University of Chicago Press, 1997.

Galland, Julien-Claude. *Le Paradis des infidèles: Relation de Yirmisekiz Çelebi Mehmed efendi, ambassadeur ottoman en France sous la Régence*. Ed. Gilles Veinstein. Paris: François Maspero, 1981.

Garcin, Jean-Claude. "The Mamlūk Military System and the Blocking of Medieval Moslem Society." In Jean Baechler, John A. Hall, and Michael Mann, eds., *Europe and the Rise of Capitalism*. Oxford: Basil Blackwell, 1988, pp. 113–30.

Geertz, Clifford. "Art as a Cultural System." *Modern Language Notes* 91, no. 6 (1976): 1473–99.

Gernet, Jacques. *China and the Christian Impact: A Conflict of Cultures*. Trans. Janet Lloyd. Cambridge: Cambridge University Press, 1985.

Ginzburg, Carlo. "Latitude, Slaves and the Bible: An Experiment in Microhistory." *Critical Inquiry* 31 (2005): 665–83.

Gliozzi, Giuliano. *Adamo e il nuovo mondo: La nascita dell'antropologia come ideologia coloniale; Dalle genealogie bibliche alle teorie razziali (1500–1700)*. Florence: La Nuova Italia, 1977.

Goertz, R. O. W. "Attack and Defense Techniques in the Siege of Chaul, 1570–1571." In Luís de Albuquerque and Inácio Guerreiro, eds., *Actas do II Seminário Internacional de História Indo-Portuguesa*. Lisbon: Instituto de Investigação Científica Tropical, 1985, pp. 265–87.

Goetz, Hermann. "Muslims in Vijayanagar, the Record of Monuments." In H. K. Sherwani, ed., *Studies in Indian Culture: Dr. Ghulam Yazdani Commemoration Volume*. Hyderabad, India: Maulana Azad Oriental Research Institute, 1966, pp. 66–70.

Gommans, Jos. "Indian Warfare and Afghan Innovation during the Eighteenth Century." In Jos J. L. Gommans and Dirk H. A. Kolff, eds., *Warfare and Weaponry in South Asia, 1000–1800*. Delhi: Oxford University Press, 2001, pp. 365–86.

———. *Mughal Warfare: Indian Frontiers and High Roads to Empire, 1500–1700*. London: Routledge, 2002.

Goonewardena, K. W. *The Foundation of Dutch Power in Ceylon, 1638–1658*. Amsterdam: Djambatan, 1958.

Gosselink, Martine. "Schilderijen van Bengaalse VOC-loges door Hendrik van Schuylenburgh." *Bulletin van het Rijksmuseum* 46 (1998): 390–409.

Green, Janet M. "Queen Elizabeth I's Latin Reply to the Polish Ambassador." *Sixteenth-Century Journal* 31, no. 4 (2000): 987–1008.

Gruzinski, Serge. "Images and Cultural Mestizaje in Colonial Mexico." *Poetics Today* 16, no. 1 (1995): 53–77.

———. *Les quatre parties du monde: Histoire d'une mondialisation*. Paris: La Martinière, 2004.

———. *The Mestizo Mind: The Intellectual Dynamics of Colonization and Globalization*. Trans. Deke Dusinberre. London: Routledge, 2002.

Guerreiro, Fernão. *Relação anual das coisas que fizeram os padres da Companhia de Jesus nas suas missões (. . .) tirada das cartas que os missionários de lá escreveram*, vol. 1. Ed. Artur Viegas. Coimbra, Portugal: Imprensa da Universidade, 1930.

Guerreiro, Inácio, and Vítor Luís Gaspar Rodrigues. "O 'grupo de Cochim' e a oposição a Afonso de Albuquerque." *Studia*, no. 51 (1992): 119–44.

Guha, Sumit. "The Frontiers of Memory: What the Marathas Remembered of Vijayanagara." *Modern Asian Studies* 43, no. 1 (2009): 269–88.

———. "Literary Tropes and Historical Settings: A Study from Southern India." In Rajat Datta, ed., *Rethinking a Millennium: Perspectives on Indian History from the Eighth to the Eighteenth Century (Essays for Harbans Mukhia)*. Delhi: Aakar Books, 2008, pp. 106–20.

Guillot, Claude, and Ludvik Kalus. "Inscriptions islamiques sur des canons d'Insulinde du XVIe siècle." *Archipel*, no. 72 (2006): 69–94.

Gurney, John D. "Pietro della Valle: The Limits of Perception." *Bulletin of the School of Oriental and African Studies* 49, no. 1 (1986): 103–16.

Hacking, Ian. *Historical Ontology.* Cambridge, Mass.: Harvard University Press, 2002.

Haidar, Navina Najat, and Marika Sardar, eds. *Sultans of the South: Arts of India's Deccan Courts, 1323–1687.* New York: Metropolitan Museum of Art, 2011.

Haig, T. Wolseley. *The History of the Nizam Shahi Kings of Ahmadnagar.* Bombay: British India Press, 1923.

Hardgrave, Robert L., Jr. *A Portrait of the Hindus: Balthazar Solvyns and the European Image of India, 1760–1824.* New York: Oxford University Press, 2004.

Hart, Roger Preston. "Translating Worlds: Incommensurability and Problems of Existence in Seventeenth-Century China." *Positions* 7, no. 1 (1999): 95–128.

Hasan, Farhat. *State and Locality in Mughal India: Power Relations in Western India, c. 1572–1730.* Cambridge: Cambridge University Press, 2006.

Hasan Shauqi. *Dīwān-i Hasan Shauqī.* Ed. Jamil Jalibi. Karachi: Anjuman-i Taraqqi-yi Urdu Pakistan, 1971.

Headley, John M. *The Europeanization of the World: On the Origins of Human Rights and Democracy.* Princeton, N.J.: Princeton University Press, 2008.

Hecker, Felicia J. "A Fifteenth-Century Chinese Diplomat in Herat." *Journal of the Royal Asiatic Society,* 3rd ser., 3, no. 1 (1993): 86–98.

Heeres, J. E., and F. W. Stapel, eds. *Corpus Diplomaticum Neerlando-Indicum: Verzameling van politieke contracten en verdere verdragen door de Nederlanders in het Oosten gesloten.* 6 vols. The Hague: Martinus Nijhoff, 1907–55.

Hellyer, Robert I. *Defining Engagement: Japan and Global Contexts, 1640–1868.* Cambridge, Mass.: Harvard University Press, 2009.

Henriques, Henrique [Antirikku Atikalar]. *Flos Sanctorum enra atiyār varalāru.* Ed. Ca. Iracamanikkam. Tutukkudi [Tuticorin], India: Tamil Ilakkiyak Kalakam, 1967.

Heras, Henry [Enric]. *The Aravidu Dynasty of Vijayanagara.* Madras, India: B. G. Paul, 1927.

Herbert, Christopher. *War of No Pity: The Indian Mutiny and Victorian Trauma.* Princeton, N.J.: Princeton University Press, 2007.

Herder, Johann Gottfried. *Reflections on the Philosophy of the History of Mankind.* Abridged, intro. Frank E. Manuel. Chicago: University of Chicago Press, 1968.

Herskovits, Melville J. *Acculturation: The Study of Culture Contact.* New York: J. J. Augustin, 1938.

Holt, P. M. "The Study of Arabic Historians in Seventeenth Century England: The Background and the Work of Edward Pococke." *Bulletin of the School of Oriental and African Studies* 19, no. 3 (1957): 444–55.

Hostetler, Laura. *Qing Colonial Enterprise: Ethnography and Cartography in Early Modern China.* Chicago: University of Chicago Press, 2001.

Hsia, Ronnie Po-chia. *The World of Catholic Renewal, 1540–1770.* Cambridge: Cambridge University Press, 1998.

Husted, Wayne R. "Karbalā' Made Immediate: The Martyr as Model in Imāmī Shī'ism." *The Muslim World* 83, nos. 3–4 (1993): 263–78.

Hutton, Deborah. *Art of the Court of Bijapur.* Bloomington: Indiana University Press, 2006.

Ibn Battuta. *Travels in Asia and Africa, 1325–1354.* Trans. H. A. R. Gibb. London: Routledge and Kegan Paul, 1929. Reprint, New Delhi: Manohar, 2001.

Islam, Riazul, ed. *A Calendar of Documents on Indo-Persian Relations (1500–1700),* vol. 2. Karachi: Institute of Central and West Asian Studies, 1982.

Jacob, Margaret C. "Bernard Picart and the Turn to Modernity." *De Achttiende Eeuw* 37 (2005): 1–16.

Jacobs, Hubert. "The Portuguese Town of Ambon, 1567–1605." In Luís de Albuquerque and Inácio Guerreiro, eds., *Actas do II Seminário Internacional de História Indo-Portuguesa.* Lisbon: Instituto de Investigação Científica Tropical, 1985, pp. 601–14.

Jesus, Tomé de. *The Sufferings of Our Lord Jesus Christ, written originally in the Portuguese by Fr. Thomas of Jesus, of the Order of the Hermits of St. Augustin.* 3 vols. London: J. Marmaduke, 1753.

———. *Trabalhos de Jesus: Compostos pelo veneravel Padre Fr. Thomé de Jesus da ordem dos eremitas de Santo Agostinho, da Provincia de Portugal, estando cativo em Berberia.* 2 vols. Oporto, Portugal: Typographia Porto Médico, 1925.

Johnson, Samuel. *The Works of the English Poets, from Chaucer to Cowper*, vol. 21. London: J. Johnson et al., 1810.

Kanbargimath, S. S. "A Study of the Battle of Talikote." *Quarterly Journal of the Mythic Society* 60, nos. 1–4 (1969): 47–55.

Katz, Nathan. "The Identity of a Mystic: The Case of Saʿid Sarmad, a Jewish-Yogi-Sufi Courtier of the Mughals." *Numen* 42, no. 2 (2000): 142–60.

Kaufmann, Thomas DaCosta. *Arcimboldo: Visual Jokes, Natural History, and Still-Life Painting*. Chicago: University of Chicago Press, 2009.

Kempers, A. J. Bernet, ed. *Journaal van Dircq van Adrichem's Hofreis naar den Groot-Mogol Aurangzeb (1662)*. The Hague: Martinus Nijhoff, 1941.

Kenseth, Joy, ed. *The Age of the Marvelous*. Chicago: University of Chicago Press, 1991.

King, J. S. *The History of the Bahmanī Dynasty, Founded on the "Burhān-i Maʾāsir."* London: Luzac and Co., 1900.

Knoppers, Laura Lunger, and Joan B. Landes, eds. *Monstrous Bodies/Political Monstrosities in Early Modern Europe*. Ithaca, N.Y.: Cornell University Press, 2004.

Koch, Ebba. "The 'Moghuleries' of the Millionenzimmer, Schönbrunn Palace, Vienna." In Rosemary Crill, Susan Stronge, and Andrew Topsfield, eds., *Arts of Mughal India: Studies in Honour of Robert Skelton*. London: Victoria & Albert Museum, 2004, pp. 152–67.

———. *Mughal Art and Imperial Ideology: Collected Essays*. Delhi: Oxford University Press, 2001.

———. "Netherlandish Naturalism in Imperial Mughal Painting." *Apollo*, no. 152 (November 2000): 29–37.

Kratzsch, Siegfried, ed. *Deex Autaer von Philip Angel: Eine niederländische Handschrift aus dem 17. Jahrhundert über die zehn Avataras des Visnu*. Halle, Germany: Verlag der Franckeschen Stiftungen, 2007.

Krishnaswami Ayyangar, S. *Sources of Vijayanagar History*. Madras, India: University of Madras, 1919.

Krstić, Tijana. *Contested Conversions to Islam: Narratives of Religious Change in the Early Modern Ottoman Empire*. Stanford, Calif.: Stanford University Press, 2011.

Kurmanatha Kavi, Gogulapati. *Simhādri-Narasimha-śatakamu*. Ed. Pantula Lakshminarayana Sastri. Simhachalam, India: Simhachalam Devasthanam, 1983.

Kurz, Otto. "A Volume of Indian Miniatures and Drawings." *Journal of the Warburg and Courtauld Institutes* 30 (1967): 251–71.

Lacombe, Paul. *Livres d'heures imprimés au XVe et au XVIe siècle, conservés dans les bibliothèques publiques de Paris.* Paris: Imprimerie Nationale, 1907.

Le Goff, Jacques. *Saint Louis.* Paris: Gallimard, 1996.

Le Gouz de la Boullaye, François. *Les Voyages et Observations du Sieur de la Boullaye-le-Gouz, gentil-homme angevin.* Paris: François Clousier, 1657.

Lemos, Jorge de. *História dos cercos de Malaca (1585).* Facsimile ed. Lisbon: Biblioteca Nacional, 1982.

Leupe, P. A. "Nederlandsche schilders in Persië en Hindostan in de eerste helft der 17e eeuw." *De Nederlandsche Spectator,* no. 33, August 16, 1873, pp. 260–63, and no. 34, August 23, 1873, pp. 165–66.

Lightbown, Ronald W. "Oriental Art and the Orient in Late Renaissance and Baroque Italy." *Journal of the Warburg and Courtauld Institutes* 32 (1969): 228–79.

Livingstone, David N. "The Preadamite Theory and the Marriage of Science and Religion." *Transactions of the American Philosophical Society,* n.s., 82, no. 3 (1992): 1–78.

Loades, David, ed. *John Foxe at Home and Abroad.* Aldershot, U.K.: Ashgate, 2004.

Loewenstein, Jean de. "A propos d'un tableau de W. Schellinks s'inspirant des miniatures mogholes." *Arts Asiatiques* 5, no. 4 (1958): 293–98.

Lombard, Denys. *Le Sultanat d'Atjéh au temps d'Iskandar Muda, 1607–1636.* Paris: Ecole Française d'Extrême-Orient, 1967.

Lopes, David, ed. *Chrónica dos Reis de Bisnaga: Manuscripto Inédito do século XVI.* Lisbon: Imprensa Nacional, 1897.

López de Gómara, Francisco. *Guerras de mar del Emperador Carlos V.* Ed. Miguel Angel de Bunes Ibarra and Nora Edith Jiménez. Madrid: Sociedad Estatal para la Conmemoración de los Centenarios de Felipe II-Carlos V, 2000.

Loureiro, Rui Manuel. *A Biblioteca de Diogo do Couto.* Macau: Instituto Cultural de Macau, 1998.

Mack, Rosamund. *Bazaar to Piazza: Islamic Trade and Italian Art, 1300–1600.* Berkeley: University of California Press, 2001.

Mackenzie, Colonel Colin. "View of the principal Political Events that occurred in the Carnatic, from the dissolution of the Ancient Hindoo
Government in 1564 till the Mogul Government was established in
1687, on the Conquest of the Capitals of Beejapoor and Golconda; compiled from various Authentic Memoirs and Original MSS, collected
chiefly within the last ten years, and referred to in the Notes at the bottom of each page." *Journal of the Asiatic Society of Bengal* 13, pts. 1 and
2 (1844): 421–68, 578–608.

Maclagan, Edward. *The Jesuits and the Great Mogul*. New York: Octagon
Books, 1972.

Malmgren, Carl D. "Self and Other in SF: Alien Encounters." *Science Fiction Studies* 20, no. 1 (1993): 15–33.

Manguin, Pierre-Yves. "Of Fortresses and Galleys: The 1568 Acehnese
Siege of Melaka, Following a Contemporary Bird's-Eye View." *Modern
Asian Studies* 22, no. 3 (1988): 607–28.

Manucci, Niccolao. *Mogul India, 1653–1708, or Storia do Mogor*. 4 vols.
Trans. William Irvine. London: J. Murray, 1907–8. Reprint. Delhi: Low
Price Publications, 1990.

Markel, Stephen, and Tushara Bindu Gude, eds. *India's Fabled City: The
Art of Courtly Lucknow*. Los Angeles: Los Angeles County Museum of
Art, 2010.

Markovits, Claude, and Sanjay Subrahmanyam. "Inde et Asie du Sud-Est:
Lendemains des empires." In Patrick Boucheron, ed., *Histoire du monde
au XVe siècle*. Paris: Librairie Arthème Fayard, 2009, pp. 232–48.

Mason, Peter. *Infelicities: Representations of the Exotic*. Baltimore: Johns
Hopkins University Press, 1998.

Matar, Nabil. *Britain and Barbary, 1589–1689*. Gainesville: University
Press of Florida, 2005.

———. *Turks, Moors, and Englishmen in the Age of Discovery*. New York:
Columbia University Press, 1999.

Matos, Luís de, ed. *Imagens do Oriente no século XVI: Reprodução do Códice
Português da Biblioteca Casanatense*. Lisbon: Imprensa Nacional, 1985.

Menzhausen, Joachim. *At the Court of the Great Mogul: The Court at
Delhi on the Birthday of the Great Mogul Aureng-Zeb; Museum Piece by
Johann Melchior Dinglinger, Court Jeweller of the Elector of Saxony and*

King of Poland, August II, Called August the Strong. Trans. Michael Horovitz. Leipzig: Edition Leipzig, 1965.

Miedema, Hessel. "Philips Angels 'Lof der Schilder-Konst.'" *Oud-Holland* 103, no. 4 (1989): 181–222.

Minissale, Gregory. "The Synthesis of European and Mughal Art in the Emperor Akbar's *Khamsa* of Nizāmī." Asianart.com, October 13, 2000, www.asianart.com/articles/minissale.

Mirza Zu'lfiqar Azar Sasani. *The Dabistan, or School of Manners.* 3 vols. Trans. David Shea and Anthony Troyer. Paris: Oriental Translation Fund, 1843.

Mitchell, Colin Paul. "Sister Shiʿa States? Safavid Iran and the Deccan in the 16th Century." *Deccan Studies* 2, no. 2 (2004): 44–72.

Mitter, Partha. *Much Maligned Monsters: A History of European Reactions to Indian Art.* Oxford: Clarendon Press, 1977.

Mohl, Jules. "Tarikh-i-Ferishta." 3 pts. *Journal des Savants,* 1840: 212–26, 354–72, 392–403.

Moreira, Rafael, and Alexandra Curvelo. "A circulação das formas: Artes portáteis, arquitetura e urbanismo." In Francisco Bethencourt and Kirti Chaudhuri, eds., *História da Expansão Portuguesa,* vol. 2: *Do Índico ao Atlântico (1570–1697).* Lisbon: Círculo de Leitores, 1998, pp. 532–70.

Murphey, Rhoads. *Ottoman Warfare, 1500–1700.* New Brunswick, N.J.: Rutgers University Press, 1999.

Muslu, E. Cihan. "Ottoman-Mamluk Relations: Diplomacy and Perceptions." Ph.D. diss., History and Middle Eastern Studies, Harvard University, 2007.

Nahrawali, Qutb-ud-Din al-Nahrawali al-Makki. *Journey to the Sublime Porte: The Arabic Memoir of a Sharifian Agent's Diplomatic Mission to the Ottoman Imperial Court in the Era of Suleyman the Magnificent.* Beirut: Ergon Verlag, 2005.

——. *Lightning over Yemen: A History of the Ottoman Campaign (1569–71).* Trans. Clive K. Smith. London: I. B. Tauris, 2002.

Naipaul, V. S. *India: A Wounded Civilization.* New York: Vintage, 1976.

Narayana Rao, Velcheru, David Shulman, and Sanjay Subrahmanyam. *Textures of Time: Writing History in South India, 1600–1800.* New York: Other Books, 2003.

Nehru, Jawaharlal. *The Discovery of India.* New York: John Day, 1946.

Neild-Basu, Susan. "The Dubashes of Madras." *Modern Asian Studies* 18, no. 1 (1984): 1–31.

Newitt, Malyn. *History of Mozambique.* London: Hurst, 1995.

Nilakantha Sastri, K. A., and N. Venkataramanayya. *Further Sources of Vijayanagara History.* 3 vols. Madras, India: University of Madras, 1946.

Nizam-ud-Din Ahmad, Khwaja. *The Tabaqāt-i-Akbarī of Khwājah Nizāmuddīn Ahmad: A History of India from the Early Musalman Invasions to the Thirty-Sixth Year of the Reign of Akbar.* 3 vols. Trans. Brajendranath De, revised by Baini Prashad. Calcutta: Asiatic Society, 1927–39.

Nordman, Daniel. *Tempête sur Alger: L'expédition de Charles Quint en 1541.* Saint-Denis, France: Bouchène, 2011.

Nunes, Leonardo. *Crónica de Dom João de Castro.* Ed. J. D. M. Ford. Cambridge, Mass.: Harvard University Press, 1936.

Nusrati. *Masnawī 'Alī Nāma.* Ed. 'Abdul Majid Siddiqi. Hyderabad, India: Salar Jang Museum, 1959.

Ogborn, Miles. "Gotcha!" *History Workshop Journal,* no. 56 (2003): 231–38.

Orme, Robert. *A History of the Military Transactions of the British Nation in Indostan from the Year MDCCXLV.* 3rd ed. London: John Nourse, 1780.

Orta, Garcia da. *Colóquios dos simples e drogas da Índia.* Ed. Conde de Ficalho. 2 vols. Lisbon: Imprensa Nacional, 1891.

Osmân Agha de Temechvar. *Prisonnier des infidèles: Un soldat ottoman dans l'Empire des Habsbourg.* Trans. Frédéric Hitzel. Paris: Actes Sud, 1998.

Overton, Keelan. "A Collector and His Portrait: Book Arts and Painting for Ibrahim 'Adil Shah II of Bijapur (r. 1580–1627)." Ph.D. diss., Department of Art History, University of California–Los Angeles, 2011.

Pagden, Anthony. *European Encounters with the New World: From Renaissance to Romanticism.* New Haven, Conn.: Yale University Press, 1993.

Parker, Geoffrey. "Europe and the Wider World, 1500–1700: The Military Balance." In James D. Tracy, ed., *The Political Economy of Merchant Empires: State Power and World Trade, 1350–1750.* New York: Cambridge University Press, 1991, pp. 161–95.

——. *The Military Revolution: Military Innovation and the Rise of the West, 1500–1800.* Cambridge: Cambridge University Press, 1987.

Parker, Geoffrey, and Sanjay Subrahmanyam. "Arms and the Asian: Revisiting European Firearms and Their Place in Early Modern Asia." *Revista de Cultura* (Macau), no. 26 (2008): 12–42.

Parkin, David. "The Creativity of Abuse." *Man,* n.s., 15, no. 1, (1980): 45–64.

Patin, Charles. *Travels thro' Germany, Swisserland, Bohemia, Holland; and other Parts of Europe describing the most considerable Citys and the palaces of Princes: Together with Historical Relations, and Critical Observations upon Ancient Medals and Inscriptions.* London: A. Swall and T. Child, 1696.

Pato, R. A. de Bulhão, ed. *Cartas de Afonso de Albuquerque seguidas de documentos que as elucidam,* vol. 1. Lisbon: Academia Real das Sciencias de Lisboa, 1884.

Paulino, Francisco Faria, ed. *Tapeçarias de D. João de Castro.* Lisbon: Museu Nacional de Arte Antiga, 1995.

Perdue, Peter C. *China Marches West: The Qing Conquest of Central Eurasia.* Cambridge, Mass.: Belknap Press of Harvard University Press, 2005.

Pereira, António dos Santos. "A Índia a preto e branco: Uma carta oportuna, escrita em Cochim, por D. Constantino de Bragança, à Rainha Dona Catarina." *Anais de História de Além-Mar* 4 (2003): 449–84.

Pereira, António Pinto. *História da Índia no tempo em que a governou o visorey D. Luís de Ataíde.* Intro. Manuel Marques Duarte. Lisbon: Imprensa Nacional, 1987.

Pia, Pascal, ed. *Voyage en Perse et description de ce royaume par Jean-Baptiste Tavernier, marchand français.* Paris: Editions du Carrefour, 1930.

Pinto, Fernão Mendes. *The Travels of Mendes Pinto.* Trans. Rebecca D. Catz. Chicago: University of Chicago Press, 1989.

Pinto, Olga, ed. *Viaggi di C. Federici e G. Balbi alle Indie Orientali.* Rome: Istituto Poligrafico dello Stato, 1962.

Pinto, Paulo Jorge de Sousa. *Portugueses e Malaios: Malaca e os Sultanatos de Johor e Achém, 1575–1619.* Lisbon: Sociedade Histórica da Independência de Portugal, 1997.

Povinelli, Elizabeth A. "Radical Worlds: The Anthropology of Incommensurability and Inconceivability." *Annual Review of Anthropology* 30 (2001): 319–34.

Prakash, Om, and V. B. Gupta, eds. *The Dutch Factories in India*, vol. 2: *1624–1627*. New Delhi: Manohar, 2007.

Rajan, Balachandra. *Under Western Eyes: India from Milton to Macaulay*. Durham, N.C.: Duke University Press, 1999.

Rajasekhara, Sindigi. "Vijayanagara Studies: A Bibliography." In Anna Libera Dallapiccola and Stephanie Zingel-Avé Lallemant, eds., *Vijayanagara— City and Empire: New Currents of Research*, vol. 2. Wiesbaden, Germany: Franz Steiner Verlag, 1985, pp. 9–65.

Ramaswamy, Sumathi. "Conceit of the Globe in Mughal Visual Practice." *Comparative Studies in Society and History* 49, no. 4 (2007): 751–82.

Redfield, Robert, Ralph Linton, and Melville J. Herskovits. "Memorandum for the Study of Acculturation." *American Anthropologist* 38, no. 1 (1936): 149–52.

Reeve, L. J. *Charles I and the Road to Personal Rule*. Cambridge: Cambridge University Press, 1989.

Reid, Anthony. *An Indonesian Frontier: Acehnese and Other Histories of Sumatra*. Singapore: Singapore University Press, 2005.

———. "Islamization and Christianization in Southeast Asia: The Critical Phase, 1550–1650." In Anthony Reid, ed., *Southeast Asia in the Early Modern Era: Trade, Power, and Belief*. Ithaca, N.Y.: Cornell University Press, 1993, pp. 151–79.

Restall, Matthew. "A History of the New Philology and the New Philology in History." *Latin American Research Review* 38, no. 1 (2003): 113–34.

Rice, Yael. "The Brush and the Burin: Mogul Encounters with European Engravings." In Jaynie Anderson, ed., *Crossing Cultures: Conflict, Migration and Convergence; The Proceedings of the 32nd International Congress of the History of Art*. Carlton, Victoria, Australia: The Miegunyah Press, 2009, pp. 305–10.

Richard, Francis. "Les manuscrits persans d'origine indienne à la Bibliothèque nationale." *Revue de la Bibliothèque Nationale*, no. 19 (1986): 30–46.

———. "Les manuscripts persans rapports par les frères Vecchietti et conserves aujourd'hui à la Bibliothèque Nationale." *Studia Iranica* 9, pt. 2 (1980): 291–300.

Robinson, Francis. "Ottomans-Safavids-Mughals: Shared Knowledge and Connective Systems." *Journal of Islamic Studies* 8, no. 2 (1997): 151–84.

Rosa, Maria de Lurdes. "Velhos, novos e mutáveis sagrados . . . : Um olhar antropológico sobre formas 'religiosas' de percepção e interpretação da conquista africana (1415–1521)." *Lusitania Sacra* 18 (2006): 13–85.

———. "Vom Heiligen Grafen zum Morisken-Märtyrer: Funcktionem der Sakralität im Kontext der nordafrikanischen Kriege (1415–1521)." In *Novos Mundos—Neue Welten: Portugal und das Zeitalter der Entdeckungen*. Dresden: Sandstein Verlag, 2007, pp. 88–105.

Rossabi, Morris. "Two Ming Envoys to Central Asia." *T'oung Pao*, 2nd ser., 62, nos. 1–3 (1976): 1–34.

Rubiés, Joan-Pau. "The Oriental Voices of Mendes Pinto, or the Traveller as Ethnologist in Portuguese Asia." *Portuguese Studies* 10 (1994): 24–43.

———. *Travel and Ethnology in the Renaissance: South India through European Eyes, 1250–1625*. Cambridge: Cambridge University Press, 2000.

Salati, Marco. "Ricerche sullo Sciismo nell'Impero Ottomano: Il viaggio di Zayn al-Dīn al-Šahīd al-Tānī a Istanbul al tempo di Solimano il Magnifico, 952/1545." *Oriente Moderno*, n.s., 9 (1990): 81–92.

Saletore, B. A. *Social and Political Life in the Vijayanagara Empire (A.D. 1346–A.D. 1646)*. 2 vols. Madras, India: B. G. Paul and Co., 1934.

Sallmann, Jean-Michel. *Géopolitique du XVIe siècle, 1490–1618*. Paris: Seuil, 2003.

Sanceau, Elaine, and Maria de Lourdes Lalande, eds. *Colecção de São Lourenço*, vol. 3. Lisbon: Instituto de Investigação Científica Tropical, 1983.

Sande, Duarte de. *Diálogo sobre a missão dos emabaixadores japoneses à Cúria Romana*. Trans. Américo da Costa Ramalho. Macao: Fundação Oriente, 1997.

Sandoval, Fray Prudencio de. *Segunda parte de la vida y hechos del emperador Carlos V.* Valladolid, Spain: Sebastian de Cañas, 1606.

Sankey, Howard. "Kuhn's Changing Concept of Incommensurability." *British Journal for the Philosophy of Science* 44, no. 4 (1993): 759–74.

Sarre, Friedrich. "Rembrandt Zeichnungen nach indisch-islamisch Miniaturen." *Jahrbuch der Königlich Preuszischen Kunstsammlungen* 25 (1904): 143–56.

Satyanatha Aiyar, R. "The Climacteric of Talikota." *Journal of Indian History* 6, no. 1 (1927): 67–78.

Sayyid Ahmadullah Qadri. *Memoirs of Chand Bibi, the Princess of Ahmadnagar.* Hyderabad, India: Osmania University, 1939.

Scalliet, Marie-Odile. "Une curiosité oubliée: Le 'Livre de dessins faits dans un voyage aux Indes par un voyageur hollandais' du marquis de Paulmy." *Archipel,* no. 54 (1997): 35–62.

Schapelhouman, Marijn. *Rembrandt and the Art of Drawing.* Amsterdam: Rijksmuseum, 2006.

Schellinkx, Willem. *Viaggio al Sud, 1664–1665.* Ed. Bernard Aikema, Hans Brand, Fransje Kuyvenhoven, Dulcia Meijers, and Pierre Mens. Rome: Edizioni dell'Elefante, 1983.

Scheurleer, Pauline Lunsingh. "De Moghul-miniaturen van Rembrandt." In Hanneke van den Muyzenberg and Thomas de Bruijn, eds., *Waarom Sanskrit? Honderdvijfentwintig jaar Sanskrit in Nederland.* Leiden: Kern Institute, 1991, pp. 95–115.

——. "Het Witsenalbum: Zeventiende-eeuwse Indische portretten op bestelling." *Bulletin van het Rijksmuseum* 44 (1996): 167–254.

——. "Mogol-miniaturen door Rembrandt nagetekend." *De kroniek van het Rembrandthuis,* no. 1 (1980): 10–40.

Schimmel, Annemarie. *The Empire of the Great Mughals: History, Art and Culture.* Trans. Corinne Attwood. London: Reaktion Books, 2004.

Schmidt, Benjamin. *Innocence Abroad: The Dutch Imagination and the New World, 1570–1670.* New York: Cambridge University Press, 2001.

Schulin, Ernst. "Rankes erstes Buch." *Historische Zeitschrift* 203, no. 3 (1966): 581–609.

Schurhammer, Georg. "O Tesoiro do Asad Khan: Relação inédita do intérprete António Fernandes (1545)." In Schurhammer, *Gesammelte Studien: Varia,* vol. 1. Ed. László Szilas. Rome: IHSI, 1965, pp. 31–45.

Scott, Jonathan. *Ferishta's History of Dekkan, from the First Mahummedan Conquests.* 2 vols. London: John Stockdale, 1794.

——. *An Historical and Political View of the Decan, south of the Kistnah; including a sketch of the extent and revenue of the Mysorean dominions,* as possessed by Tippoo Sultaun, to the period of his latest acquisitions of territory, and commencement of the present war in 1790. London: J. Debrett, 1791.

Screech, Timon. *The Shogun's Painted Culture: Fear and Creativity in the Japanese States, 1760–1829.* London: Reaktion Books, 2000.

Sewell, Robert. *A Forgotten Empire (Vijayanagar): A Contribution to the History of India.* London: S. Sonnenschein and Co., 1900. Reprint, New York: Barnes and Noble, 1972.

Seyller, John. "The Inspection and Valuation of Manuscripts in the Imperial Mughal Library." *Artibus Asiae* 57, nos. 3–4 (1997): 243–349.

——. *Workshop and Patron in Mughal India: The Freer Rāmāyana and Other Illustrated Manuscripts of ʿAbd al-Rahīm.* Zurich: Artibus Asiae Publishers, 1999.

Shahnawaz Khan, Nawwab Samsam al-Daula. *Maʾāsir al-Umarāʾ.* Ed. Maulavi ʿAbdur Rahim and Maulavi Mirza Ashraf ʿAli. 2 vols. Calcutta: Asiatic Society of Bengal, 1888–90.

——. *Maʾasir-ul-Umara, being Biographies of the Muhammadan and Hindu Officers of the Timurid Sovereigns of India from 1500 to about 1780 A.D.* Trans. H. Beveridge and Baini Prashad. 3 vols. Calcutta: Asiatic Society of Bengal, 1911–52.

Shareef, Mohammed Jamal. *Dakan mein urdū shāʿirī Wali se pahle.* Ed. Mohammad Ali Asar. Hyderabad, India: Idarah-i Adabiyat-i Urdu, 2004.

Sherwani, Haroon Khan. *History of the Qutb Shāhī Dynasty.* New Delhi: Munshiram Manoharlal, 1974.

Silva Rego, António da, ed. *Documentação ultramarina portuguesa,* vol. 3. Lisbon: Centro de Estudos Históricos Ultramarinos, 1963.

Silveira, Francisco Rodrigues. *Reformação da milícia e governo do Estado da Índia Oriental.* Ed. B. N. Teensma, Luís Filipe Barreto, and George D. Winius. Lisbon: Fundação Oriente, 1996.

Skelton, Robert. "Indian Art and Artefacts in Early European Collecting." In Oliver Impey and Arthur Macgregor, eds., *The Origins of Museums: The Cabinet of Curiosities in Sixteenth- and Seventeenth-Century Europe.* Oxford: Clarendon Press, 1985, pp. 274–80.

Slatkes, Leonard J. *Rembrandt and Persia*. New York: Abaris Books, 1983.

Sousa, Francisco de. *Oriente conquistado a Jesus Cristo pelos padres da Companhia de Jesus da Província de Goa*. Ed. Manuel Lopes de Almeida. Oporto, Portugal: Lello e Irmão, 1978.

Speelman, Cornelis. *Journaal der reis van den gezant der O.I. Compagnie Joan Cunaeus naar Perzië in 1651–1652*. Ed. A. Hotz. Amsterdam: J. Müller, 1908.

Stein, Burton. *Vijayanagara: The New Cambridge History of India*, vol. 1, pt. 2. Cambridge: Cambridge University Press, 1989.

Stewart, Devin J. "The Humor of the Scholars: The Autobiography of Niʿmat Allāh al-Jazāʾirī (d. 1112/1701)." *Iranian Studies* 22, no. 4 (1989): 47–81.

———. "The Ottoman Execution of Zayn al-Dīn al-ʿĀmilī." *Die Welt des Islams*, no. 48 (2008): 289–347.

Stolte, Carolien. *Philip Angel's Deex-Autaers: Vaisnava Mythology from Manuscript to Book Market in the Context of the Dutch East India Company, ca. 1600–1672*. New Delhi: Manohar, 2012.

Stooke, Herbert J., and Karl Khandalavala. *The Laud Ragamala Miniatures: A Study in Indian Painting and Music*. Oxford: B. Cassirer, 1953.

Strathern, Alan. *Kingship and Conversion in Sixteenth-Century Sri Lanka: Portuguese Imperialism in a Buddhist Land*. Cambridge: Cambridge University Press, 2007.

Stronge, Susan. "'Far from the arte of painting': An English Amateur Artist at the Court of Jahangir." In Rosemary Crill, Susan Stronge, and Andrew Topsfield, eds., *Arts of Mughal India: Studies in Honour of Robert Skelton*. London: Victoria & Albert Museum, 2004, pp. 129–37.

Strzygowski, Josef, and Heinrich Glück. *Die indischen Miniaturen im Schlosse Schönbrunn*. Vienna: Wiener Drucke, 1923.

Subrahmanyam, Sanjay. "Dom Frei Aleixo de Meneses (1559–1617) et l'échec des tentatives d'indigénisation du christianisme en Inde." *Archives de Sciences Sociales des Religions*, no. 103 (1998): 21–42.

———. "Monsieur Picart and the Gentiles of India." In Lynn Hunt, Margaret Jacob, and Wijnand Mijnhardt, eds., *The First Global Vision of Religion: Bernard Picart's "Religious Ceremonies and Customs of All the Peoples of the World."* Los Angeles: Getty Research Institute, 2010, pp. 197–214.

———. "O gentio indiano visto pelos Portugueses no século XVI." *Oceanos*, nos. 19/20 (1994): 190–96.

———. "Palavras do Idalcão: Um encontro curioso em Bijapur no ano de 1561." *Cadernos do Noroeste* 15, nos. 1–2 (2001): 513–24.

———. "Par-delà l'incommensurabilité: Pour une histoire connectée des empires aux temps modernes." *Revue d'Histoire Moderne et Contemporaine* 54, no. 5 (2007): 34–53.

———. "Pulverized in Aceh: On Luís Monteiro Coutinho and His 'Martyrdom.'" *Archipel*, no. 78 (2009): 19–60.

———. "A Roomful of Mirrors: The Artful Embrace of Mughals and Franks, 1550–1700." In "Globalizing Cultures: Art and Mobility in the Eighteenth Century," ed. Nebahat Avcioğlu and Finbarr Barry Flood. Special issue, *Ars Orientalis* 39 (2010): 39–83.

———. "Sobre uma carta de Vira Narasimha Raya, rei de Vijayanagara (1505–1509), a Dom Manuel I de Portugal (1495–1521)." In Isabel de Riquer, Elena Losada, and Helena González, eds., *Professor Basilio Losada: Ensinar a pensar con liberdade e risco*. Barcelona: Universitat de Barcelona, 2000, pp. 677–83.

———. *Three Ways to Be Alien: Travails and Encounters in the Early Modern World*. Waltham, Mass.: Brandeis University Press, 2011.

Syndram, Dirk. *Der Thron des Grossmoguls im Grünen Gewölbe zu Dresden*. Leipzig: E. A. Seemann, 2009.

Tabataba, Sayyid ʿAli [bin ʿAzizullah]. *Burhān-i Maʾāsir*. Ed. Sayyid Hashmi Faridabadi. Delhi: Matbaʿ Jamiʿa, 1936.

Tarassuk, Leonid. "Model of a Basilisk by Petrus de Arena." *Metropolitan Museum Journal* 24 (1989): 189–97.

Tavakoli-Targhi, Mohamad. "Contested Memories of Pre-Islamic Iran." *Medieval History Journal* 2, no. 2 (1999): 245–75.

Tavernier, Jean-Baptiste. *Les six voyages en Turquie et en Perse*. Ed. Stéphane Yerasimos. 2 vols. Paris: F. Maspero, 1981.

———. *Travels in India by Jean-Baptiste Tavernier, Baron of Aubonne*. 2nd ed. Ed. and trans. V. Ball and W. Crooke. 2 vols. London: Oxford University Press, 1925.

Teensma, B. N. "An Unknown Portuguese Text on Sumatra from 1582." *Bijdragen tot de Taal-, Land- en Volkenkunde* 145, nos. 2–3 (1989): 308–23.

Teixeira, Pedro. *Relaciones de Pedro Teixeira d'el origen, descendencia, y succession de los reyes de Persia, y de Harmuz, y de un viage hecho por el mismo autor desde la India oriental hasta Italia por tierra.* Antwerp: H. Verdussen, 1610.

Thomaz, Luís Filipe F. R. "A Crise de 1565–1575 na História do Estado da Índia." *Mare Liberum,* no. 9 (1995): 481–520.

———. "As cartas malaias de Abu Hayat, Sultão de Ternate, a El-Rei de Portugal, e os primórdios da presença portuguesa em Maluco." *Anais de História de Além-Mar* 4 (2003): 381–446.

———. "The Image of the Archipelago in Portuguese Cartography of the 16th and Early 17th Centuries." *Archipel,* no. 49 (1995): 79–124.

Tinguely, Frédéric, ed. *Un libertin dans l'Inde moghole: Les voyages de François Bernier (1656–1669).* Paris: Chandeigne, 2008.

Toby, Ronald P. *State and Diplomacy in Early Modern Japan: Asia in the Development of the Tokugawa Bakufu.* Princeton, N.J.: Princeton University Press, 1984.

Todorov, Tzvetan [Tsvetan]. *The Conquest of America: Perceiving the Other.* Trans. Richard Howard. New York: Harper and Row, 1984.

———. "Cortés et Moctezuma: De la communication." *L'Ethnographie* 76, nos. 1–2 (1980): 69–83.

Toomer, G. J. *Eastern Wisedome and Learning: The Study of Arabic in Seventeenth-Century England.* Oxford: Clarendon Press, 1996.

Twain, Mark. *A Connecticut Yankee in King Arthur's Court.* New York: Harper, 1889.

Unger, Willem S., ed. *De oudste reizen van de Zeeuwen naar Oost-Indië, 1598–1604.* The Hague: Martinus Nijhoff, 1948.

Valensi, Lucette. *The Birth of the Despot: Venice and the Sublime Porte.* Trans. Arthur Denner. Ithaca, N.Y.: Cornell University Press, 1993.

———. *Fables de la mémoire: La glorieuse bataille des trois rois.* Paris: Seuil, 1992.

Van den Boogaart, Ernst. *Civil and Corrupt Asia: Image and Text in the "Itinerario" and the "Icones" of Jan Huygen van Linschoten.* Chicago: University of Chicago Press, 2003.

Van der Krogt, Peter, and Erlend de Groot. *The Atlas Blaeu-van der Hem of the Austrian National Library.* 7 vols. 't Goy-Houten, The Netherlands: HES Publishers, 1996–2008.

Van der Willigen, A. *Les artistes de Harlem: Notices historiques avec un Précis sur la Gilde de St. Luc.* Nieuwkoop, The Netherlands: B. de Graaf, 1970.

Vasumati, E. "Ibrahim Qutb Shah and the Telugu Poets." In S. M. Qadri Zore, ed. *Qutb Shahi Sultans and Andhra Samskriti.* Hyderabad, India: Idara-e-Adabiyat-e-Urdu, 1962, pp. 28–42.

Vélez de Guevara, Luis. *La mayor desgracia de Carlos V.* Ed. William R. Manson and C. George Peale. Newark, N.J.: Juan de la Cuesta, 2002.

Venkataramanayya, Nelatur. *Studies in the Third Dynasty of Vijayanagara.* Madras, India: University of Madras, 1935.

———. *Vijayanagara: The Origin of the City and the Empire.* Madras, India: University of Madras, 1933.

Vignati, Antonella, ed. "Vida e Acções de Mathias de Albuquerque, Capitão e Viso-Rei do Estado da Índia." 2 pts. *Mare Liberum*, no. 15 (1998): 139–245; no. 17 (1999): 267–360.

Villiers, John. "Aceh, Melaka and the *Hystoria dos cercos de Malaca* of Jorge de Lemos." *Portuguese Studies* 17, no. 1 (2001): 75–85.

Vogt, John. "Saint Barbara's Legion: Portuguese Artillery in the Struggle for Morocco, 1415–1578." *Military Affairs* 41, no. 4 (1977): 176–82.

Voigt, Lisa. *Writing Captivity in the Early Modern Atlantic: Circulations of Knowledge and Authority in the Iberian and English Imperial Worlds.* Chapel Hill: University of North Carolina Press, 2009.

Von Wyss-Giacosa, Paola. *Religionsbilder der frühen Aufklärung: Bernard Picarts Tafeln für die "Cérémonies et Coutumes religieuses de tous les Peuples du Monde."* Bern: Benteli Verlag, 2006.

Wachtel, Nathan. "L'acculturation." In Jacques Le Goff and Pierre Nora, eds., *Faire de l'histoire*, vol. 1. Paris: Gallimard, 1974, pp. 126–33.

Wagoner, Phillip B. "Fortuitous Convergences and Essential Ambiguities: Transcultural Political Elites in the Medieval Deccan." *International Journal of Hindu Studies* 3, no. 3 (1999): 241–64.

———. "Precolonial Intellectuals and the Production of Colonial Knowledge." *Comparative Studies in Society in History* 45, no. 4 (2003): 783–814.

———. "'Sultan among Hindu Kings': Dress, Titles and the Islamicization of Hindu Culture at Vijayanagara." *Journal of Asian Studies* 55, no. 4 (1996): 851–80.

——. *Tidings of the King: A Translation and Ethnohistorical Analysis of the "Rāyavācakamu."* Honolulu: University of Hawaii Press, 1993.

Wicki, José [Josef]. "Dokumente und Briefe aus der Zeit des indischen Vizekönigs D. Antão de Noronha (1563–1568)." *Aufsätze zur portugiesischen Kulturgeschichte,* no. 1 (1960): 225–315.

——. "Duas cartas oficiais de Vice-Reis da Índia, escritas em 1561 e 1564." *Studia,* no. 3 (1959): 36–89.

——. "Duas relações sobre a situação da Índia portuguesa nos anos 1568 e 1569." *Studia,* no. 8 (1961): 133–220.

Wicki, Josef, and John Gomes, eds. *Documenta Indica.* 18 vols. Rome: Monumenta Missionum Societatis Iesu, 1948–88.

Wilkinson, J. V. S. "An Indian Manuscript of the *Golestān* of the Shāh Jahān Period." *Ars Orientalis,* no. 2 (1957): 423–25.

Wilks, Mark. *Historical Sketches of the South of India, in an attempt to trace the History of Mysoor,* vol. 1. London: Longman, Hurst, Rees and Orme, 1810. Reprint. Madras, India: Higginbotham, 1869.

Wills, John E., Jr. *Embassies and Illusions: Dutch and Portuguese Envoys to K'ang-hsi, 1666–1687.* Cambridge, Mass.: Harvard Council on East Asian Studies, 1984.

Wilson, Bronwen. *The World in Venice: Print, the City, and Early Modern Identity.* Toronto: University of Toronto Press, 2005.

Wormser, Paul. *Le Bustan al-Salatin de Nuruddin ar-Raniri: Réflexions sur le rôle culturel d'un étranger dans le monde malais au XVIIe siècle.* Paris: Editions de la Maison des Sciences de l'Homme, 2012.

Wright, Elaine, et al. *Muraqqaʿ: Imperial Mughal Albums from the Chester Beatty Library, Dublin.* Alexandria, Va.: Art Services International, 2008.

Xavier, Ângela Barreto. *A invenção de Goa: Poder imperial e conversões culturais nos séculos XVI e XVII.* Lisbon: Imprensa de Ciências Sociais, 2008.

Yermolenko, Galina I., ed. *Roxolana in European Literature, History and Culture.* Farnham, U.K.: Ashgate, 2010.

Zainuddin Makhdum, Shaikh. *Tuhfat al-Mujāhidīn: A Historical Epic of the Sixteenth Century.* Trans. S. Muhammad Husayn Nainar. Kuala Lumpur: Islamic Book Trust, 2006.

Zebrowski, Mark. *Deccani Painting*. Berkeley: University of California Press, 1983.

Zir, Alessandro. *Luso-Brazilian Encounters of the Sixteenth Century: A Styles of Thinking Approach*. Lanham, Md.: Rowman and Littlefield, 2011.

Zubairi, Mirza Ibrahim. *Tārīkh-i Bījāpūr musammā bi-Basātīn us-Salātīn*. Hyderabad, India: Sayyidi, 1880.

Županov, Ines G. *Missionary Tropics: The Catholic Frontier in India*. Ann Arbor: University of Michigan Press, 2005.

Index

Note: Page numbers followed by *f* and *t* indicate figures and tables.